From Feast to Famine

From Feast to Famine

Official Cures and Grassroots Remedies to Africa's Food Crisis

Bill Rau

Zed Books Ltd
London & New Jersey

From Feast to Famine was first published by Zed Books Ltd,
57 Caledonian Road, London N1 9BU, UK and 171 First Avenue,
Atlantic Highlands, New Jersey 07716, USA, in 1991.

Copyright © Bill Rau, 1991.

Cover designed by Sophie Buchet.
Typeset by Opus 43, Broughton-in-Furness.
Printed and bound in the United Kingdom
by Biddles Ltd, Guildford and King's Lynn.

British Library Cataloguing in Publication Data

Rau, Bill
From feast to famine : official cures and
grassroots remedies to Africa's food crisis.
1. Africa. Food supply
I. Title
338.196

ISBN 0-86232-926-4
ISBN 0-86232-927-2 pbk

Library of Congress Cataloging-in-Publication Data

Rau, Bill.
From feast to famine : official cures and
grassroots remedies to Africa's food crisis/
Bill Rau.
p.   cm.
Includes index.
ISBN 0-86232-926-4. – ISBN 0-86232-927-2 (pbk.)
1. Africa – Economic conditions.   2. Africa –
Dependency on foreign countries.   1. Title.
HC800.R38   1990
338.96 – dc20   90-38990
                                                       CIP

Contents

v

Acknowledgements

Many peple have been important in the creation of this book. Nick Mottern suggested the concept and has been a creative and honest friend throughout. Sjef Donders, Ted Hayden and Maura Brown of Africa Faith and Justice Network in Washington, DC, provided a forum to raise and share many of the ideas elaborated in this book. I have appreciated for several years their support and commitment to convey to the US public the message that we have one element of the power to alter US policies toward Africa.

A very special and warm thank you to Susan Roche. Susan provided numerous examples of women's activities in Africa, drawn from her own experience and research. She has been caring and insightful, dividing her busy schedule to free up time fc.˙ my writing.

Doug Hellinger took the initiative to suggest the book to Robert Molteno at Zed Books. Doug organized several critical discussions of ideas developed in this book. In his work he offers the flattering compliment of incorporating some of those ideas on the process of popular development into the structures of US foreign aid.

Maghan Keita and Fantu Cheru contributed ideas, examples and critical comments to the book on several occasions. Both of them represent the best of academia — involved in both African and US struggles for change, and committed to forms of development education that reflect African realities.

A number of other people have provided the time, enthusiasm and critical insight an author needs to sustain the writing. I want to thank Margie Weber, Ben Wisner, Ben Hoskins, Sara Talis, Tim Lind, Dominic Ntube, Sarah Sehnert and Malkia M'buzi who provided the inspiration for the title, Newman Fair, Tony Barnett, Nick Abel, Michael McCoy, Chris Matthews, and John Daniel and Robert Molteno of Zed Books.

For

Robert B. Kent

an invaluable counsel and friend as he
enters retirement after leaving an
indelible mark on legal education in
the USA and Zambia: our gratitude is
as great as our debt

1 The Food & Development Crises in Africa

Late in 1984 the world's attention was drawn to famine victims in northern Ethiopia. For the second time in a decade people in the Horn of Africa faced drought and famine. And twice since then, in 1986/87 and 1989/90, famine conditions have affected people in Ethiopia. The famine which began in 1983 was more severe and widespread than that which occurred across the Sahel region from Senegal to Ethiopia in 1973/74. Probably no other food-related crisis generated as much public interest and concern as the 1983–85 Ethiopian famine. Literally tens of millions of dollars in public and private contributions from people and nations in the northern hemisphere were given with the intent of addressing the immediate food need problems of the region. During the response to the immediate needs of hundreds of thousands of destitute and starving people — primarily children, women, the rural poor in general — a question often asked was: Why has this happened again?

The question remains both vital and valid, yet often the answers elicited are limited, lacking in historical perspective and understanding of African conditions. Some observers talk about the famines as an outcome of some twenty years of mismanaged independence in African countries. For these people, Africa's complex relationships with Europe and America, reaching back centuries, are ignored. Other analysts suggest the famines are an outgrowth of a natural event; drought has indeed affected large parts of the continent and destroyed food crops and livestock. But famine is not a natural occurrence nor an act of nature; famine is a social and political process. Famine, hunger and poverty result from decisions about the control of resources and who shall benefit by that control.

This book provides an historical and analytical view of the current food crisis in Africa. Special attention is given to descriptions of the innovative efforts of African people to address food and development problems. The book seeks to go beyond headlines and the immediacy of parched fields. It examines major factors which have made Africa's rural poor extremely vulnerable to famine while demonstrating that those same people provide the means to address Africa's development crisis.

1

Part I looks back several hundred years to trace the origins of Africa's current conditions. Its internal dynamics and history are as complex, varied and vital as those of other regions, but from the time that the first slavers carried away Africa's people to serve external interests, the continent has also been subject to tremendous disruption from outside. The loss of independence at the end of the nineteenth century to European imperial powers — Britain, France, Germany, Belgium and Portugal — intensified the distortion in Africa's economic and political development that began with the slave era. African resources — human, mineral and agricultural — were used to strengthen the economies of the colonial powers. Force was commonly used: from scorched earth wars designed to starve out resistance to kidnapping of family members in order to coerce obedience from others.

Independence brought the promise of improved living conditions and development, expectations that were not matched by effective policies for integrated development within Africa itself. Scattered projects, based on European and North American models and often on Northern money and technical expertise, have done little to stimulate agricultural production. But even more, those projects have strengthened the trend which began in the colonial era toward producing crops and minerals for overseas markets. African wealth was, and remains, at the service of others.

Independence did not contribute to greater African control over African resources. Rather, there was a rapid rise of self-interested elites. In league with multinational firms and development agencies, these elites have enriched themselves by impoverishing their compatriots. Decisions effectively directing resources away from the vast majority of Africans for the benefit of a few inside and outside Africa are now accepted, albeit unspoken, components of much development planning and financial assistance. Military spending is significant and wars — now sponsored by the major industrial powers — add to the hardship, poverty and hunger of millions of African people. The rural areas of Africa have provided human and agricultural resources which have enabled wealthy groups, often living in Africa's cities and towns and Northern nations, to expand their riches and power. The rural areas and people there have not, however, received an equal return in services or income.

Foreign aid (including food aid) has, in many instances, allowed African governments to import relatively cheap commodities rather than rely upon the development of their own resources. Exports from Africa are overwhelmingly in primary commodities, and prices and demand are externally determined. Imports of consumer goods (especially for the elite) or inappropriate industrial equipment have tremendously increased African debt. And as the International Monetary Fund (seconded by the World Bank, the United States

Agency for International Development and European aid agencies) adds a new form of coercion by pressuring African governments to reduce social expenditures and increase exports, the continent is, in general, no more in control of her resources and her future than in the past. Where once slave ships pulled away from Africa's coast with her wealth in humans, so today ships, planes and electronic transfers depart with Africa's wealth in the form of minerals, agricultural products and savings. Thus, for 400 years Africa has been exploited to serve external, primarily Northern, interests.

Part II examines the reactions of Northern contributors and African leaders to the food and development crises. From the North come solutions that incorporate the common images of a continent in chaos and collapse — a charity case, yet one ungrateful for attention and handouts from benevolent donors.

Those images are blessed by the oft-repeated statistics worked up by the United Nations agencies: 100 million people chronically hungry; 30 million people in 24 countries at risk of starvation in 1984; 25 per cent of Africa's food needs being met through imports, reflecting the reportedly steady decline in per capita agricultural output over two decades. Half the world's 10 million refugees are Africans, people in flight from wars, drought and internal oppression. Rapid population growth places ever increasing demands on already strained social services and arable land. Sub-Saharan Africa carries a debt burden of over $200 billion, owed primarily to Northern creditors, with the result that there is now a net outflow of cash resources from African countries to Northern 'donor' agencies.

In other cases, the images are ones of decay and neglect. For example, we hear about the movement of the Sahara Desert into formerly productive lands, of roads and transportation systems collapsing for want of maintenance, of health centres opening without medical supplies and schools operating without pencils, paper or desks. Development projects — from water pumps to agricultural credit schemes — have been abandoned as hopeless failures.

These images depict conditions that require careful analysis, free from the burdens that distort much Northern writing: the paternalism of charity, the arrogance of assumed racial and technical superiority and the blinkered vision of exploitative economic and political power. Countering the Northern analysis are the programmes and initiatives designed by African political, religious and intellectual leaders. While not uniform, the views from these perspectives within Africa offer a more solid and realistic basis for addressing the food and development problems of the continent.

African leaders have become far less complacent about the unhappy outcomes of development projects and about models of development which outsiders feel are appropriate for Africa. However, their approaches often ignore the needs of farmers and workers and the sustained and comprehensive skills that those groups have brought to the development process. In short, national elites, like their international counterparts, define development in their own image and interests and far too rarely reflect the interests and views of the poor.

Part III of this book moves beyond the largely official cures for Africa's problems and offers a more realistic and positive image of African people that is grounded in innumerable popular actions, small and large, occurring in every country, if not in every community. It is a reality that we rarely see or hear about, but one that commands ready recognition. We argue that among the people who have faced starvation in Ethiopia and elsewhere, a vast energy exists that asserts dignity, ingenuity and dedication to constructive change. For centuries people have been utilizing and adapting their skills and knowledge to remain solvent and act together within coherent communities. That starvation did occur between 1983 and 1990 in parts of Africa is a result not of the failure of people's systems of survival, coping and problem-solving, but of decisions beyond their control which undermined food production and the ability of people to obtain food. Those external constraints remain and continue to cause hunger, but within a year after images of famine flooded the North in 1984, many African communities also had succeeded in renewing their food production. This book seeks to place the current food situation of Africa in a wider, positive framework.

It is true that many development projects in Africa have fallen into neglect or have been abandoned by external donors. In their place, however, a more legitimate and sustainable form of change is evident. People across Africa are redefining the meaning and intent of development. This has meant that new popular organizations have emerged to clarify people's needs and skills and to create programmes and projects that build upon local resources in ways that outside programmes have rarely attempted in the past.

Similarily, the seeming political chaos in South Africa is in fact a broad popular response to the oppression of apartheid. Although the struggle against South African oppression has long existed, the continuous pressure against apartheid's structures in the 1980s represents a major initiative by poor and middle-class Africans to seize control for themselves, thereby setting the stage for a transfer of political and economic power. Few commentators suggest that the struggle in South Africa is almost won, but the significant gains that have occurred have been the result of increasingly sophisticated organization and mobilization by people there. The growth of African labour unions and the attempts by local communities to move from boycotting schools to gaining control over the operation of those schools represent progressive efforts by people to determine their own futures.

We conclude by adopting the appeal of many African and other Third World people to concerned people in the North: work to change the conditions emanating from your countries which inhibit our struggles for change! It is a challenge too easily ignored when we are accustomed to defining hunger, poverty and inequality as 'their problems', not ones demonstrating our complicity. However, concerned citizens in the North have numerous political and economic opportunities to organize and work for changes in the policies and structures of their societies. Utilizing those opportunities joins us intimately with African people in the struggle for popular change. Those struggles are not easy, but in the words of the people of Mozambique who have fought for many decades against the destruction wrought by Portuguese colonialism and South African apartheid: '*La Luta Continua* — The Struggle Continues!'

Part I

A History of Food Security & European Intervention in Africa

2 Centuries of Diversity & Self-Sufficiency

Africa's destiny has been entwined with that of Europe and western Asia for thousands of years. The early contacts were primarily through northern Africa. At least from 7000 B.C. in what is now northeastern Niger people had invented pottery, patterned with intricate designs. Grain grinding tools have also been discovered that date from that period. Taken together, the archaeological evidence suggests the likelihood that the domestication of grain had occurred. It has long been assumed that the planting and harvesting of seeds began in the Middle East and spread to other areas. We now know that African people developed the pottery making technology and domestication of grain independently and perhaps the discoveries spread outward, to the Middle East.[1] The Egyptian dynasties from the fourth millennium B.C. regularly traded with western Asia. The Egyptian courts imported commodities, such as ivory and hardwoods, from lands to the south. Other African states (i.e., Nubia and Kush) emerged along the Nile in the pre-Christian era, contributing to an exchange of ideas and resources throughout northeast Africa and the Middle East. For some 600 years from the second century B.C. onwards, the Romans ruled over North Africa and the area became a major granary for the empire. Agricultural systems for the production of export crops were imposed. Nomadic populations were settled on the newly opened agricultural lands. The material impact of the Romans on Africa was not lasting but, it can be suggested, the concept of colonialism entered European philosophy from this period.

The next invasion of the continent began in 639 A.D. Inspired by a new religion, Muslim Arabs swept into Egypt and over the next hundred years overran all of Africa north of the Sahara Desert. Islamic religion and culture have had a lasting impact on much of northern and West Africa and along the East African coast. The Muslim expansion into western Africa — both peacefully over hundreds of years and militarily — provided an additional cohesive element to existing political entities. The spread of Islam also strengthened trade links between the Sahel (the region between the southern edge of the Sahara Desert and the northern edge of the savannah) and the Arabic states of North Africa and western Asia. Soninke traders who travelled

9

through western Africa were among the first social groups to adopt Islam. These traders, along with their commercial goods, also brought the religion of Mohammed to peoples of West Africa. In time, Islam was gradually adopted by the traders and rulers of African states of the Sahel and throughout the second millennium it has been adopted and adapted by millions of people in West and northeastern Africa.[2]

At least from the beginning of the fifth century major state systems existed in West Africa. However, our knowledge of these states before the tenth century is sketchy. The first states appeared in the Sahel, along the northern edge of the savannah. The most prominent were Ghana, located between the Senegal and Niger rivers, Gao, to the east of the great city of Timbuktu, and Kanem on the eastern shores of Lake Chad. Ghana's renown was based on its extensive trade in gold; the kingdom of Gao rested on a more diversified agricultural, fishing, hunting and trade economy; Kanem grew out of the settlement of formerly nomadic groups, using its location as a central terminus for traders from north, south and west to sustain its economy and political position.[3]

In East and southern Africa large states emerged somewhat later than in West Africa — from the twelfth to the eighteenth centuries. These tended to be smaller than in West Africa but no less complex and elaborate. Many were firmly grounded in religious authority, composed of complex networks of local healers whose credibility stemmed from their roles as intermediary messengers for the opinions and advice of ancestor spirits. Through various hierarchies of spirit mediums a common belief system and culture, often overlapping with or co-opted by political authority, spread across many societies. The kingdom centred on the stone city of Great Zimbabwe (in what is now southern Zimbabwe) illustrates the merger of religious and secular authority and the adoption of new technologies into a major state system. At least from the tenth and until the fifteenth century, the spread of iron technology in the production of tools encouraged the consolidation of agriculture and the adoption of new crops. Cattle-keeping became more sedentary. Gold mining and trade provided a means for rulers to acquire and control wealth. The religious culture of the region provided a common overlay for state growth. During the fifteenth century, the kingdom of Great Zimbabwe went into sharp decline, perhaps because it could no longer support a large population. Meanwhile, other state systems in southern Africa continued the pattern of linking secular and religious authority. The strength of this culture was evident during the liberation struggle in Zimbabwe in the 1960s and 1970s when soliders in the liberation armies readily sought out and consulted with local spirit mediums as a way to strengthen ties with local people and with the spiritual 'owners of the land'.[4]

Most people in sub-Saharan Africa lived within stateless societies, that is, societies without centralized authority of leaders. Statelessness did not imply smallness, however, nor lack of complexity in political, economic and social relationships. Extensive trade could and did occur within the context of such societies. Ibo traders, in what is now southern Nigeria, utilized the vast network of local markets and the protection of religious authority to link into the long-distance trade of the region. Statelessness was a choice of some societies, reflecting both social and political values. It was recognized that

> state administration may only serve to draw off part of the social product for officials and courtiers who contribute little or nothing to that product. Many Africans apparently reached this conclusion, for states and stateless societies have existed side by side over nearly two millennia, without stateless people feeling a need to copy the institutions of their more organized neighbours.[5]

African state systems were constantly adapting to meet new situations. Societies designed complex mechanisms to link together vast and diverse areas and peoples. Trade was a key factor in generating wealth for states and rulers; religious beliefs and institutions often provided a cultural coherence to both social and political functions. Trade also served ordinary people and strengthened social relations. It has been argued:

> The importance of the [pre-colonial] market rested ... in the fact that women met as partners in a total economy to equalize, through exchange, the differences arising from individual production methods. In addition, the exchange provided variety to the diet and disposed of perishable surpluses. Thus, the traditional food market was oriented to distribution, not profit.[6]

Changes in Europe

In Europe, also, the nature of the state was undergoing change, this in response to economic changes from the fifteenth century onwards. Trade, land consolidation and manufacturing were emerging, especially in western Europe, as the means for individual advantage. These initiatives existed outside of the direct control of the feudal state, but later the new economic order was guaranteed by the state which was itself transformed by the economic revolution. Individual businessmen and firms assumed control over production, acquiring financial profits for their own benefit and as a means of expanding business. Gradually, land that had been held for common use was consolidated into private holdings; trade that had previously enriched the states came to benefit private merchants; manufacturing led to the emergence of large industrial complexes which were controlled or run for private and later corporate gain. Labour became the primary commodity available for workers to sell and thus began a long struggle between workers and owners of capital to control the value derived from labour.

Capitalism, as these economic forms of production and control came to be called, was in the process of transforming first Europe and, over several centuries, much of the rest of the world. The political state gradually changed in character and the power of the church was reduced. By the late eighteenth or mid-nineteenth century, the royalist state systems of much of western Europe had been taken over by a new group of people — or their representatives — who wielded economic power in the form of capitalistic businesses and services. The dual economic and political transformation became the impetus for the creation of the modern state system in Europe, in North America and eventually in colonial Africa. The expectation of ever-increasing profits stimulated the age of imperialism in the nineteenth century. The expansion of the imperial state system reflected the creation of a global economy designed to serve the interests of European elites.

Change and continuity within Africa

The capitalist system arose out of a set of unique features in western European history. Similarily, Africa's internal political and economic systems reflected conditions on that continent. The empires of the Sahel provided long periods of political, economic and social development. Agricultural systems evolved that were highly adapted to their locale and based on crops highly productive for their environment, thus providing food security and social stability. New crops were occasionally adopted if they proved suitable and beneficial. African societies were not totally egalitarian, but they did develop mechanisms of communal sharing of labour and goods, of trade and transfer, and of central grain storage against periods of shortage. Many societies share a view of well-being that assumes cultural and economic security within a whole community.

For the most part, African societies were internally self-sufficient. Political authority and legitimacy were based on the economic well-being of the community and social stability, not simply on power. While technology was relatively simple by standards used in the North today, it matched and served the needs of communities. Further, the technology was integrated to serve social needs, whether it be to control diseases or promote the cultivation of crops. Over centuries these African societies learned to utilize their environment for their own needs. Soils, weather, the response of various types of seeds to different conditions and labour inputs, as well as effective storage techniques were all intimately understood. Knowledge acquired from experience — trial and error, and demonstration — was passed down to, and adopted by, new generations.

From the fifteenth and sixteenth centuries new crops — such as corn (maize), bananas, cassava and peanuts — were introduced from outside and were absorbed into Africa's granaries. These crops offered new sources of food and permitted expanded production, gradually complementing, but not replacing, existing crops such as millet and sorghum. While corn and cassava did become the predominant staples in many areas over time, they were cultivated along with other crops: varieties of potatoes, grains such as millets and sorghum and many leafy vegetables. These were supplemented with wild and domesticated fruits and vegetables, meat and seasonally available products. The African agricultural systems were deeply rooted in decades and centuries of experience, were adaptable, were integrated and were productive.

Here [in Timbuktu in *c.* 1500] are many wells containing most sweete water; and so often as the rivers Niger overfloweth they conveigh the waters thereof by certain sluces into the towne. Corne, cattle, milk and butter this region yieldeth in great abundance.....
— Leo Africanus, *History and Description of Africa.*

While internally productive and self-sufficient, most African states and societies also engaged in trade. Historians have emphasized the importance of long-distance trade for the development of major African states. But much local trade also occurred. The exchange of products from one group to another was frequent, reflecting differing needs and resources and the variations in environmental zones. Some agricultural trade occurred, most usually at a local level, but large markets also existed and attracted substantial surpluses. Areas endowed with iron ore were able to produce hoes and axes and trade them to others. Groups of people were recognized for special skills, in iron-working and hunting, for example. Trade revolved around practitioners with iron-working skills and occasionally those technical experts travelled from community to community to repair iron tools. In the nineteenth century, itinerant gunsmiths moved across East Africa, repairing and even manufacturing firearms. Major trading links existed along several routes across the Sahara Desert which made Africa known in Europe and Asia. Products considered luxuries — such as ivory, gold, ebony, cloth and salt — were regularly exchanged by various peoples across the Sahara region. Islamic converts travelled to Mecca from Africa. Thus, trade in goods and ideas was a constant feature in African life. The continent was dynamic, innovative and adaptive.

Entering the world economy: cheap labour, racism and the slave trade

It is one of the tragic elements of global history that Africa has been considered a 'logical' source of cheap labour. The logic is ideological, and takes for granted Western assumptions about the primacy of capitalism as an economic and social system and the racial inferiority of African people. Over the past four centuries, this logic was played out by incorporating tens of millions of people, through violence and coercion, into Western economic systems. The precedents set by the ancient North African empires — Egyptian and Roman — in utilizing slave labour from sub-Saharan Africa continue to be exhibited in contemporary South Africa and in the policies of international agencies such as the World Bank which are aimed at reducing the value of labour while opening African economies to European and United States corporate investment.

The era of the exploitation of African labour for external benefit can be said to have now lasted over a millennium, beginning in the ninth century. From the mid-ninth century A.D. black Africans were transported across the Sahara and dispersed into northern Africa, southern Europe and western Asia. The trade in slaves was a part of a wider trading system linking sub-Saharan West Africa to the north. From the East African coast, Arab city states organized a small trade in slaves from the thirteenth century. This trade grew substantially in later centuries, but the Arab influence was confined to a few coastal settlements.

In addition to these early instances of slave trading for external markets, some African societies practised forms of slavery. Chattel slavery, as found in the Americas, was the exception in Africa. Far more common were forms of clientage, indenture, indebted servitude. Political leadership was gained and retained by attracting followers and by demonstrating an ability to provide for their welfare and control the wealth they generated. African forms of servitude allowed leaders to expand the number of their followers and their patronage. Slaves were employed in food and craft production and trade, and thereby helped enhance the power of slaveholders. Unlike most forms of Western slavery, African servitude often permitted clients and serfs to gain their freedom after one or two generations of service. The incorporation of slaves into the social and political systems of the receiving societies was common, and often fostered. For example, the House system practised in the states of the Niger Delta 'was designed to turn a foreign slave into a member of his community and kin to all other members of the House'. Slaves went through an initiation of re-birth and acquired new mothers and new names, these rituals integrating them into the kinship network. In their new homes, former slaves were encouaged to become quickly acculturated, to become full, loyal and productive members of their new society.[7] In many cases, slaves could attain positions of political influence once integrated into their new societies. In essence, slavery in Africa reflected existing social relationships in which kinship was the major way by which people were connected with one another. The task in societies in which slavery grew was to incorporate slaves into an intricate system of social dependency.

The expansion of the Portuguese mercantile empire in the fifteenth and sixteenth centuries not only brought Africa more directly into contact with Europe but introduced forms of economic, political and technical relationships that were inordinately unequal and exploitative in character. The Portuguese empire was unashamedly extractive, drawing from Africa — and colonies in Latin America and Asia — human, agricultural and mineral resources for the enrichment of a small metropolitian elite. During the mid-fifteenth century, Portugal established trading posts around Africa's coasts. Gold and ivory were initially more important export items than slaves for the Portuguese. From 1492, when Columbus identified for Europe the continents of the western hemisphere, Africa was progressively drawn into the European economic system — as a place to sell shoddy products and as a supplier of human and mineral resources. A few years later, the Spanish began importing African slaves into the Americas. 'And in 1510,' Basil Davidson has observed, 'there came the beginning of the African slave trade in its massive and special form: royal orders were given for the transport first of fifty and then two hundred slaves for *sale* in the [West] Indies.' [8] In the sixteenth and seventeenth centuries, the trade in slaves progressively grew as mines and plantations were established in the Americas and the Caribbean. The riches from the Americas, as well as from the extensive trade in moving human beings, returned to Spain's royal court and small mercantile class. By the mid-seventeenth century Britain, France and the Netherlands had joined the Portuguese and Spanish as the major extractive powers. Patterns were emerging that would influence Africa to the present. Of that long period, historian Walter Rodney has written:

> dependency automatically came into existence when parts of Africa were caught up in the web of international commerce. On the one hand, there were the European countries who decided on the role to be played by the African economy; and on the other hand, Africa formed an extension to the European capitalist market. As far as foreign trade was concerned, Africa was dependent on what Europeans were prepared to buy and sell.[9]

Differentiated by size, political systems and different expectations of advantage or threat from trade with Europeans, many African states were drawn into the slave-trading economy based on the trans-Atlantic trade. In about 1630 the Angolan state of Matamba (under Queen Nzinga) resisted Portuguese intrusions into their areas. However,

Portugal's material goods were a sufficient attraction to neighbouring states which opposed Matamba's position. By 1656 those opposing factions commanded sufficient strength to threaten Matamba's position: the state faltered, allowing an expansion of the slave trade. Seventy years later, in the early 1700s, the kingdom of Dahomey in West Africa began to recognize the economic losses and dependency it was suffering because of its involvement in the slave trade. Dahomey attempted to stop the slave trade but, like Matamba, was prevented by European-led opposition among competing African societies. Without greater coordination of policy and greater internal strength, African states alone could not stop the loss of their people. Africa's internal economic and political events were being strongly influenced by the demands of European capital development.

Numbers

It will never be known how many Africans were landed in the western hemisphere or reached North Africa and Asia, nor how many were put aboard ships for the voyage but died en route, nor how many found their lives, villages and cultures disrupted by the four-century search for human chattels. Diverse and scattered documents have been reconstructed to suggest the magnitude of the trans-Atlantic slave trade, but even those records are uneven and incomplete. Attempts to assess the magnitude of human losses within African societies depend on yet more fragmentary evidence. Thus, we are left with the knowledge that the exact size and overall impact of the slave trade era on population growth and internal development can never be fully measured and assessed.[10] Even the most radically conservative figures — offered, incidentally, by those who minimize Africa's suffering — trace a human suffering and tragedy that far exceeds the major calamities of recent decades.

As the numbers have been refined by research over the past two decades, a complex picture emerges which shows not only a long history of slave trading from many parts of Africa, but a trade at its most intense in the eighteenth century in West Africa and between 1750 and 1880 in East Africa. Although the incompleteness of the evidence leaves many gaps in quantifying the size of the slave trade, there is now some agreement that the number of Africans exported is roughly as follows:

In the Atlantic trade	11.7 million
North across the Sahara	7.4 million
In the Indian Ocean trade	3.8 million
Total	22.9 million[11]

There is also a wide range of difference in estimates of the number of people affected by slave trading and slave wars within Africa. It is reasonable to suggest that somewhere between 50 and 100 per cent more people died or were seriously displaced than the number who actually reached their intended destinations during the slave trade era. Taking the larger percentage, an estimated 45 million people were directly lost to their societies. Young men and women — people in the prime of their lives — were the core group of the slaving diaspora. Without their reproductive contribution, the overall growth of the continent's population was very low for nearly four centuries from 1500 to 1870.

Issues

1. The demographic gap: The slave trade has left Africa with wounds that continue to handicap its development. First, the sheer number of people involved — 23 million exported, another 10 to 25 million dead, injured or displaced — created a demographic gap on the continent. Historians debate the importance of this gap. Some have argued that the loss of people retarded internal growth and development; others have said that a subsequent population surge followed the gap. But, as other continents were growing through an interplay of agricultural, industrial, technological and population expansion, the slave trade denied Africa the physical and mental energies of young, strong people who would have contributed to the overall development of their continent. Instead, slavery forced Africans to produce for the wealth and power of others. This was further reinforced by the fact that slavery within African societies was not sustainable as slaves did not biologically reproduce themselves in sufficient numbers to replace losses. Thus, slave-holding societies had to obtain fresh recruits from outside, intensifying the wars and exploitation that produced slaves, whether for internal or external use.

2. Foundations of imperialism: Second, the slave trade laid the foundation for further European expansion into the continent — and into the Americas, as well. The exploitative nature of the trade, and the underlying racial thinking, encouraged Europeans to treat Africans as inferiors, their land, bodies and souls open to manipulation and use by self-styled 'superior' peoples. For example, while David Livingstone abhorred the trade in slaves, his solution was to substitute trade in so-called legitimate products (cloth, manufactures) to fill the African market. Without European goods and moral values, Livingstone felt that Africa would remain the 'Dark Continent'. Similarily, the slave trade reinforced European and American racial attitudes toward Africans. Racism and economics became closely bound together. And racism sanctioned further exploitation in the name of mutual improvement.

We are guilty of keeping up slavery by giving increasing prices
for slave-grown cotton and sugar. We are the great supporters of
slavery — unwittingly often, but truly.
— David Livingstone, 1859.

3. Internal differences intensified: The slave trade intensified
differences within African societies. The expanding demand for
slaves in the Americas from the sixteenth to the eighteenth centuries
affected social structures within African states, particularly those
that became functionaries in the export trade. We have seen that
forms of servitude existed within some African states. And while
African societies were not ideal egalitarian regimes, the major
differences between socio-economic groups that emerged in Europe
did not exist in Africa. The hierarchy found in Africa was based on
prescribed factors — birth, demonstrated leadership or skills — while
in the West material wealth and possessions became the symbols of
success and position. In Africa, status emerged out of social relations.
In Europe and America the control of resources for individual
enhancement became the basis of organizing society. As the external
demand for slaves began to be felt in Africa, many of the established
mechanisms for exercising authority began to break down in favour of
personal greed. Violence increased, not only the violence of wars and
raids, but that of social manipulation. In return for material rewards,
tribal leaders might distort their authority to accuse followers of
crimes which resulted in enslavement and sale. As a few leaders used
the slave trade to increase their power, the social distinctions between
people became more pronounced. People became commodities
rather than followers. Individuals who were the most vulnerable, those
who were least able to defend themselves or retain the assistance and
good will of others, were most likely to be pulled into the slaving
economy.

In the nineteenth century, as commercial (then termed 'legitimate')
trade began to blend with and then surpass the trade in slaves, African
merchants and warlords 'demanded more from their slaves'. Slaves
were used internally for production of export crops and minerals and
in some cases — such as the Asante state in contemporary Ghana,
Dahomey in current Benin and the Tanzanian island of Zanzibar —
plantation systems were established to assure extensive production of
kola nuts, palm oil, cloves or gold. In the process, commodity
production from within Africa for export — as opposed to the export
of slaves for external production — merged with the capitalist economic forces of the North.[12]

4. Food production affected: With respect to food security, the unsettled conditions caused by slave raids severely affected agricultural production and output. Farming cycles were disrupted by raids; people feared going to their fields, and planting or harvesting were severely curtailed. Food insecurity fell hardest on younger and elderly people, on those already vulnerable. This is not to suggest that those parts of Africa affected by slaving suffered chronic disruption or famine. Slaving activities moved from area to area, over time, as did the immediate impact on local economies. It is to suggest that at its most intense and most destructive, the slave trade contributed to increased social and economic discrepancies in Africa's population and undermined the ability of societies to meet their own needs.

5. Distorting communities and cultures: Finally, although people were drawn from all over the continent, for over four centuries, the slave trade had a differential impact over time and place. Some societies collapsed under the violence and loss of people, others were forced to adapt to new ways of life. In other instances, some states expanded in size and power. Thus, change did occur — the slave era did not cause Africa's history to stop. But it did distort that history and exposed Africa as never before to the world economy, an economy that was increasingly being dominated by capitalist demands within Europe for individual and corporate profit and national strength to facilitate and protect those profits.

Notes

1. J-P. Roset, 'Ten thousand years ago in the Sahel', *The Courier*, no. 116 (July–August 1989), pp. 91–98.
2. Nehemia Levtzion, 'The early states of the western Sudan to 1500', in J. F. A. Ajayi and Michael Crowder (eds), *History of West Africa*, Vol. 1, 2nd edition (Columbia University Press, New York, 1976), pp. 116–118.
3. Philip Curtin, *et al.*, *African History*, (Little, Brown and Co., Boston, 1978), pp. 86–87.
4. Peter Garlake, *Great Zimbabwe* (Thames and Hudson, London, 1973); David Lan, *Guns & Rain: Guerrillas & Spirit Mediums in Zimbabwe* (Zimbabwe Publishing House, Harare, 1985).
5. Curtin, *et al.*, *op. cit.*, pp. 82–84.
6. Helge Kjekshus, *Ecology Control and Economic Development in East African History: The Case of Tanganyika, 1850–1950* (University of California Press, Berkeley, 1977), p. 114.
7. E. J. Alagoa, 'The Niger Delta states and their neighbors, to 1800', in Ajoyi and Crowder (eds), *op. cit.*, pp. 343–345.
8. Basil Davidson, *The African Slave Trade*, revised edition (Little, Brown and Co., Boston, 1980), p. 64.

9. Walter Rodney, *How Europe Underdeveloped Africa* (Howard University Press, Washington, D.C., 1981), p. 76. Rodney also writes: 'Throughout the seventeenth and eighteenth centuries, and for most of the nineteenth century, the exploitation of Africa and African labour continued to be a source for the accumulation of capital to be reinvested in Western Europe. The African contribution to European capitalist growth extended over such vital sectors as shipping, insurance, the formation of companies, capitalist agriculture, technology, and the manufacture of machinery.' (p. 84).

10. For a review of existing arguments and evidence on the numerical impact of the slave trade see David Henige, 'Measuring the immeasurable: the Atlantic slave trade, West African population and the Pyrrhonian critic,' *Journal of African History*, Vol. 27 (1986), pp. 295–313.

11. Paul E. Lovejoy, *Transformations in Slavery: A History of Slavery in Africa* (Cambridge University Press, Cambridge, 1983).

12. *Ibid.*, pp. 163–165, 276–278.

3 Africa in the Nineteenth Century

Although the slave trade drew millions of people away from Africa, and other millions away from their homes, Africa nevertheless remained much its own continent well into the nineteenth century. European goods — such as textiles, iron and steel tools, discarded firearms — were finding their way into the interior. But African families, villages and societies continued to live within well-defined dynamic systems that reflected community integrity and supportive social orders. In many instances, values, customs and procedures had been disrupted by slaving's multiple intrusions. But crops continued to be grown, and interaction with the physical environment was deeply embedded in traditional knowledge. Political structures grew or contracted. Thus, African people lived their own history although the economic structures of the continent were increasingly influenced by external forces. By the end of the nineteenth century that history would again be altered with the introduction of colonialism, a starker and more intense form of Northern capitalism, and its expropriation of more of Africa's resources for external interests. Before reviewing the European intrusion into Africa it is useful to briefly examine the state of African agriculture and food security in the late nineteenth century.

Everywhere food is abundant — bananas, plantains, sweet potatoes, cassava ... corn, beans, peas, millet and other seeds, wild fruits, wild grapes, tobacco, honey, milk, fowls, and beef. I have been able to collect over twenty different species of bananas, all known and named and put to different uses. This tree furnishes the black man with paper and twine; from the leaves he makes mats and blankets; from the fruit he makes flour, porridge, bread, and wine.
— European explorer in Central Africa, 1889.

The basis of food self-sufficiency in Africa

The most striking picture of pre-colonial Africa was its ability to feed itself, except in times of extreme natural or political disaster. The ability of African people to feed themselves was based on an intimate knowledge of the resources needed for agricultural production. Political and social structures reinforced that knowledge. African farmers knew which soils were most productive, which seeds would respond to different soil and planting conditions, how various crops would nurture one another and protect the soil if planted together, how crop rotations and fertilization enhanced food production. Major African crops, such as sorghum, millet, rice and maize, had been adapted to local conditions. These crops provided grain even in rain-short years and stored well.

An excellent study from Tanzania provides a number of examples of the complexity of African agricultural systems in the nineteenth century. Rice and other grains and vegetables were produced in substantial surpluses on the fertile alluvial soils of rivers, often taking advantage of the residual moisture for dry season cultivation. These surpluses were sold to neighbouring groups, to traders and to merchants in the coastal urban centres. In some areas, ridges and irrigation works testified to the very labour-intensive forms of agriculture being practised. The Sambaa people of northeastern Tanzania were described as 'excellent water technicians because of the extensive irrigation channels they had built and maintained'. Grain production followed a three-year production cycle, followed by one year of fallow. Maize, sorghum and rice were traded with coastal settlements in exchange for fish. To the west of the Sambaa, around Mount Kilimanjaro, irrigation systems assured three cropping seasons, practically eliminating food shortages in the area. Both ash from burned refuse and cattle manure were used as fertilizer on fields. A final example from what is now Tanzania, which does not complete the picture of the diversity of that region, is from the western part of the country. The Matengo people lived in a very hilly region and developed an elaborate system of anti-erosion ridges within their agricultural system. The use of green manure (vegetation turned over into the soil and left to decompose) was the basis for sustaining a dense population with maize, peas, beans, cotton and other crops. Tree-planting provided material for cloth, firewood and building materials.[1]

Intercropping (the mixing of various crops within the same field) was, and remains, widely practised by African agriculturalists. The method offers several advantages: various crops ripen at different and progressive times in the year, providing a regular diet; in the event one crop fails, others would survive and be available for consumption; crops often are symbiotic, providing nutrients, shade or other growing advantages to one another; the extra ground cover reduces soil erosion and helps maintain soil fertility. African farming methods regularly produce surpluses. These are stored, processed into other foods (millet into beer, for example), sold to towns or passing traders, or provided as relief to other peoples whose crops may have suffered for various reasons.

There is little we can teach the Kano [Nigerian] farmer ... they have acquired the necessary precise knowledge as to the time to prepare the land for sowing; when and how to sow; how long to let the land be fallow; what soils suit certain crops; what varieties of the same crop will succeed in some localities and what varieties in others ... how to ensure rotation; when to arrange with Fulani herdsmen to pasture their cattle upon the land.
— E. Morel, *Nigeria: Its People and Problems,* 1911.

The fertility of the lands lying between the Mahoro land Rufiji [rivers in modern-day Tanzania] is extraordinary. Maize, rice, millet, ground-nuts and peas are largely cultivated, and heavy crops are garnered every year, the periodical inundations bringing fresh life to the soil. Sheep, cattle, and goats are in sufficient numbers to be bought for export....
— J. F. Elton, *Travels and Researches among the Lakes and Mountains of Eastern and Central Africa,* 1879.

The crops that were grown and consumed were of great variety, providing a nutritionally varied and balanced diet and security against crop diseases. Among the crops grown were basic grains (over 40 varieties of rice were identified in one local area in West Africa) and starches, numerous tubers, legumes and vegetables.[2] Fresh fruit was widely available and occasionally meat. Cattle-keeping peoples had milk and blood. European travellers were struck by the intensity and diversity of many African agricultural systems in the nineteenth century. These rich and varied economies provided well for people in most cases. During the thirty years in which he travelled in eastern and southern Africa in the mid-nineteenth century, David Livingstone rarely mentioned nutritional diseases or problems among the people he saw. The goal of African farmers was to feed themselves and sustain their social systems, and people worked hard, utilizing skills and knowledge acquired over time to achieve that goal.

Political and social systems reinforced production. In western Zambia, for example, the Lozi royalty enforced the annual clearing and maintenance of a vast system of channels, designed to drain low-lying land and contribute to its fertility.[3] In the Sokoto Caliphate of what is now northern Nigeria, cooperative arrangements for sharing labour at critical periods allowed households to engage in an extensive agriculture and craft system. In addition, a range of other labour relations existed, including slavery, wage labour and share-cropping arrangements. Agricultural production was enhanced in this area of high population density by fertilization of crops, drainage of low-lying areas and crop rotation. The political hierarchy sustained itself through an intricate system of taxes on agricultural production, manufacturing and trade.[4]

Agriculture provided the economic base for states in the Niger delta region of modern-day Nigeria in the first half of the nineteenth century as the slave trade was coming to an end. Palm oil and palm kernels were in increasing demand in Europe as raw materials for manufacturing. Demand for palm products in the Bight of Biafra commanded prices that exceeded the value of slaves in the 1830s. By the end of the nineteenth century, the export of palm products was worth over one million pounds sterling. In turn, the trade in palm products stimulated surplus production of food, often on plantations controlled by African merchants and worked by slaves, to support the large numbers of people engaged in the palm trade operations.[5]

Around Lake Victoria in East Africa, there were intricate systems of trade in agricultural commodities. Markets existed along the boundaries separating wetter and dryer zones, thus encouraging the exchange of food crops, salt, livestock and fish. Along both the eastern and western shores of Lake Victoria trade in agricultural commodities provided wealth to traders and political leaders who controlled exchange, but also assured food to people in areas where shortages occurred due to disruption or bad weather. To the east, in central Kenya, diverse micro-environments influenced crop production and contributed to a lively exchange of commodities. Trade permitted the 'redistribution of agricultural (including livestock) products to diversify diets, alleviate regular inequalities, ease temporary shortfalls and to ensure adequate sustenance in areas facing chronic shortages'.[6]

A fascinating example of a society growing because of its prime role in food production is that of Ukerebe, centred on an island in the southeast of Lake Victoria. Late in the eighteenth century, and stretching well into the nineteenth, Ukerebe greatly expanded the production of cassava, maize and new varieties of millet and sorghum. Ukerebe produce made up for occasional food shortages in the dryer regions to the south of the lake and facilitated further trade in cattle and manufactured goods, such as hoes. In the latter half of the nineteenth century, the Ukerebe food trade network was disrupted by rising demands by Swahili and Arab traders from the East Coast for slaves and ivory and the expansion of the Buganda state along the east side of the lake.[7]

The magnitude of surplus crop production often was very striking.

For example, in the 1890s, at a trade depot in central Kenya, 30,000 pounds of foodstuffs were sold to just one caravan. Many other trade caravans obtained food there also, suggesting the strength of the agricultural economies which served this market.[8]

In southern Africa, in the region encompassed by modern Zimbabwe, most societies were based on substantial grain production. Millet, sorghum, rice and maize were all grown and consumed. Surpluses allowed trade in agricultural commodities. Both Shona and Ndebele people also held livestock — cattle, goats and sheep. Prior to major losses to disease and European confiscation at the end of the nineteenth century, the Shona were estimated to have 300,000 head of cattle alone and the Ndebele 200,000.[9]

Political leaders achieved and maintained their legitimacy by assuring ample food for their people. This was achieved with prayers and rituals for timely and well-distributed rains, by propagating the spirits of the land and by collecting grain and storing it in central storage units against periods of shortage. The religious and political authorities were closely allied, providing institutional mechanisms for meeting community needs. The rituals also provided a check and balance against self-serving leaders. Failure to provide for rural welfare could have direct political costs. For example, in the Sahel area of West Africa, urban rulers who were in collaboration with unscrupulous grain traders became the target of rural reformists and revolutionary movements in the nineteenth century.

A division of labour also existed. Women were then, as now, largely responsible for basic food production and preparation. Within most societies men were responsible for clearing fields; preparation of the land for planting could be the responsibility of either men or women, or could be shared, depending upon the society. Women would sow, share in weeding, and harvest. Young boys might guard the fields against birds and other predators. Food processing and preparation was the responsibility of women. Gathering was primarily women's role; hunting was a shared activity. Labour-sharing groups were a feature of many societies, particularly at critical times in the growing season, such as during weeding and harvesting. These groups provided a socially defined means of increasing production and assuring food security for everyone. In addition, women were the primary collectors of water and firewood.

In the pre-colonial era, many societies and people engaged in non-agricultural activities. In the off-season, women, men and children in Zimbabwe panned for alluvial gold to place in international trade.[10] Skilled artisans, such as weavers, potters and iron workers, sustained local economies, their goods often being traded across long distances. We have mentioned the itinerant iron workers and gunsmiths of the nineteenth century. In central Kenya, some people hired out their labour to others, and by the middle of the nineteenth century

Mozambican workers were travelling to South Africa to work on sugar plantations and later in the diamond and gold mines.

Among pastoralists — a large segment of the Sahel population — an intimate knowledge of the environment allowed them to live with their animals on lands that were marginal for crop production. Pasture land was sought out in the dry season near wells and other sources of water. Herd size was determined by the amount of grazing land in the dry season, and it was common that increased off-take occurred in especially dry years — a crucial coping mechanism. Pastoralists also used agricultural lands in the dry season, their animals eating the stubble from harvested crops, manuring the fields and moving on as the rains brought forth the grass in the wild. Trade with agricultural people provided grain and some pastoral groups also cultivated the land. There was a range of actions open to pastoralists, allowing them flexibility in coping with the harsh Sahel environment.

In summary, throughout much of their history African communities were self-sufficient in food. They were often able to produce or acquire surpluses that provided security against bad years or could be distributed to others who were short of food. Diets were varied and balanced. It may not have been an ideal situation, but it was generally a self-sustaining one.

Inequalities and poverty

Despite the integrated and adaptable nature of African societies in meeting people's needs, distinctions based on wealth and social conditions did exist between groups of people. Slavery continued into the early twentieth century in some areas, but the forms of slavery normally differed from those found in European colonies in the western hemisphere and in the United States and the system was mitigated as slaves became integrated into society. In some societies, such as Ethiopia and parts of West Africa, people who were physically disabled or alienated from land or otherwise unable to work and provide for themselves tended to be stigmatized as poor. In the Darfur area of western Sudan, people were regarded as destitute if they were unable to live at a socially recognized standard that met their basic needs. Such people could include slaves, farmworkers, blacksmiths and those who depended upon gathering wild foods; they subsisted on the margins of society in both an economic and a social sense.[11] The feudal system of irregular but heavy tribute collection in Ethiopia left many people in poverty. In other cases, the armies of the various Ethiopian rulers confiscated both food and labour from peasant households and communities, throwing them into long-term poverty. In East Africa, the impact of an expansion in the slave trade and resultant social disruption in the nineteenth century probably resulted in increased insecurity and poverty conditions for large numbers of people. Rural poverty was often a result of inadequate household labour to invest in productive activities — agriculture, crafts and household maintenance. Households could be short of labour because of the untimely death, illness or loss of family members. In East Africa, the expansion of the slave trade in the nineteenth century particularly contributed to labour shortages and poverty, although we do not know the extent of such poverty in particular societies or during specific periods of time. The demand by the Portuguese for slaves for work in Brazil and by French planters for labourers on the Indian Ocean island of Reunion were met by increased shipments of people from Mozambique. The expansion of the slave trade caused the loss of people and set in motion changes that extensively disrupted agricultural production and social security in the lower Zambezi River valley. Local famines became common, causing people to attach themselves to patrons who could provide food.[12] Drought, flooding, cattle disease and locust invasions all presented periodic crises for people in the savanna region of West Africa, thereby contributing to insecurity and potential inequalities.[13]

Poverty, whether structural or due to an immediate crisis, was addressed by most societies. The Christian tradition in Ethiopia and Islamic beliefs that existed in West Africa provided for charity to poor people. Accepting a client/patron relationship — temporary or long-term — was a not uncommon reaction for people who lost their crops or faced insecurity for other reasons. A person's or household's benefactor thus acquired potential labour or followers, and the insecure household could generally be assured of protection and provision of basic necessities. In Central African societies, chiefs had the obligation to maintain grain stores for distribution in times of need. Nevertheless, people in poverty relied overwhelmingly upon themselves and their own social networks to survive.[14] The sharing of labour for crop production and sharing of food with families suffering from shortages were commonly practised. Whether it was through patronage relationships or the structures of given societies, poor people and households sought to retain their social alliances and thus their social dignity.

In essence, people were distinguished by social identity — their place in a complex of social relationships — and ability to live a sustainable life in community. Those people who acquired wealth often did so within the social framework, so that it was not simply a matter of accumulating material wealth for its own sake, but utilizing that wealth to attract, care for, support and influence other people, thereby maintaining a social order and perhaps enhancing the power and prestige of given individuals and groups. In turn, individual wealth was tempered by the political and social conditions prevailing at any time. The means by which people were defined and related to one another, by which access to resources was determined, continued through the colonial era into the present.[15]

We have seen that there were periods of extreme hardship, often affecting societies as a whole. Major droughts, followed by famine, have been documented in Ethiopia in the sixteenth century and in the Sudano-Sahelian region of sub-Saharan Africa in the seventeenth and eighteenth centuries. In the mid-seventeenth century, following several decades of erratic weather, drought induced a famine that was said to have cost the lives of half the population of Timbuktu. In the late nineteenth century, the Great Ethiopian Famine claimed one third of the total population — a scale equivalent to the reported number of people at risk in Ethiopia in the mid-1980s. Some areas north of Addis Ababa, the capital, suffered mortality rates of 50 to 60 per cent, both from starvation and the effects of disease. Drought, rinderpest (a disease that kills cattle and some wild animals) and locust invasions which devoured crops were precipitating factors in the Great Ethiopian Famine of 1888−92. In neighbouring Sudan, conscription of rural people to expand the army of the new state resulted in the depletion of workers from fields. With the onset of the drought which also affected Ethiopia, food production suffered and famine ensued.[16] Rinderpest entered Ethiopia in the mid-1880s with cattle imported from India. The disease assumed epidemic proportions and over the next decade spread rapidly from north to south across the eastern side of Africa. This event set the stage for European intrusion in some areas, such as Eritrea and eastern Zambia, as people were too scattered or preoccupied with searching for food to resist.

These historical pandemics were catastrophic for the people involved. By the early twentieth century drought or locust could trigger food-crop declines, but they need not have led to famine. However, political events changed the character of nature's course. With the advent of European colonial domination, Africa's agricultural systems became badly disrupted. The diversity and flexibility to deal with food insecurity became threatened and within a short space of time, two to three decades, households and whole communities curtailed or abandoned mechanisms which had formerly protected them. Agricultural production under colonial rule altered from generally serving internal needs to serving European commercial and extractive interests. As a result, in the twentieth century, hunger became a structural factor in Africa.

European imperialism and the conquest of Africa

Africa's initial incorporation into the world economy through the slave trade rapidly intensified in the late nineteenth century. The increasing demand and competition for both resources and markets among Europe's capitalist economies led them to carve out territories in Africa that offered the prospect of vast mineral and agricultural wealth.

We have there [in West Africa] a vast and immense domain which is ours to colonize and to make fruitful; and, I think that . . . as foreign markets are closing against us, and we ourselves are thinking of our own market, I think, I repeat, that it is wise to look to the future and reserve to French commerce and industry those outlets which are opened to her in the colonies and by the colonies.
— Eugène Etienne, French Minister for Colonies, *c.* 1890.

The capitalist economies of late nineteenth-century Europe were increasingly industrialized. Maintaining profits depended upon expanding markets — for acquiring raw materials and for selling finished goods. Attitudes that justified such a rapid and intense exploit-ation of natural resources for private gain supported these economic activities. Industrialization, technological refinement, personal gain and mass consumerism became the ethical criteria of capitalist Europe. By contrast at this time, the economies of most African societies were based on the use of resources for communal well-being (or for household well-being within a wider community). Private profit was not a basic motivating factor in African economies. Varying degrees of wealth existed, but social and political mechanisms existed to assure a broad fulfilment of basic needs. Labour was central to production, which was overwhelmingly agricultural, while in Europe labour became subordinate to machines and the value of labour and machines was redirected to the owners of capital. Most African households and communities possessed the resources for creating all of their needs — labour, tools, land and natural resources. However, in late nineteenth-century Europe most people largely had lost control over tools and land and possessed only their labour as a productive resource, and that had to be sold in order to live. The basic differences between the European and African systems were rarely appreciated by European imperial agents (whether military, missionary or trader), but for them the superiority of their system was taken for granted and became an explanation for the colonial takeover of Africa.

As the slave trade drew to a close, the British and French, especially, were finding major economic advantage in other African products. Vegetable oils were in great demand in Europe for making soap and margarine. In 1830, Britain bought 10,000 tons of palm oil from what would later become southeast Nigeria. Exports contined to grow throughout the century, as other areas along the coast responded to the demand. In Senegal, French demand for vegetable oil stimulated peanut production. By the 1890s annual exports exceeded 60,000 tons, a figure that was six times greater thirty years later. Cocoa was first exported from Ghana in 1891, having been introduced by Europeans. Output rapidly increased to 175,000 tons — nearly half the world's total — three decades later. The initial expansion of these cash crops demonstrated the productive capacity and adaptability of African farmers within their economic systems.[17]

European colonialism was unwilling, however, to maintain those levels of balanced production of which African agriculture was capable. European industry demanded far higher outputs of African cash crops. Colonialism became the instrument for assuring that European home-market demand was met. The quest for commercial advantage by European states in Africa had its competitive problems, however. Thus, in November 1884 the major European powers met in Berlin to discuss their related commercial interests and differences in West and Central Africa. The conference set the framework for formalizing colonial territorial divisions in Africa. It was largely a paper exercise. European presence in Africa at that time was limited to exploration, to a few trading posts along the West African coast, to French political control along the Senegal River, a few Portuguese settlers in Angola and Mozambique, and the presence in South Africa of descendants of Dutch and British settlers. Mission stations were scattered through the continent, primarily close to the coast. Not surprisingly, there were no Africans involved in the Berlin Conference. The economic forces of imperialism were integrated with perceived moral issues — saving African 'pagans' from their 'idolatry' for Christianity — and highly charged psycho-emotional motivations. Racism was the prime emotional issue, but military and nationalistic prestige also motivated many individuals. The varying importance of these factors in European imperialism has long been debated by historians. There is general agreement that African interests were progressively subsumed to those of Europe. African agriculture, mineral resources, values and political systems were considered inferior and in need of control by Europe. Africa, it was felt, was a *tabula rasa*, subject to European needs and demands. The arrogance of the European conquerors was seen at all levels, among people of all backgrounds. Missionaries denied the existence of African spiritual values and undermined African concepts of self and worth. Colonial administrators denied African knowledge of complex agricultural systems, insisting instead on monocrop production of exports such as peanuts, cotton, tobacco and palm oil. European traders and business concerns denied the coherence, security and economic importance of African households, communities and trading systems by drawing away men for low-paying work on commercial farms and in mines. In essence, the strengths of Africa were challenged at their core by European imperialism.

You know, long ago they used to say, '... the missionaries came to Africa and they had the Bible and we had the land. And then they said, "Let us pray." And when we opened our eyes, we had the Bible and they had the land.'
— Desmond Tutu, 1984 Nobel Peace Prize winner.

Many African political systems were relatively small, or decentralized with a diversity of social forms and controls that met communities' needs. European imperial agents were able to take advantage of these factors of size and diversity to play one group off against another (as they had with those states which opposed the slave trade) and by imposing authority over one society at a time. Small material inducements backed by the threat of force served to persuade many Africans to accept European takeover. Military force was widely used to intimidate and overpower African states, and the firepower Europeans brought to bear had a major impact on decisions to accommodate European rule instead of attempting overt resistance. And, as noted earlier, large areas of eastern and southern Africa had been disrupted by rinderpest and food shortages late in the nineteenth century, coinciding with the arrival of colonial forces in some cases.

This is not to suggest that Africans passively accepted European takeover. There are numerous examples of African resistance to imperialism — some of which later inspired nationalist movements. Italian forces were routed by an Ethiopian army in 1896. The African leader, Samori Ture, successfully resisted the French military in the western Sahel for over a decade and a half in the 1880s and 1890s, with a highly organized, well-equipped army of nearly 40,000 foot and cavalry troops. The trading state of Nembe, in the Niger delta region, in 1895 openly fought the economic incursions of the Royal Niger Company. In southern Africa, the Zulu kingdom wiped out a British expeditionary force. Mozambican peoples vigorously resisted the military build-up by the Portuguese as the latter sought to gain greater economic control over the colony in the last three decades of the nineteenth century. German imperialism was strongly resisted by people in modern Tanzania. Individual states fought German forces in the 1880s and 1890s, but it was two 'national' wars that were particularly noteworthy. In 1888—89, at least 100,000 people from various parts of inland Tanzania travelled to the coast to resist the establishment of German settlement along the coast. In the end, German military power prevailed, but the resistance set the stage for numerous struggles by individual leaders and states in the subsequent two decades. In 1905 the exploitative and repressive nature of German rule led to a massive uprising known as the Maji-Maji revolt. Religious cults and messengers provided a means of communication and co-ordination between people spread over hundreds of miles. To suppress the revolt, the Germans carried out a scorched-earth war so devastating that three years of famine followed. Numerous other instances, larger and smaller, of resistance occurred across the continent.[18] In fact, Ranger argues that 'virtually every sort of African society resisted, and there was resistance in virtually every region of European advance'.[19] European success depended on its military technology and organization, a zeal to conquer and prevail and an economic system willing and able to sustain those efforts over two decades, in anticipation of major returns. Further, initially, the European presence was not always perceived as a threat. The export of select cash crops yielded substantial economic rewards for some interests within Africa while the early missionary settlers were often used by African rulers in the pursuit of foreign policy. Complaints or promises to mission groups could induce them to put pressure on their European military and administrative peers to alter policies toward Africans. The presence of Europeans had to be measured and assessed as part of a process of seeking advantage, of adapting to new circumstances, but of retaining the cultural essence of society.

I would like to know how many independent villages of France have been destroyed by me, king of Dahomey. Be good enough to remain quiet, carry on your commerce . . . and like that we will remain at peace with each other as before. If you wish war, I am ready. I will not end it even if it lasts a hundred years. . . .
— King Behanzin of Dahomey [Benin] in a letter to the French governor at Porto Nova, 1892.

In summary then, the spur to imperialism was the European desire to control production of African resources and create a captive market for European manufactured goods. It is occasionally suggested that the colonial era was a positive, developmental step for Africa, an introduction to the modern world. That view is highly suspect and does not stand up under close study. The colonial era was not Africa's introduction to the modern world — assuming that the West holds a monopoly on what is 'modern'. A world economy existed at least from the sixteenth century that closely bound Africa and her people to external economic forces.[20] Colonialism intensified that relationship, substituting the export of agricultural and mineral products for people. Further, colonialism introduced the dimension of external political control to better facilitate resource control and market access. Colonialism intensified the social divisions within Africa, creating distinct socio-economic groups. Thus, as a facilitator of modernity, colonialism offered few positive examples, images or structures for Africa.

Notes

1. Helge Kjekshus, *Ecology Control and Economic Development in East African History: The Case of Tanganyika, 1850–1950* (University of California Press, Berkeley, 1977), Chapter 2.
2. Paul Richards, 'Ecological change and the politics of African land use', *African Studies Review*, Vol. 26, No. 2 (June 1983), pp. 1–72.
3. Laurel Van Horn, 'The agricultural history of Barotseland, 1840–1964', in Robin Palmer and Neil Parsons (eds), *The Roots of Rural Poverty in Central and Southern Africa* (University of California Press, Berkeley, 1977), p. 140.
4. Michael Watts, *Silent Violence: Food, Famine & Peasantry in Northern Nigeria* (University of California Press, Berkeley, 1983), pp. 66–69.
5. Patrick Manning, 'Slave trade, "legitimate" trade, and imperialism revisited: the control of wealth in the Bights of Benin and Biafra,' in Paul E. Lovejoy (ed.), *Africans in Bondage* (African Studies Program, University of Wisconsin, Madison, 1986), pp. 203–233.
6. Charles H. Ambler, 'Population, social formation and exchange: central Kenya in the nineteenth century,' *International Journal of African Historical Studies*, Vol. 18, No. 2 (1985), p. 204.
7. David William Cohen, 'Food production and food exchange in the pre-colonial Lakes Plateau region,' in Robert I. Rotberg (ed.), *Imperialism, Colonialism, and Hunger: East and Central Africa* (Lexington Books, Lexington, MA, 1983), pp. 1–18.
8. Ambler, *op. cit.*, p. 219.
9. David Beech, 'The Shona economy: branches of production', in Palmer and Parsons (eds), *op. cit.*, pp. 37–65.
10. For a brief description of women's activities in pre-colonial Zimbabwe, see Elizabeth Schmidt, 'Farmers, hunters, and gold-washers: a reevaluation of women's roles in precolonial and colonial Zimbabwe,' *African Economic History*, Vol. 17 (1988), pp. 45–80.
11. Alexander De Waal, *Famine that Kills: Darfur, Sudan, 1984–1985* (Clarendon Press, Oxford, 1989), pp. 55–58.
12. Leroy Vail and Landeg White, *Capitalism and Colonialism in Mozambique* (University of Minnesota Press, Minneapolis, 1980).
13. John Iliffe, *The African Poor: A History* (Cambridge University Press, Cambridge, 1987), chapters 2 and 3.
14. *Ibid.*, p. 47.

15. Sara Berry, 'Social institutions and access to resources', *Africa*, Vol. 59, No. 1 (1989), pp. 41–55.
16. Richard Pankhurst and Douglas H. Johnson, 'The great drought and famine of 1888–92 in northeast Africa', in Douglas Johnson and David M. Anderson (eds), *The Ecology of Survival: Case Studies from Northeast African History* (Westview Press, Boulder, CO, 1988), pp. 47–70.
17. A.G. Hopkins, *An Economic History of West Africa* (Longman, London, 1975), p. 174.
18. For a summary of African resistance see the chapters in A. Adu Boahen (ed.), *General History of Africa, Vol. VII: Africa under Colonial Domination 1880–1935* (UNESCO, Paris, 1985).
19. T. O. Ranger, 'African initiatives and resistance in the face of partition and conquest' in Adu Boahen, *op. cit.*, p.47.
20. L.S. Starvianos, *Global Rift* (William Morrow, New York, 1981).

4 The Early Colonial Period: Africa Becomes Europe's Plantation

As we have seen, there was a strong demand in European industries for select African crops and minerals from at least the mid-nineteenth century. While the colonial state was being established early in the twentieth century, the means to expand the extraction of crop and mineral resources in the colonies also solidified. Coercive political and economic policies, often enforced with overt violence, were applied against the colonial subjects. In eastern and southern Africa land was confiscated for distribution to white settlers. Africans were assigned to less productive, marginal and overcrowded areas. In turn, settlers needed African labourers to work the alienated lands and the colonial governments complied to enforce the movement of men into the European commercial economy.

Taxation was at the core of the colonial system of inducing African involvement in the cash economy. An annual tax, as well as other use taxes, was required from each person or head of household. Initially, in some areas taxes could be paid in produce or livestock, but soon cash payment was the basis of the system. To earn that cash, crops could be raised for which there was a demand in the colonial market economy; alternatively, men would leave their homes to work on European settler farms or in the mines owned by European interests. In West Africa, cash crop production for the European market was more common, although labour migration also occurred. In eastern and southern Africa, migration was the major source of cash income, particularly as sales of major crops were usually restricted to protect white settlers from competition.

In West Africa the colonial state provided an umbrella for European trading firms to conduct business exclusively in certain areas or in certain crops, to buy and sell at fixed prices, and to force African farmers to produce crops for the market. Thus, Africans grew the crops that were in demand in Europe — cotton, peanuts, cocoa, palm kernels, and later, coffee. Many farmers turned to growing these export crops. Early in the twentieth century in many parts of West Africa, people responded to market conditions and colonial taxation policy by rapidly expanding crop production. Sale of crops provided cash to pay the taxes imposed by the colonial state and to purchase material goods imported from Europe.[1] Those imports often replaced African products. For example, many areas of West Africa had manu-factured cloth in the pre-colonial era. Cheap industrial imports, closed markets and colonial neglect of indigenous manufacturing resulted in the collapse of African manufacturing. Farmers also found their production threatened by the colonial economy. For example, as prices for agricultural products were set very low, producers often found themselves in debt — the cost of production exceeding their returns. Farmers had to sell some or all of their land to others who were better off, or remained tied to foreign trading companies as a result of their agricultural debt.

This linkage between agricultural production and European com-mercial exploitation was exemplified in colonial Zaire. This large colony was the personal holding of King Leopold of Belgium from 1885 to 1908. He granted unbridled access to the resources of the colony to businesses and individuals. These in turn enforced cash-crop production in the most violent manner. Rubber production and sales epitomize the violent incursion of capitalism in Zaire in the early colonial era. Slave raiding and trading continued, serving the colonial demands for labour to collect and process rubber and to work the copper in the mines of Shaba Province in southern Zaire.[2] The tremendous profits Belgian traders and agents made from the rubber trade were directly related to their extremely harsh exploitation of Zairean people. People were required to pay their tax in rubber. Failure to pay the tax or actively collect rubber could result in retribution: enforced labour for weeks at a time; kidnapping of village leaders until a rubber ransom had been paid; the cutting off of hands, not only of those who did not comply, but of children as well. To feed workers, taxes payable in food were regularly demanded of rural people. European and U.S. missionaries reported (although their home offices rarely acted on the reports from the field) throughout the 1890s and the first decade of the twentieth century that the well-being of Zaireans was seriously eroded by Belgian company colonialism. Towns of several thousand people declined to several hundred in the space of a decade, as people fled or fell before the violence used to enforce the collection of labour and agricultural products. Speaking to a commission of inquiry in 1903, people who lived in King Leo-pold's own region summarized their experiences:

> It used to take ten days to get the twenty baskets of rubber. We were always in the forest, and then when we were late we were killed. We had to go further and further into the forest to find the rubber vines, to go without food, and our women had to give up cultivating the fields and gardens. Then we starved.... [W]hen we failed, and our rubber was short the soldiers came up [to] our towns and shot us. Many were shot; some had their ears

cut off; others were tied up with ropes round their neck and bodies and taken away. Our chiefs were hanged, and we were killed and starved and worked beyond endurance to get rubber. . . .[3]

In 1919, over a decade after Leopold's personal hold over Zaire had ended, an official Belgian commission of inquiry found that the population of the colony had declined by half during the 23 years of Leopold's rule. In the French-held areas which now comprise Chad, Cameroon, Gabon and the Central African Republic similar corporate forms of colonialism were utilized, with similar devastating results for the African population.[4]

As there were few alternatives for earning needed cash, crops had to be grown. But, for many Africans, earning cash led to increased impoverishment. The rapid and major expansion of peasant cash-cropping for export had two further implications for long-term poverty. First, as farmers concentrated on cash-crop production their ability to produce food was constrained. There simply was not enough time nor household labour to produce food and cash crops at the levels required, this despite the increased burden that most rural women assumed to maintain household food supplies and contribute to the males' cash crops. Household and community surpluses, a feature of the pre-colonial period, gave way in the first decade of the twentieth century to more limited household food production and availability. In some cases, household food consumption declined, in other cases food had to be purchased, often at high rates, in turn reinforcing the cash-crop syndrome. Thus, food deficits and increased vulnerability to hunger became more closely associated with conditions of poverty.

Second, households that produced cash crops often required extra labour to work their fields at critical times in the season. The demand for labour was met by people who did not regularly produce commodities for export — such as poor households in Niger, Mali and Burkina Faso — at that time. Seasonal and long-term workers migrated to the cocoa areas of Ghana or the peanut regions of Senegal and the Gambia. The households and areas from which men migrated experienced economic disruption, as their own agriculture was neglected, establishing a pattern that continues into the present. Migrant workers in Ghana's cocoa farms were often exploited, but also over several decades workers were able to impose labour contracts that allowed them to manage farms in return for a portion of the crop, thereby increasing their income and security on the land.[5]

In eastern and southern Africa, land alienation for use by white settlers was an added burden for people. From the mid-1600s Europeans had been taking more and more land in South Africa. Early in the twentieth century, the South African government legalized the inequities in landholdings, providing whites with 87 per cent of the total land area and nearly all of the best land for agricultural purposes. Under the so-called Natives Land Act of 1913 the African population which represented nearly 80 per cent of the total in South Africa, was consigned to just 13 per cent of the land. The events that led up to the legislation of land alienation in South Africa include both agricultural and industrial changes and both internal and external market forces. The expansion of gold and diamond mining in the late 1800s required, from the mine owners' standpoint, a regular and cheap source of labour. At the same time, white commercial farmers experienced competition in the sale of their agricultural products from both United States suppliers and more efficient and diligent African farmers. Thus, white farmers and industrial interests converged in seeking a steady supply of workers whose wages would be controlled at low levels. Along with other legislation, the Natives Land Act effectively removed Africans from farming for profit, assigning them to 'reserves', later to be termed 'homelands'. Under the Act the land available to them was too scarce and only marginally fertile. Africans were expected to emigrate out of the reserves for the duration of employment within white-owned enterprises. At the end of employment contracts or when they retired or became disabled, workers were expected to return to their assigned 'homelands' where families retained their subsistence living. The system required occasional tinkering, but worked for whites, who even believed the myth of subsistence homelands. In fact, the lands available for African agriculture quickly became overcrowded and overworked; it was impossible either to grow enough food or to sustain a livelihood within the reserves. But then, that was the purpose of segregation all along, to assure that self-sufficiency was not available to Africans and to design a system that forced Africans to contribute to the economic wealth of whites.[6]

The white occupation of Zimbabwe late in the nineteenth century had the goal of exploiting the perceived mineral wealth of the country. When that expectation collapsed, vast tracts of land were set aside for the benefit of a white settler population. In Zambia, Malawi and Tanzania land was set aside for colonial occupation and use, while in Kenya the extremely fertile lands around Nairobi were settled by whites. The pattern of extensive settler farms, worked by African labour at marginal wages, was well established by 1920.

European settlement policies in eastern and southern Africa had significant ecological and environmental repercussions. The early colonial policies of defining limits on human settlement, of delineating 'native' from settler land for purposes of political and economic control, led to rapid changes in land use. Land was more intensively occupied than previously, as more people were crowded into limited areas. The results were a greater strain on the land, with fewer options for promoting its regeneration and sustainability. Soil fertility rapidly declined in some areas as fallow periods were reduced and trees were cut more intensively to use available land. Hillsides were cleared and farmed in the search for land. Irrigation and conservation works fell into disrepair and disuse for lack of labour and policies to maintain these systems. Erosion rapidly followed, turning otherwise productive areas into arid and sterile zones which were unable to support people.

In parts of eastern and central Africa, limitations on African settlement allowed tsetse fly to spread into areas where the fly had previously not existed or had been controlled. Tsetse fly carried a disease fatal to cattle and humans and was carried by wild animals. Early in the twentieth century, the disease claimed the lives of tens of thousands of people in Uganda and Tanzania. In the pre-colonial era, African people had controlled wild animal movements and populations. Wildlife preservation (at least for the benefit of whites) became the colonial norm and restrictions were placed on Africans hunting and controlling animals.

Taxation and social disintegration

Colonial governments imposed taxes almost universally on Africans as a means to force people out of their villages into the commercial economy controlled largely by Europeans. As we have seen above, that system was highly successful. Taxation had the added intention of making the administrations self-sufficient, without relying for financial support on the European home governments. Initially the tax could be paid in kind, but in most cases by 1910 the tax had to be paid in cash. In order to meet their tax obligations, rural Africans sold cash crops, grain or their labour.

Resistance to taxation and forced labour was common. Men went into hiding when colonial tax collectors approached their villages. Often, these same officials would burn the houses of defaulters or arrest family members until the men gave themselves up. In other instances, labourers deserted their workplaces or engaged in petty forms of sabotage. In Kenya, a major millenarian religious movement grew out of disaffection with tax and labour demands.[7]

Despite widespread resistance to taxation, in eastern and southern Africa taxation was the major means of pulling men out of their communities to work on settler farms and in the gold, silver and copper mines. In several areas, tax payments initially could be made in kind, such as food crops or livestock. This stimulated crop production as smallholders sought to meet tax demands and serve a growing market created by mining, administrative, construction or infrastructural development. For example, rice — introduced in the nineteenth century by Swahili traders — temporarily flourished in northern Zambia until the colonial government refused to accept the grain as payment for taxes. Near the mining centres of colonial Zimbabwe, peasant producers rapidly adopted new varieties of maize to cater to the active market, although millet remained the staple food of the producers for another three decades because women resisted providing the additional labour required in hand-processing the maize.[8] However, the pattern of legal coercion that emerged in South Africa was emulated in similar forms in other parts of southern and eastern Africa. In order to meet the tax requirements men had to move out of their own local economy and into the European-controlled economy of mining and settler agriculture.

As early as the first decade of the twentieth century men were travelling hundreds of miles to obtain employment in the mines in Zimbabwe, Zambia, South Africa and Zaire. Minimizing African labour costs in order to increase profitability was a compelling factor in the mining industry. The mines often provided rations for their workers as a means to promote a stable workforce, but to save money those rations were given grudgingly and at sub-standard levels throughout the 1920s. Workers' health suffered terribly, in part from accidents, but over-whelmingly from poor food, housing and sanitary conditions on the mines. In 1906, for every 1,000 mine workers in Southern Rhodesia (now Zimbabwe), 66 lost their lives to non-accidental causes. The rate fell to less than 10 non-accident deaths per 1,000 workers only after 1930.[9]

By the early 1920s the mining industry had consolidated and standards for food rations were more firmly in place, but those rations could be supplied only by a select group of producers. African farmers who had supplied food to mines in the early years of operation were often legally excluded from further selling of food to these markets. European settlers, using African labour and land acquired by conquest and confiscation, served the lucrative mining market.

Migrant workers were initially away from their homes for relatively short periods — two to six months — depending upon the type of job obtained. However, the tendency of men to return to their homes in order to help prepare the fields for planting conflicted with settlers' demands for labour. Gradually, both industrial and agricultural capitalism sought to stabilize their labour forces, not always successfully, by demanding longer contracts from their workers. Increasingly, men were away from their homes and local economies for long periods of time. Economic, social and cultural structures in the rural areas necessarily began to change.

The young men go to the mines and elsewhere so we old men and women just grow enough food for our own needs. The young men returned and ate up our food, so now we are hungry.
— Zambian peasant, 1914.

Undermining food production

The process set in motion by colonial taxation and labour migration can be illustrated by village histories from southern Africa. The absence of men from the agricultural production cycle — clearing and preparing the land for planting, assisting with protecting crops from pests and in harvesting and storage — significantly curtailed the output from that cycle. The ability of rural people to meet their domestic food needs was regularly threatened and often required extraordinary efforts to sustain social and production systems under stress. An increasingly heavy burden fell on women to maintain household food production. However, there were limits to their abilities to run all aspects of the farming system: less land was cleared and cultivated; less attention was given to vital farming tasks like weeding; and storage facilities deteriorated. The result was less food in rural areas. Further, women were often expected to contribute labour to the cash crops which were grown by men, but they were excluded from access to the money earned. It was (and remains) common that women with extensive household responsibilities would sell a small amount of produce at harvest time in order to raise cash for household essentials, only to be short of food later in the year. A distinct feature of twentieth-century Africa had its roots in this initial period of declining food production. Less grain was grown and stored, resulting in 'hunger periods' in the weeks and months before new crops became available. Village life slowed down as people struggled to survive. The image of the 'lazy native' had nothing to do with laziness, but a lot to do with undernutrition. Seasonal food shortages did occur in pre-colonial Africa, but were managed through socially acceptable methods such as communal storage and sharing. However, seasonal hunger periods became both longer in duration and structurally determined under the drag of colonialism.[10]

The crops grown also changed. The diversity of crops that were grown narrowed in the twentieth century as less labour was available to engage in the entire agricultural cycle. There were also changes in the major staples available to people. Sorghum and millet were the primary staple grains grown by Africans prior to the twentieth century. These crops continued to be grown, but people began to substitute others that were easier to cultivate. Cassava and maize — long grown on the continent — assumed a larger proportion of cultivated area. Cassava was relatively easy to cultivate and its tubers provided a ready store of food that could remain in the ground until needed. As early as the second decade of the twentieth century, women in Zambia were increasing plantings of cassava as a substitute for major grains. Without the labour of men, often away at work, cassava production became an alternative that could be managed exclusively by women while ensuring a basic food supply. As for maize, it matured earlier than other grains and could be eaten green (on the cob), thus providing food earlier than other, longer maturing grains. Also, maize demands less intensive labour inputs than millet and sorghum, an important consideration for women when male labour was serving the farms and mines of colonialists. Also, some varieties of maize were somewhat easier to prepare into ground flour which was the basis of many African meals. Both cassava and maize, however, were less nutritious (maize not substantially so) than either millet or sorghum.[11]

Smaller areas cultivated, less food grown and consumed, new crops entering the diet and fewer foods available to overcome seasonal shortages and provide diversity — such were the effects of the colonial takeover. Malnutrition, as it is known and seen today, based on structural deprivation among producing households, only emerged in African societies in the early stages of the colonial era. Although food production remained the central concern of rural households, vulnerability to hunger occasioned by slight changes in the economic or natural environment effected millions of people. Variations in household food production could be affected by such factors as out-migration of male workers, sickness at critical times in the production cycle, and rains that arrived too late or were too heavy, flooding fields.

An additional implication of this process was declining health standards. The European presence brought new diseases to Africa: tuberculosis, sand jiggers (a flea that became imbedded in the feet, leading to severe infections) and venereal diseases are prime examples. The movement of people — European traders, military caravans and African migrant labourers — greatly increased the spread and risk of disease. A degree of isolation in pre-colonial societies had allowed communities to develop immunities. Curative and preventative measures had been regularly practised by African societies in the pre-colonial era, including immunization against diseases such as smallpox, but this knowledge confronted an exclusive system that ignored and discredited such abilities.

As population movements broke down the relative isolation of local communities, new diseases and new strains of illnesses entered. Epidemics of smallpox, measles, syphilis, tick-born relapsing fever and other diseases swept the continent. The confiscation of land and the resettlement of people had disastrous results in Uganda, Kenya and Tanzania. Areas that African societies had isolated as a way to contain the impact of tsetse fly — a threat to both cattle and people — were opened to forced settlement. In the early years of the twentieth century, an estimated one third of the population of southern Uganda died of tsetse-induced sleeping sickness. Combined with the effects of undernutrition due to the changes in food production, these diseases created for people 'the unhealthiest period in all African history' between 1890 and 1930.[12] By that latter date, African communities had developed new immunities and new methods of coping. To a far lesser degree, and up until the 1950s, Western forms of medicine offered little advantage to Africans.

Declining living standards and rural vulnerability

A number of historians have identified the first three decades of the colonial era (*c.* 1890–1920) as a particularly hard period for African people. The loss of land and livestock, the displacement of agricultural labour, the harsh imposition of administrative structures, changes in crops, settlement patterns and the intensification of disease, all combined to make rural areas particularly vulnerable to threats to food supplies. Although there was a strong demand for West African agricultural exports, providing people with cash, overall living standards actually declined in the early colonial era. Security against food shortages, previously provided by extensive and integrated agricultural systems and community structures, was threatened by these changes. The coping mechanisms of the past were breaking down and new methods were not easily found.

[The peasants] have suffered greatly ... [due] to our not having realized how great was their want, and for the last few months the old people, the women and the children have literally been starving.
— Colonial officer on the 1908 famine in northern Nigeria.

The famine of 1913–14 in northern Nigeria and Niger illustrates the vulnerability of rural areas. The sale of grain reserves by households and the out-migration of men seeking cash wages in order to pay taxes clearly contributed to the famine. Another factor was the completion of a railway to northern Nigeria in 1912 which stimulated increased peanut production. The railway allowed cheap and ready export of the crop and traders encouraged plantings and sales. There was a ten-fold increase in marketed peanut production between 1912 and 1913. Sales meant cash but definitely at the expense of food production. The immediate cash rewards from peanut sales were lost in the ensuing famine as there was insufficient food for sale in the region. The famine fell particularly hard on the rural poor, the smaller households with fewer resources and assets to manage through hard times. To survive, it was necessary to go into debt to patrons, merchants or better-endowed farmers. Ironically, the escape from debt was through further production of cash crops. As one authority has noted,

> Groundnut [peanut] production doubled every year in the post war [the First World War] years, and famine actually seemed to have intensified and consolidated the very developments that were instrumental in its genesis.[13]

The First World War and intensified change

The era of the First World War intensified these changes in Africa. Men, livestock and crops were requisitioned by French, British and German military commands in the colonies. As never before, men were pulled out of their villages to serve in the European war efforts as soldiers and as carriers of food and materials. The French recruited over 100,000 West Africans to serve on the Western Front in Europe. Over 30,000 Africans were recruited into the King's African Rifles and served the British empire in its war efforts in East Africa, Europe and western Asia. But it was primarily as carriers of foodstuffs, military equipment and other war materials that Africans served the colonial powers. An estimated two million Africans from across the continent saw service in the war, as soldiers or labourers.[14] Military recruitment was widely unpopular and placed many chiefs in the difficult position of defying either local opinion and opposition or the colonial authorities. There were numerous instances of chiefs protesting to the government about recruitment and cases of open opposition.[15] However, many African local authorities did comply with the recruitment effort — often because they were beholden to the colonial government for their positions. Nevertheless, they were not popular. For example, there is the fascinating case of 'lion-men' in southeastern Zaire, guerilla fighters whose earlier resistance to the establishment of colonial rule and collaboration was revived to punish people who profited from their alliance with the colonial authorities during the war.[16]

In many areas of central and east Africa wildlife was greatly reduced by European hunters paid to supply food to the military forces. Further, many communities were forced to provide food well beyond their internal needs, resulting in extensive malnutrition and related illnesses, especially among women and children. There were numerous reports from across the continent of the inability of the local populations to meet their own food needs in addition to providing the food demanded by the war authorities. In such circumstances, external demands usually prevailed. The 1914–15 famine in the Sahel was occasioned, in part, by extensive French requisition of food, cattle and camels. Widespread starvation occurred in east central Africa in 1915–17 as people went without food which had been required by British and German forces. In Kenya, inflation resulted in a decline in real incomes of African people of nearly 40 per cent between 1914 and 1916, despite increased employment and agricultural sales. Resistance to recruitment for war service found an outlet in Africans taking employment on the rapidly growing estates of white settlers. The result, in Kenya, was an undermining of what generally had been sustainable and flexible agricultural systems. The withdrawal of male labour and the heavy demand for foodstuffs placed extra burdens on women and children. Two things happened: food consumption declined among most rural people as crops were sold beyond internal needs; and care of crops and crop land deteriorated in the absence of adequate labour. For example, the on-farm storage of grain to guard against seasonal shortfalls was abandoned by many households and weeding of crops became sporadic in the absence of sufficient labour. Further, inequalities between groups of people became more pronounced. Farmers with larger areas, who were able to retain sufficient labour for production, were able to take advantage of the increased demand for agricultural products, but they were a small minority of rural inhabitants. Most people became worse off during the war.[17]

The excessive demands for food combined with an intensified period of disease produced prolonged famine from 1918 to 1926 in modern-day Chad.[18] One authority estimates that a quarter of a million African people lost their lives during the war years, but this figure does not seem to take into account the severe local hardships experienced by communities in the Sahel, the Cameroon, Chad and central Africa.[19] By 1918–19 in Africa, as in Europe, the population was especially weakened and susceptible to disease. The pandemic of Spanish influenza which swept the world, taking an estimated 20 million lives, can be blamed on the vulnerable status of people whose resources had supported a massive war. The death rate from the disease in Africa cannot be ascertained — neither colonial nor African records account for the figures. Data from local areas suggest very widespread incidence of the disease — literally tens of millions of people suffered — and mortality rates ranging from 2 to 60 per cent. A recent estimate places the number who died in Africa at between one and two million people.[20] As with other disasters, the poor, including those made poor by the impact of the war, suffered inordinately.

The war also occasioned significant political change, primarily in attitudes, but also in the rise and consolidation of African political organizations that emerged in the wake of the war. The inequities and extreme suffering under the colonial systems had been intensified by the practices used during the war. Rectification of those inequities was foremost in people's minds. Also, there were the expectations raised by rewards of land and money offered as an inducement to Africans to join the military effort. In the post-war era, however, few of these promises were kept and the inequities were institutionalized. Colonial governments increased the tax rate. In east and southern

Africa, the efficiency of the military recruitment systems was emulated to channel men into work in the settler and mining economies. Governments, settler farmers and businesses conspired to hold down wages. These conditions, as well as the harshness of the war experience, further undermined European claims for the civilizing mission of colonialism. For many African participants, the war experience was perceived as an equalizer in human relations — between Europeans and Africans and between Africans of varying social classes. Expectations of equality in political relations and wealth were strong and were channelled into African political organizations that sought greater opportunities and an end to discrimination. These organizations were made up primarily of educated and employed Africans, and represented their interests, with little reference to the conditions of rural and poor people.

At the end of the First World War, Africa began to emerge from a period in which people experienced some of the harshest conditions and most rapid changes imaginable. The early colonial period, roughly 1890—1920, brought new economic opportunities for some people, but for most others it occasioned the break-up of integral economic and social systems, and the introduction of difficult and highly exploitative work, searches for new ways to live — or survive — from the land and new and disastrous diseases.

The threat to their survival was resisted in many ways, from passive resistance to labour recruitment, to desertion from onerous employment, to sabotage and open warfare. Massive revolts against the colonial systems occurred in Namibia, Zimbabwe, Tanzania, Somalia and many other countries as people sought to recover land lost to white settlers or to regain control over agricultural production from a system which had deprived them of basic foodstuffs. The revolts were brutally crushed, although some of the worse excesses of colonial extraction were modified in the aftermath. However, the concessions to African needs were small as the colonial concern was to assure a steady movement of agricultural and mineral products out of Africa to the European markets. European concern over African food security, health, social structures and well-being was usually confined to occasional statements by missionaries or isolated colonial officers. However, neither the metropolitan powers nor the local colonial administrations showed such concern unless conditions threatened to disrupt production. In short, Africa and the people there were bound tightly to powers and structures which ignored their interests and needs.

Notes

1. Michael Watts, *Silent Violence: Food, Famine and Peasantry in Northern Nigeria* (University of California Press, Berkeley, 1983).
2. Jean-Luc Vellut, 'Rural poverty in western Shaba, *c.* 1890–1930', in Robin Palmer and Neil Parsons (eds), *The Roots of Rural Poverty in Central and Southern Africa* (University of California Press, Berkeley, 1977), p. 302.
3. E. D. Morel, *Red Rubber: The Story of the Rubber Slave Trade which Flourished on the Congo for Twenty Years, 1890–1910*, revised edition (B. W. Huebsch, Inc., New York, 1919), p. 52. First edition: 1906.
4. Basil Davidson, *Africa in History*, revised edition (Collier Books, New York, 1974), p. 249.
5. Gareth Austin, 'The emergence of capitalist relations in South Asante cocoa-farming, *c.* 1916–33', *Journal of African History*, Vol. 28 (1987), pp. 259–279.
6. Martin Legassick, 'Gold, agriculture, and secondary industry in South Africa, 1885–1970: from periphery to sub-metropole as a forced labour system', in Palmer and Parsons (eds), *op. cit.*, pp. 175–187.
7. Robin Cohen, 'Resistance and hidden forms of consciousness among African workers', *Review of African Political Economy*, No. 19 (1981), pp. 8–22.
8. Elizabeth Schmidt, 'Farmers, hunters, and gold-washers', *African Economic History*, Vol. 17 (1988), pp. 45–60.
9. Charles van Onselen, *Chibaro: African Mine Labour in Southern Rhodesia, 1900–1933* (Pluto Press, London, 1976).
10. Bill Rau, 'The underdevelopment of Zambia's northern province', paper prepared for the Zambia Geographical Association, 1977; Steven Feierman, 'Struggles for control: the social roots of health and healing in modern Africa', *African Studies Review*, Vol. 28, Nos. 2/3 (June/September 1985), pp. 100–101.
11. Jelle van den Berg, 'A peasant form of production: wage-dependent agriculture in southern Mozambique', *Canadian Journal of African Studies*, Vol. 21, No. 3 (1987), pp. 379–380.
12. Gerald W. Hartwig and K. David Patterson (eds.), *Disease in African History* (Duke University Press, Durham, NC, 1978), p. 4; John Ford, *The Role of Trypanosomiases in African Ecology: A Study of the Tsetse Fly Problem* (Clarendon Press, Oxford, 1971).
13. Watts, *op. cit*, p. 297.
14. The most comprehensive study of the impact of the First World War on Africans is Melvin E. Page (ed.), *Africa and the First World War* (Macmillan, London, 1987).
15. David Killingray, 'Military and labour policies in the Gold Coast during the First World War', in Page, *op. cit.*, pp. 152–170.
16. Allen F. Roberts, ' "Insidious conquests": wartime politics along the south-western shore of Lake Tanganyika', in Page, *op. cit.*, p. 198.
17. John Overton, 'War and economic underdevelopment? State exploitation and African response in Kenya 1914–1918', *International Journal of African Historical Studies*, Vol. 22, No. 2 (1989), pp. 201–221.
18. Mario Joaquim Azevedo, 'Epidemic disease among the Sara of southern

Chad, 1890–1940,' in Hartwig and Patterson (eds), *op. cit.*, pp. 118–152.
19. Page (ed.), *op. cit.*, p. 14.
20. *Ibid.*, p. 16.

5 The Later Colonial Period: 1920–1960

Africa became thoroughly integrated into the world economy during the colonial era. Yet during that period leaders within the colonial states gradually acquired the means to assert an independent political stance. Those political tools were developed in the context of widespread and popular disgust at the inequities occurring under colonial rule and at European hypocrisy about the civilizing effects of colonial rule amid the active exploitation of African labour and resources for European benefit. The harsh means by which Europeans expected Africans to survive belied European claims of developing Africa. The exploitative nature of racism, which was experienced by Africans at all levels in their daily lives, contradicted the Christian message of universal equality. The disparities between European affluence and African misery were seen by Africans as interrelated. Africans recognized that their own poverty and vulnerability were due to the special conditions Europeans had created. The very nature of colonialism provided Africans with the increased consciousness and impetus to seek to overthrow it. However, while the later colonial period was one of major African political initiatives to gain advantages from the colonial system and then to replace that system, it was also a time when the economic aspects of colonial dependence deepened and strengthened. These two interrelated threads will be followed in this chapter.

Political consciousness and nationalism

The colonial era altered the political, economic and social relations among Africans but it did not totally rend the basic fabric of community relationships that have been a basis for continued survival. Local (so-called 'traditional') authorities often retained significant influence in the lives of their people. Even when the colonial governments incorporated these local authorities into the administrative system or replaced them with puppets, local politics retained significant influence from below. These local authorities often reflected the opinions of their people in voicing discontent with colonial taxation, labour and land practices and administrative decrees that interfered with their lives and limited their options for political and economic change. Throughout the colonial period there was a steady disavowal by rural peoples of colonialism's impact. Although eventually most African states gained independence without a major war, the severity of fighting in Algeria, Kenya, Mozambique, Angola, Guinea Bissau and Zimbabwe gives a clear statement of the commitment of rural peoples to throwing off the pressures of colonial exploitation.

You inhabitants of the palace you had better reduce your swaggering. . . . You cannot show off on an empty stomach. The children went to get relief but there was none. The elders were thinking that it was due to the children's lack of strength. But the whole issue is not concerned with strength.
— Proverb from famine in Nigeria, 1942.

While rural discontent was strong and continuous, the rural voice was rarely heard in the centres of power. Food insecurity, malnutrition and ill-health, rural areas drained of agricultural and human resources — these were not the issues that determined the course of African nationalism, although rural people hoped that independence would alleviate their problems.

African involvement in the Second World War helped prepare the way for Africa's thrust toward independence. Over 100,000 African troops were sent to France following the fall of the Vichy regime in 1943. But more than military recruitment, both Vichy and Free France looked to their African colonies to supply French industries with agricultural commodities. Although marketed production of peanuts and cotton in the French colonies declined in the war years because marketing conditions were disrupted, French administrators in the colonies were particularly harsh in enforcing the production that did occur. The British recruited about 200,000 African soldiers, many to serve in Burma. In order to ensure a continued supply of agricultural products, the British set up agricultural marketing boards which after the Second World War became the standard (as they remain today) for setting prices and controlling markets. All of these efforts intensified pressure on rural Africans, contributing to their growing discontent. Also, many of the Africans who had acquired a Western form of education saw through the Allies' appeals for loyalty and promises of post-war self-determination. The hypocrisy and racism of the colonial powers in speaking about independence, but refusing to act, gave a significant impetus to the disillusionment of Africans and led them into new forms of political action.[1]

The nationalist movement originated in the inter-war years with the articulation of grievances by Africans who, as a group, had been originally incorporated into the colonial system. They were civil servants and teachers, overwhelmingly men, who sought greater benefits from the colonial state. Pragmatic colonialism sought to maintain itself by co-opting Africans, including many of these men, while the colonial ideal urged gradual education for Africans in order to introduce them to the lower and middle levels of administration in anticipation of eventual independence in the twenty-first century.

But the European timetable for an 'orderly' transfer of government was speeded up by the Second World War. In its aftermath, African leaders pushed for a more rapid change in government; they learned and applied the language and political methods of the colonizers in order to struggle for independence. These nationalist leaders were sincere and dedicated, but not always conscious of, or willing to deal with, the larger economic system of which their countries were a part. It is not surprising, then, that the independence struggle and negotiations often involved elements of constitutional reform, power-sharing in 'representative' councils or assemblies, elections and the use of other political structures that originated in the imperial homelands. For the most part, the nationalist leaders were willing to work with the colonial powers to install new African-led governments which were then modelled on the institutional forms of London or Paris. By the early 1950s there was an open or an assumed understanding on each side that independence would be attained within recognizable political structures which, not incidentally, had long served the interests of the colonial powers themselves. In 1957 Ghana became independent; in the next decade much of Africa followed.

We need schools in Africa, but schools in which we show the native the way to the dignity of man and the glory of the [Portuguese] nation which protects him. We want to teach the natives to write, to read, and to count, but not to make them learned men.
— Cardinal Cerejeira of Lisbon, in his Christmas message of 1960.

Social divisions in the colonial state

The African political elite that evolved through the nationalist movement was one group in an African social spectrum defined by colonialism's economic activities.

Labour migration to industrial and agribusiness centres appears to have had a dual effect on stratification of working people. On the one hand, many migrants earned only enough money to pay their taxes and meet limited material needs. Their condition in rural communities may even have declined as farm land and storage facilities were neglected. Many migrants died or were severely injured or became ill while in waged employment. In southern Africa tuberculosis was evident among industrial workers early in the twentieth century, but from the late 1930s the disease spread rapidly among migrant workers who also carried it back into their rural homes. The families of migrant labourers suffered equally; then, as now, women and children have made up the majority of rural poor. On the other hand, some migrant labourers were able to acquire some capital and to invest in land or small businesses, becoming larger peasant farmers or petty traders. This group of larger-scale farmers was later enhanced by a handful of beneficiaries of token rural development projects undertaken by the colonial governments. This small stratum of rural elite was joined by rural-based civil servants — such as teachers, clerks and agricultural inspectors — who lived in rural areas but did not identify with the majority of rural people.

The migrant labour system created one other group: industrially based urban workers. From the late 1930s and early 1940s, mining companies sought to stabilize their work forces. Living conditions at or near work sites were improved and, in some cases, families were provided for. Governments adopted a similar policy. As a result towns began to assume a new character from that of earlier years. The colonial towns were bureaucratic centres, for organizing and regulating the affairs of the state. The towns also served as commercial centres for the generally small white population. Petty trade was often carried on by another group — Asians in eastern and southern Africa, Middle Easterners in western Africa. Africans generally were excluded from urban settlement in the period before the 1930s, unless employed and with the expectation that they were only temporary inhabitants. The move in the 1940s toward stabilizing workers meant that by the next decade most colonies had a distinct African urban population tied to government or business or industry, accustomed to urban conveniences and material goods and a regular salary. In the same period, African workers were organizing to improve their wages and working conditions. The struggle to unionize and push for greater well-being contributed to the growth of urban centres. The core of an urban working class was founded, sometimes collaborating with its political and bureaucratic counterparts, but occasionally in conflict with those segments of the national elite.

The urban dwellers were heavily exposed to the most conspicuous operations of capitalist enterprise — trade, small-scale businesses and manufacturing, mining and government. They acquired and developed their craft, business and educational skills while employed. But

Africans were largely excluded from real control in these activities; management was closed to them and upward mobility was severely restricted. From the African perspective, these enterprises were hierarchical and exclusive. Capitalism's lessons of individual initiative and rewards had little relationship to the way most Africans encountered it. Yet the promise of those rewards was not lost from view by a minority who eventually came to exercise political and economic power in the urban, and national, setting.

Only an insignificant minority have any political awareness. . . . It must be realized now and for all time that this articulate minority are destined to rule the country.
— Chief Obafemi Awolowo of Nigeria, 1947.

The rural population was both absolutely and relatively poor in comparison to those who had steady salaries in urban areas. Poverty was especially acute among women left behind or abandoned by male migrant workers. They, their children and the elderly were especially vulnerable to food shortages, being on the margin of food production in the first place. The rural poor were like those who were found by one researcher in the 1940s to exist during the 'hunger season' on one major meal every other day.[2] They were often unable to cultivate a large enough area to feed themselves and their immediate dependants. They often worked for larger and wealthier farmers for food or cash, at the expense of production on their own fields.

Agricultural production by the rural poor remained especially susceptible to external disruption. In southern Tanzania, it appears that overall yields of major subsistence crops declined in the 1930s and 1940s as women, children and the elderly struggled to grow their food. In this area, where neither drought nor famine were experienced, the British imposed regulations for cultivation of cassava as a precaution against hunger. Yet the result was the exact opposite, for cassava was not as nutritious as the grains that people had grown and resulted in a less diverse and flexible agrarian system than that which in the past had sustained people.[3] In areas where crops were grown for the market, malnutrition also was extensive. The land and labour required to produce the cash crops drew time away from food crops. The cash derived from the sale of crops was either too little to compensate for lost food production or was not shared by men (who often controlled the use of household labour for cash crop production and the disposal of income from sales of those crops). Women especially assumed an increased burden. The multiple tasks of food and cash crop production and processing, marketing, household maintenance and child care placed an impossible burden on rural women. The prevalence of nutritional disorders and increases in susceptibility to diseases due to lowered nutritional well-being were a common feature of this period — and subsequently.

It has been suggested by some scholars that there were dual African economies: a modern, urban economy of industry and services and a stagnant, poor rural economy of limited agricultural production. It is argued that these two economies existed independently of one another. One goal of development, then, was to upgrade the rural economy to 'modern' standards.[4]

Improving our country for us, are you? Railways, roads, mines, indeed! For whose benefit are they? You can take them all away so far as I'm concerned. What are you leaving us with? A sucked orange!
— Zambian chief, late 1930s.

The idea of dual economies does not justly characterize either colonial or independent Africa. Just as the centuries of the slave trade were the beginning of the extractive era and Africa's integration into the global economy, so the colonial period offered a new phase in that process. The pressures of linking rural and urban Africa, and these areas to the imperial economy, altered and probably intensified throughout the six decades of colonial rule in the twentieth century. There is no doubt that rural areas are poor, with limited agricultural production entering the market system. However, there are not separate and independent rural and urban economies. Urban Africa, with its wage-earning elite, exists because of the poverty of rural Africa. Rural areas, as we have seen, have supplied industry, mining, settler plantations and the civil service with cheap labour, allowing those sectors to expand and grow. Rural areas have supplied the urban populations with food deliberately priced low by government marketing policies. And rural areas have produced the cash crops — often at the expense of food crops — which governments have taxed or purchased at low prices, later to be exported for higher prices and for the benefit of foreign businesses and Western consumers. If rural areas in Africa are poor, stripped of their resources and producing cash crops for minimal returns, it is because of deliberate policies to withdraw that wealth in order to enrich other sectors of the economy. It was particularly in the latter part of the colonial era that those policies were implemented. And they were largely adopted by the governments of independent Africa.

South Africa

We have seen that in 1913 legislation enacted in South Africa denied Africans ownership of 87 per cent of the land of the country. The law legitimized a long-standing process of land alienation, impoverishment and formal discrimination against Africans (and people of mixed race and Asian immigrants brought in as labourers in the late 1800s) by the white minority of the country. The remaining land was not conducive to even subsistence food production and overall agricultural production may have declined in the 1930s and 1940s. Africans on the land were thus dependent upon cash income to purchase food produced by the white farming population. Not surprisingly, chronic malnutrition   and susceptibility to nutritionally related diseases became common.[5]

Income was largely derived from work within the white dominated economy, on farms of white settlers or the mining sector. Wages in the cash ecomony were low but employers rationalized that workers' needs were low and partially met by family members who remained in the rural reserves, generally forbidden to join men in the work areas. Wages for farm workers were (and are) notoriously low. A survey in the late 1930s found that the annual income of farm workers was about £20; the wages of mine workers were about twice that amount. Not only did the low wages keep people on the edge of survival, but the chance of unemployment and destitution was ever-present. The cyclical nature of the capitalist economy of South Africa resulted in periodic recessions. The early 1930s saw thousands of Africans out of work, and vast suffering. One writer spoke of how the 'whole Native population simply sagged down to a still lower sub-economic level'.[6]

Despite the severe material deprivation experienced by a large portion of the South African population, common forms of support and sharing existed. The culture (known as *marabi*) of the urban shantytowns encouraged a sense of unity, a collective survival spirit. Sharing of food and cash allowed people temporarily adrift to survive. Informal sector jobs, such as self-employment in sales of consumer goods, small-scale manufacturing and repair, beer brewing by women, frequently enabled people to survive transitions between more formal employment. In fact, the informal economy expanded rapidly in the 1930s: its potential as a basis for economic strength and growth for Africans, however, was severely limited by the South African government and business community. Similarly, the perpetual poverty of most rural and urban people placed considerable strains on systems of sharing. For example, during a particularly difficult time in 1980 people in one rural reserve shared only under duress, their own stocks being in critically short supply.[7] It is significant for this study, however, to stress the adaptability of African social systems, the ability of people to redefine social relations to meet new circumstances, and the existence of socio-economic differences within societies.

Limited economic options

A major factor in both rural and urban popular discontent with the colonial systems was the active discrimination practised against African people. Wage levels for urban workers were set low, numerous restrictions were placed on African agricultural production and educational opportunities were usually limited to basic literacy or vocational courses designed to serve the European economy. A small segment of the educational system catered to creating an African middle class, including running classes for the wives of educated African men on 'proper' European ways to set dinner tables, to serve tea and to sew Western-style clothing.

At a more structural level, policy decisions were made in this later part of the colonial era which have continued to influence African rural and national development. A case study from the Belgian Congo (now Zaire) illustrates the process and consequences of channelling African agriculture to better serve colonial interests and thereby limiting African economic choices over both the short and long term.[8]

The Katanga (now Shaba) region of the southern Belgian Congo was valued for its natural rubber and extensive copper deposits. By the end of the First World War, the latter had become more important to Belgian industrialists and assuring both a stable African labour force and adequate food at low prices to feed those workers was a key consideration in colonial policy. The expansion of the mining industry in the 1920s put pressure on local food supplies and allowed prices paid to rural producers to increase. The colonial government experimented with establishing a European settler population in Katanga — as had occurred in the colonies of southern Africa — but this gave way in the early 1920s to a policy of compulsory cultivation by African producers to provide much of the food for the mining industry. Events in the 1930s, at the time of the Great Depression, further fixed the structure of the rural economy. Two major decisions were crucial. The first was that the colonial state should manage the economy, thereby rescuing the capitalist investments from collapse and losses. The second was that the state would organize food production within the perceived structure of rural villages. Food production and sales quotas were set for sub-regions within Katanga, these quotas based on assessments of African household size, nutritional needs and labour inputs into agricultural production. 'Just' prices were fixed for sales of produce and in 1933 a governmental decree reinforced the demand for compulsory cultivation of basic food and cash crops. Taken together, the price and production decisions assured the urban markets of low-priced, regular supplies of foodstuffs.

The impact on rural society was significant and long-lasting. Not only were men expected to provide the labour for the Katanga mines, but from the early 1930s rural households were expected to provide the food for those workers. Agricultural incomes were set by prices determined by administrative decisions and industrial traders to favour the mining sector, thereby preventing any form of capital accumulation and growth among rural producers and undercutting the potential that existed in the mid-1920s for rising rural incomes, living standards and demand for manufactured goods. 'The choice of unequal development, to the detriment of African agriculture, became entrenched during the Depression and was in fact maintained through the rest of the colonial period.'[9] Indeed, the model of rural exploitation to serve industrial and capitalist interests is one widely inherited by African states at independence and a model which continues to command wide influence in African economies.

There were efforts to move beyond the changes induced by colonial policies. An example from Mozambique illustrates the analytical and innovative nature of rural people, but also demonstrates the severe constraints imposed by colonialism.[10]

In 1926 the Portuguese colonial authorities began a system of forced cotton production in northern Mozambique. Perhaps three-quarters of a million adults and children were involved by the mid-1940s. Chiefs and state agents vigorously enforced production, requiring ever longer periods of time in cotton production. Peasants resisted in subtle ways by withholding their labour at key times and cultivating smaller areas than ordered, but living standards and food consumption did suffer.

Borrowing from the independent peasant cooperatives in neighbouring Tanganyika (now mainland Tanzania), where many Mozambican peasants worked, the Mozambique African Voluntary Cotton Society was formed in 1957. Within two years, the cooperative had grown to about 3,000 members. Its goals were several. Most overtly, it provided members with a structure to balance food and cotton production, to market their crop without the shortchanging by buyers that normally occurred, and to increase prices for cotton through collective bargaining. Also, the cooperative became a base for people to voice anti-colonial sentiment and to organize to protest colonial rule. Fairly quickly, the framework of the cooperative merged with the strong anti-colonial feelings among people. In 1961 a number of cooperative members joined a non-violent demonstration, demanding national independence. The Portuguese responded by ordering police and army troops to open fire; 600 people were killed and in the aftermath the cotton cooperative was banned.

The Mozambique African Voluntary Cotton Society was not without problems, notably the concentration of wealth in the hands of several larger farmers and society officials. However, as a movement for greater African economic and political autonomy, the Society proved an important stage in organizing a popular grassroots movement that helped stimulate the independence struggle and influenced the ideology of the nationalist movement by rejecting rural exploitation.

Expanding agricultural exports

As African nationalists were organizing politically to challenge the colonial system, that system was expanding its economic role in Africa. The exceptionally harsh labour conditions of the earlier colonial era often gave way to a more systematic and regularized process of utilizing African labour to extract wealth. As European industries and economies recovered from the impact of the Second World War, the export of commodities from the colonies increased. Peanut production in Senegal increased by about 50 per cent in the decade after the end of the war. In Niger peanut sales were seven times greater in the 1953–54 season than in 1944–45.[11] The period was also one during which the colonial powers adopted a more acceptable rhetoric and spoke of Africa's development. Such 'development,' it turned out, strengthened the economic dependence of Africa on Europe. Development for Africa meant increased cash crop production, either for export or for use by urban populations, and manufacturing dependent upon Western techniques and materials.

Two mechanisms existed for stimulating export crop production: control of marketing by private trading companies or state marketing boards; and an emphasis on improving the productivity of cash cropping.

The European Merchant is my shepherd,
And I am in want;
He maketh me to lie down in cocoa farms;
He leadeth me beside the waters of great need.
— Ghanaian soldier, 1940s.

The influence of state marketing agencies and private companies on agricultural production has been significant. Firms like Unilever and Brooke Bond not only purchased crops from small-scale farmers, but also controlled the export trade of those crops and any local processing involved; increasingly, moreover, they have moved into direct production by establishing company growers, supplying crop inputs and setting growing standards. In the colonial period, major crops associated with these multinational companies were peanuts and palm oil, tobacco, tea and cotton. By controlling marketing at both ends of the production phase, the companies were able to ensure that output met their needs. In Nigeria, the United Africa Company, a subsidiary of Unilever, accounted for over 40 per cent of the import-export trade of the colony. In addition, UAC and other British and European firms controlled the banks, insurance business and shipping agencies that were involved in financing and transporting commodities. There was little if any room for the expansion of African entrepreneurs in these major industries and the well-being of farmers was dependent upon the marketing criteria and prices set by the companies, often in collusion with governments. In some instances, the companies paid a small subsidy to growers to assure a steady flow of commodities. More often, farmers and plantation labourers were paid low prices. Their debts mounted as they were obliged to accept controlled prices while also paying for productivity enhancements introduced by the company, such as mechanical cultivation, pesticides and fertilizers. Once involved in the cash economy created by export production, most farmers remained bound to the system. Strengthening the system were the 'development' projects conceived and implemented by governments. Governments provided or subsidized many of these production schemes by developing roads and dams, and providing agricultural supervisors to the export sector.[12]

In other instances, government controlled the marketing process. Like the multinational companies, these state agencies were linked to production from the planning stage through to the sale of the crops. Unlike the companies which controlled production for corporate profit, the state marketing agencies extracted a surplus from the crop sales in order to invest elsewhere or to cover the running expenses of the colonial state. In other words, peasants were being taxed (with low producer prices) in order to subsidize other public activities. In itself, such taxation may appear appropriate; investable capital has to be generated from some source. But low producer prices were an inequitable form of taxation. Further, low producer prices resulted in little interest or ability on the part of farmers to expand production and prevented peasants themselves from accumulating capital for their own well-being and expansion. The operation of colonial agricultural price and marketing policies was designed to ensure that production served European interests and that any 'development' would be determined by the colonial authorities.

The colonial system showed little interest in improving the productive efficiency of the vast majority of peasants. Across Africa, when independence arrived, most rural producers were using implements for cultivation very similar to those of their ancestors — only now the hoe and axe were imported from Europe rather than being locally produced. Research was overwhelmingly designed to improve the productivity of cash crops; basic food crops and the social and technological systems which supported them were not accorded research status. As far as women were concerned, the colonial authorities were generally indifferent to their conditions, and ignored the major changes occurring in women's roles. During this period, control of land became more concentrated and formalized in the hands of men and the limited agricultural projects were designed almost exclusively for and by men. Women were ignored, except that they were expected to respond passively to the male household head's decisions. Yet women, in fact, assumed increased responsibilities for food production in the colonial period as many men left their homes to work on settler farms or the mines. One researcher refers to the contradiction 'between women as producer-nonowners and men as nonproducer-owners' of farm land.[13] As cash crops gained in importance, the disparity between women's work and control over resources became wider. Women experienced both the loss of some of the land they had controlled for food crop production, with implications for both household food security and the income women could gain from the sale of crops, and additional demands on their time to work on their husbands' lands.

The second feature of crop production was the emphasis given to cash crops by companies, government and, from the late 1940s, development agencies. A steady flow of African raw materials to finishing plants in Europe was not only the objective of colonialism, it became the ideal model of development — as defined by Western 'experts'. In the aftermath of the Second World War, new technologies were developed to expand agricultural production — tractors, chemical fertilizers and pesticides, for example. The development model of the period emphasized production for export. The means to achieve increased exports was to expand crop production and, not incidentally, the sales of chemical and technical inputs being manufactured in the industrial countries. In Africa, the targets for this application of industrial technology to agriculture were white settlers and a handful of 'progressive' or 'advanced' African farmers. By helping to create a class of modern African farmers, the colonial development policy hoped to achieve two goals, one political and the other economic. First, the integration of a rural capitalist class into the national economy was expected to defuse the anti-colonial and national activism that pervaded rural Africa in the latter 1940s and the 1950s. On this count, colonial-style elite development quickly failed. The strength of the nationalist movements rapidly overrode the stalling tactics of the imperial countries. Second, it was widely assumed that the example of these 'progressive' farmers would sufficiently impress other, resource-poor farmers so that they too would gradually take up the new techniques, thereby contributing to both rural and national economic growth. In fact, the focus on providing benefits to select farmers widened the disparities between richer and poorer rural people. A variety of production schemes using the new technologies sprang up in the late colonial years. In some, the peasants were little more than labourers, conforming to externally planned directions. Those farmers who were able to conform and take advantage of the schemes, often were able to further enhance their positions by hiring labour or acquiring more land. Many peasants, however, went deeply into debt through participation in such projects, thereby increasing the degree of rural differentiation.[14]

The new technologies were designed to circumvent the constraints on production imposed by rural poverty and inequalities; they were not designed to alleviate that poverty. The technological approach to agricultural production was sometimes carried out through marketing cooperatives and/or state farms, an approach often adopted by independent African governments as well. Few of these schemes succeeded — whether they originated in the colonial or post-colonial era. They failed for a variety of reasons: lack of support from the central government or from a coordinating bureaucracy; over-emphasis on technical solutions which were as inappropriate to local social situations and environments as they were widely popular among funding sources; overall low producer prices; peasant scepticism about the 'benefits' to be gained from centrally established production units. Some of the colonial projects were colossal failures: $100 million was lost in a peanut scheme in Tanzania, for example. Yet two patterns were apparent in these production schemes. One was that they ignored the social and physical conditions of Africa and, thus, were very prone to failure. And that failure was inevitably at the expense of overall rural improvement and, eventually national food self-sufficiency. Second, the pattern was set of linking technologies developed largely in Europe with cash crop production in Africa, to be applied by both better-off smallholders and large farms. Despite repeated failures and tremendous capital and human costs, the pattern largely remains in place today.

... [W]hilst we cannot afford to neglect the subsistence cultivator we must place much greater emphasis on cash crops, thus avoiding the dispersal of effort which a programme for the improvement of subsistence agriculture always entails. Since the internal market is limited in the case of many [agricultural] commodities we must pay special attention to those which have an export value.
— Rural development report by the colonial government of Zambia, 1960.

The result of these policies for most rural people was further impoverishment and food insecurity. Increasing emphasis and resources were placed on cash crop production at the expense of securing a firm food production base with technologies and research that reflected peoples' needs and experiences and aimed at improving rural nutrition. It was widely assumed by colonial authorities that people in rural areas provided sufficiently for their own food needs. However, the few nutrition studies conducted in colonial Africa repeatedly pointed to the precarious nutritional status of rural peoples — undernutrition in terms of inadequate calorie consumption and specific vitamin deficiencies was endemic to the lives of the rural poor.[15]

The relationship between colonial agricultural policies and increasing malnutrition among rural women and children is insufficiently studied. However, as we have argued in the previous chapter and according to other research relating to the colonial era as a whole:

> much of sub-Saharan Africa crop regimes have changed over the past century so as to intensify seasonal food shortages, and also to intensify seasonal variations in the demands on women's work time. This led in turn to higher seasonal peaks of both malnutrition and death among infants and children.[16]

Feierman argues that during periods of peak labour demand on farms, women have less time for caring for their children. Their time and energy is already thinly stretched. The earlier part of the rainy season is also a time of general food shortages, so that food is scarce for both women and children, and malnutrition rates rise.[17]

The norms of exploitation from the early colonial era and of structural inequalities and hunger in the post-colonial period were firmly linked by the 'development' policies in the two or three decades after the Second World War. Food production became secondary to cash crop production, and more and more land was opened up to cash crops as colonial development activities increased in the 1940s and 1950s. In Mali, for example, the French had been gradually expanding irrigated cash crop production along the Niger River since 1919. By the end of the Second World War 20,000 people had been settled on about 55,000 acres in order to grow cotton and rice. Expansion proceeded rapidly after the war. The area under irrigated production exceeded 124,000 acres by 1964, with nearly 33,000 settlers. Between 1948 and 1960 rice and cotton output increased by about 300 per cent. Despite these trends, or perhaps because of them, the scheme demonstrated repeated problems: incompatibility between the stipulated production methods and required labour inputs of the two crops; frequent irrigation breakdowns which stranded farmers; inappropriate technical approaches demanded of farmers; and shortage of labour for integrated production. Thus, the scheme did not contribute to the collective well-being of its settlers; neither were they able to move out of the scheme because of financial dependence.[18]

Similiarly, in the Machakos district of Kenya, cultivation of coffee was opened to Africans in the early 1950s. Production steadily climbed, reaching a value ten times greater in 1962 than it had been with the first harvest in 1957. While coffee production provided financial benefit to some African producers and integrated those households into the cash crop economy, the vast majority of farmers in Machakos lacked the land and other resources to use the incentive of increased crop income to improve their local conditions or further expand production. Rather, what was occurring in the area was a rapid expansion of population and demand for land. In-migration by people from surrounding areas who had lost land to white settlers, or as a result of new colonial policies to formalize land tenure/ownership, placed extreme pressure on existing land. Small plots became the norm, and tree cover was cleared for land use and fuel. Soil exhaustion and erosion followed rapidly. Information on the nutritional impact on households of the colonial emphasis on cash crops and individual land tenure is not available. But by the mid-1970s, ten years after Kenyan independence and an intensification of many of the colonial policies, over one third of Machakos children between one and four years old were chronically malnourished. There was little difference between children of families heavily engaged in cash crop production and those who were only marginally involved in market sales. The implication is that, despite rhetoric to the contrary, entry into the market economy through substantial agricultural sales is no guarantee of improved nutrition for most rural households. As was the case in colonial Katanga (see above), the structure of the rural economy worked against the well-being of people.[19]

The expansion of crops occurred at the expense of maintaining a sound ecological balance — forests were destroyed to make way for more farm land and fragile soils were spoiled by monocropping. In West Africa, agriculturalists began to move into areas long used by pastoralists, depriving the latter of grazing land and forcing them into more marginal areas. This was the case in the irrigated cash crop areas of Mali, noted above, but as climatic conditions were relatively mild during this period the negative ecological impact of marginalized livestock and crop production was not immediately evident. Although the money from crop sales provided some people with material goods, the economy of cash cropping was not integrated into rural development programmes that served the needs of all rural people. Instead, rural areas continued to provide crops and people to meet external demands — either from overseas or increasingly from the urban areas of Africa itself. The promotion of western forms of technology for production aggravated ecological imbalances and rural stratification. Further, the expansion of peanut and cotton production in parts of West Africa relied on migrant labour from other areas, continuing the depletion of labour in some areas and contributing to growing inequalities between groups of people. Throughout this period leading up to independence, the official assumption of colonial governments was that rural people would take care of themselves — an assumption based on wishful thinking and wilful neglect, but little empirical evidence.

The commercialization of rural areas — by introducing cash crops and creating needs (such as for taxes and consumer goods) that could only be met with cash — made food self-sufficiency more difficult. Most rural households preferred — and still prefer — to meet most of their basic food needs from household production rather than relying on the market. However, that preference became more difficult to balance with other demands of farm labour. Some families reduced food production in favour of cash crop production, then relied on the market to make food purchases. For most households, especially those that were resource poor, that option was very risky. Because of the cash demands on households, it was not uncommon that part of the annual crop was sold at the time of harvest in order to raise money for school fees, medical expenses, clothes or household utensils. The poorest households — notably those headed by women — often followed this pattern. However, later in the season food had to be repurchased. Occasionally cash would be available for those purchases; at other times people worked for other, larger farmers for food or cash or found off-farm, part-time and temporary jobs. In a number of cases documented in recent years (but probably applicable in the colonial era), the burden of food production fell increasingly on women.[20] Where households also had cash crops, women were expected to contribute labour there, in addition to growing and processing household food supplies, household maintenance and child rearing.

I have much difficulty as a woman. I work hard on the farm and yet get nothing at all. We wives are taken only as labourers.
— Zimbabwean woman, 1981.

Balancing labour demands of food and cash crops became a highly complex affair, usually requiring additional time within an already heavy schedule. What is important in terms of the ability to produce sufficient food is that women, in particular, have had to assume far greater burdens than in the past. In a perfectly stable situation, balancing crop and household labour demands might be possible, although very hard. However, illness, the absence of one or more members of the household, extra cash needs, external effects on crop prices, or drought could easily upset that balance. Unfortunately for rural Africa the edge for survival in difficult circumstances was increasingly narrowed during the colonial era. Poor rural women and their children were the closest to the edge — and remain so.

Colonialism drew to a close for most African countries in the late 1950s and early 1960s. The sophistication of political leadership guided African states to independence, but at the cost of retaining close identification with European concepts of government and development. Most African nationalists received a major impetus from the fears and concerns of rural people about the loss of their land and the exploitation of marketing agencies and companies. But the new leaders often opted to gain the political high ground (independence) first and deferred dealing with the complex problem of economic dependency, rural exploitation and class inequalities.

In retrospect, the naivety of some African leaders in the politics of economics is astonishing, although it can be argued that their choices were limited by their position within the global economy. For, while nationalism was taking its course, the external economic structures that controlled African resources were expanding and being strengthened. Further, the international system was defining the meaning and forms of Third World development with minimal African discussion. By 1960, development schemes, projects, plans and thinking reinforced the processes of extraction that were crippling Africa. By and large, the independent states of Africa accepted such approaches to 'development' or remained powerless to alter them. In the process the rural poor and food issues were largely ignored.

Notes

1. Thomas Hodgkin, *Nationalism in Colonial Africa* (New York University Press, New York, 1957).
2. Audrey Richards, *Land, Labour and Diet in Northern Rhodesia* (Oxford University Press, London, 1939).
3. Meredeth Turshen, 'The impact of colonialism on health and health services in Tanzania', *International Journal of Health Services*, Vol. 7, No. 1 (1977), p. 23.
4. One of the early proponents of the concept of 'dual economies' was William J. Barber, *The Economy of British Central Africa: A Case Study of Economic Development in a Dualistic Society* (Oxford University Press, London, 1961). The concept remains in use, along with its analytical flaws, particularly in mainstream development and funding agencies, such as the World Bank.

5. John Iliffe, *The African Poor: A History* (Cambridge University Press, Cambridge, 1987), p. 124.
6. *Ibid.*, p. 130, citing Ray Phillips, *The Bantu in the City* (Lovedale, nd.).
7. Christine Obbo, 'Food sharing during food crisis: case studies from Uganda and Ciskei', in Johan Pottier (ed.), *Food Systems in Central & Southern Africa* (School of Oriental and African Studies, University of London, London, 1985), pp. 270–278.
8. This section draws heavily upon Bogumil Jewsiewicki's 'Unequal development: capitalism and the Katanga economy, 1919–40', in Robin Palmer and Neil Parsons (eds), *The Roots of Rural Poverty in Central and Southern Africa* (University of California Press, Berkeley, 1977), pp. 317–344.
9. *Ibid.*, p. 333.
10. This example is drawn from Allen Isaacman, 'The Mozambique cotton cooperative: the creation of a grassroots alternative to forced commodity production', *African Studies Review*, Vol. 25, Nos. 2 and 3 (June–September 1982), pp. 5–25.
11. Finn Fuglestad, *A History of Niger, 1850–1960* (Cambridge University Press, Cambridge, 1983), pp. 168–169.
12. Barbara Dinham and Colin Hines, *Agribusiness in Africa* (Earth Resources Research, London, 1983); Robin Cohen, *Labour and Politics in Nigeria 1945–71* (Heinemann, London, 1974), p. 38.
13. Fiona Mackenzie, 'Local initiatives and national policy: gender and agricultural change in Murang'a District, Kenya', *Canadian Journal of African Studies*, Vol. 20, No. 3 (1986), p. 389.
14. John C. de Wilde, *Experience with Agricultural Development in Tropical Africa*, Vol. 2 (Johns Hopkins University Press, Baltimore, 1967). This volume contains several useful case studies of development schemes which overlap the colonial and post-colonial eras.
15. Two such studies were Betty Preston Thomson, *Two Studies in African Nutrition* (Manchester University Press, Manchester, 1954); and Margaret Read, 'The basis of nutrition in tribal society', *Man*, Vol. 41, No. 64 (July–August 1941).
16. Steven Feierman, 'Struggles for control: the social roots of health and healing in modern Africa', *African Studies Review*, Vol. 28, Nos. 2 and 3 (June–September 1985), p.99.
17. See also a summary of recent studies by Alanagh Raikes, 'Women's health in East Africa', *Social Science and Medicine*, Vol. 28, No. 5 (1989), pp. 447–459.
18. De Wilde, *op.cit.*, pp. 245–300.
19. *Ibid.*, pp. 84–120; Ben Wisner, *Power and Need in Africa: Basic Human Needs and Development Policies* (Earthscan and Africa World Press, London and Trenton, 1988), pp. 208–216.
20. See the essays and references in *Review of African Political Economy*, Nos. 27 and 28 (1983).

6 The Post-colonial Heritage: Famines & Underdevelopment

African countries and people attained their independence amid high hopes and expectations. The euphoria of the political struggle suggested that many things were possible. Politicians talked of the expanding opportunities for all people. And that rhetoric seemed based on reality, for in the early years after independence governments and economies did indeed expand rapidly. New jobs became available at all levels, new offices, houses and roads were required, and construction boomed. Gross National Product grew at 7 to 10 per cent annually in some countries. Social services, such as education and health facilities, long denied Africans, were now provided. Agricultural commodity production increased as farmers, too, were caught up in the expectations for improved futures. The weather was particularly good in most years in the late 1950s and the 1960s. Development agencies poured in resources — money, personnel, ideas, new projects and equipment. Rarely was there a clearer indication of the constraints of colonialism than the contrast produced by the economic growth of the early independence period. Those years were important because of the sense of identity and hope that political independence inspired. The expansion of schools, clinics, agricultural services, housing and water systems were all very real achievements. But many of these achievements were not evenly distributed. Rural areas received far fewer services than urban areas. The cost of building and running a large teaching hospital in an urban centre often was equal to or more than the amount of money and staff put into all rural health centres, this despite the fact that 70 to 90 per cent of national populations lived in the rural areas. Development plans and projects were formulated in central ministries or overseas capitals and were set up without consultation with rural constituencies. And almost inevitably the new projects and plans envisioned rural areas transformed by commercial agriculture. The containment of African agriculture to meet the needs of urban labour and national treasuries was updated and placed within the context of modernizing rhetoric. Rural areas were expected to continue to grow crops to feed the cities and to raise foreign exchange through the export of crops. Many of the resources that went to 'develop' rural Africa were designed to serve those external interests.

Development thought

On both sides, African and European, planners and politicans worked with insufficient information and often naive ideas to promote the 'modernization' of African economies. The concept of development was narrowly defined, essentially in terms of the building of physical structures, usually to expand commodity production. There was little experience in relating social change and human well-being and participation to the complex processes of development. The models for modernization, the term commonly used in the 1960s to describe development, were specific to Northern experiences and expectations. The common base of experience was the Marshall Plan, in which massive amounts of money were injected into Europe after the Second World War for reconstruction of the industrial and infrastructural base of national economies.

We . . . have failed in Africa, along with everybody else. We have not fully understood the problems. We have not identified the priorities. We have not always designed our projects to fit the agro-climatic conditions of Africa and the social, cultural, and political frameworks of African countries. . . . We, and everybody else, are still unclear about what can be done in agriculture in Africa.
— Ernest Stern, Vice President for Operations, World Bank, 1984.

The limitations of such experience are readily evident in Africa. For example, both European and African development thinkers in the 1960s and 1970s — and many well into the 1980s — have considered subsistence farming (another term for self-sufficiency) a reflection of the primitive nature of rural society. Literally billions of 'development' dollars have gone into completing the thrust of colonialism: rendering rural economies into commercialized replicas of Europe. It is one of the great ironies of the modern world that feeding oneself, one's household or community had come to be viewed as primitive and insufficient for national growth. The methods of most farmers were questioned as being backward and unproductive. Farmers' knowledge of their environment and of the complex farming operations were dismissed as non-scientific and non-Western. The structural constraints to making rural communities more productive, including the policy constraints, were rarely understood or addressed.

Underlying these thoughts was the overwhelming desire of African leaders and bureaucrats and Northern development planners to make rural agricultural production a market-oriented activity. Crops produced by farmers for home consumption were rarely figured into national accounts; those crops were considered 'lost' to the economy, irrelevant to national needs. Farmers were exhorted to be patriotic and to produce for the market. Agricultural extension workers, government planners and politicians all agreed that farmers could only be 'modern' by selling food which was sought in the urban areas or agribusiness crops which would be sold overseas. However, 'modern' production methods entailed the use of chemical fertilizers and of cultivation practices which have now come to be assessed as inappropriate to the vast majority of smallholder producers.

At the international level, the World Bank led the pressure for changing peasant production toward a market economy. A Bank position paper argued that rural development

> is concerned with the modernization and monetization of rural society, and with its transition from traditional isolation to integration with the national [and world] economy.

That integration can be accomplished by

> greater interaction between the modern and traditional sectors, especially in the form of increased trade in farm produce and in technical inputs and services.[1]

This view of a dual economy (a concept dating from the colonial era, as noted earlier) has little respect for rural producers and their continuous inputs into, and losses to, the 'modern' sector of the economy. The approach assumes that urban, national and international needs all take precedence over rural 'traditional isolation'.

Over the past two decades the World Bank has contributed as much to agricultural disaster in Ethiopia as the governments themselves.
— Yonas Deressa, Ethiopia Refugees Education and Relief Foundation, 1987.

The United States Agency for International Development (USAID), the European Economic Community (EEC) members' bilateral aid programmes and the EEC's multilateral Development Fund (EDF) and other development agencies generally followed the ideological lead of the World Bank. USAID funding to Africa was to large, centrally planned, commercially oriented projects. These included road building (so commodities could be more easily moved), irrigation systems for cash crop production, and other agricultural projects using tractors and chemical inputs. The U.S. and EEC aid has involved significant food aid transfers, while over 80 per cent of EDF project aid to Africa is spent on large projects, often transportation schemes. The United Nations system of development agencies — for example, the Food and Agriculture Organization (FAO) and International Labour Office (ILO) — were a part of this system which defined 'development' in monetary terms. The FAO, for example, maintained a clearing-house for agribusiness firms during the 1970s in order to facilitate their penetration into Third World countries implementing FAO-funded agricultural projects.[2]

The rhetoric of development

The central core of development thinking and related policy — stimulating rural commodity production and sales to meet the needs of urban dwellers and overseas markets — was often obscured by pronouncements in favour of rural development, small-scale farmers, the poor, women and the otherwise disadvantaged. Every decade brought another focus, ushered in with great fanfare as *the way* to promote development but then quietly downgraded or abandoned as problems arose. Rarely was rhetoric matched by effective action. Several reasons for this lapse are apparent.

First, the development establishment sought to integrate the poor or women into the monetary economy. The lack of money, no matter how earned, is the common definition of poverty and said to be the cause of hunger. For the majority of rural dwellers, the sale of agricultural products or their labour was the only means to acquire cash. However, as has been pointed out, investing time and resources into producing cash crops is highly risky when balanced against farming to meet food needs. The disadvantaged groups are those least able to risk the vagrancies of the market economy. A failed crop, debt acquired because of low producer prices, inefficient delivery systems for crops or inputs — all can place the poor in an even more precarious position. Survival with dignity and overcoming the lack of productive resources while maintaining social cohesiveness are key considerations for the rural poor; feeding the towns does not easily fit into that equation.

Second, projects aimed at the rural poor and/or small-scale farmers promised increases in income but failed to address a variety of other concerns of farmers. Some of those concerns were: insufficient household labour to meet production requirements for various crops; relatively low producer prices; and lack of consumer goods for purchase in rural areas. Many rural people felt that projects and policies discriminated against them. They distrusted the promises made by project advocates. Rarely did project planners seek out the opinions of rural constituents or even use widely accepted knowledge about strengths and weaknesses of rural communities to guide their work, much less give control of projects to rural people. Thus, projects and programmes for the 'rural poor' often alienated those people by being imposed on them, isolating rural communities from the real world or threatening their limited security.[3]

Third, almost exclusively those projects were channelled through governments and had to conform to the policies, organizations and political and class structures of those governments. Perhaps it was both appropriate and logical to work through governments. For international development and lending agencies to circumvent those official structures would have been blatant arrogance and interference. However, governments often were not dedicated to the real needs of their low-income citizens, whether rural or urban. Like the development and lending agencies on the international scene, African governments were dedicated to expanding commodity production. Cash crops fed the cities, helped to fill the national coffers and produced foreign exchange. No African government effectively altered these urban-based priorities in order to secure national food security based upon effective development of rural areas. Further, the nature of the bureaucratic state resulted in an exclusive hierarchy of authority. Knowledge, power and resources were assumed by national elites to reside in the state. There were few sincere attempts to promote empowerment of rural populations, along lines defined and accepted by those populations growing out of their own knowledge, skills and resources. Instead of empowerment and development, governments and aid agencies in traditional imperialistic style adopted a position of 'blaming the victim'; the poor were responsible for their own poverty because of their laziness and their conservative resistance to new ideas and technologies. The poor are poor and hungry, the argument went, because they have failed to join the cash economy. It was an argument that was self-serving to special interests, those articulate and powerful enough to blame the poor for their own starvation!

A vast continent, located strategically between the U.S. and the Middle East and sitting astride the sea lanes of communication between the Middle East, Europe and North America, Africa is rich in natural resources — minerals in southern Africa and petroleum in West and Central Africa . . . U.S. interests in Southwest Asia and the Indian Ocean have led to increased military and economic cooperation with countries in East Africa.
— The view of Africa from the U.S. Department of State, GIST, May, 1984.

Finally, there is another level at which development rhetoric must be measured. Northern assistance activities in Africa — especially U.S., British and French initiatives — involved a strategic element, with strong military overtones. Assurance of the continued Western consumption of oil had placed northeast Africa and South Africa in key positions because of their proximity to sea lanes from the Middle East. Increasing levels of foreign assistance to countries in northeast Africa reflected U.S. priorities. In the early and mid-1980s half of all U.S. Economic Support Fund payments for Africa (used for balance of payments and import purchase use by recipient countries) went to Kenya, Somalia and Sudan, countries strategically placed in terms of East-West politics in the oil-rich Middle East. Between two-thirds and three-quarters of all U.S. military assistance to Africa in the 1980s went to the same three countries. The coercive posturing and direct military involvement in maintaining the status quo in this geo-political environment differs only in scale and time from the practices of the earlier colonial powers in 'persuading' African peasants to conform to the demands of external interests.

What has been happening to poverty? What has been happening to inequality? What has been happening to unemployment? . . . [I]f these are getting worse it would be strange to call the result development, even if per capita income had soared.
— Dudley Seers, *From Thought to Practice,* 1972.

Two brief case studies will help illustrate trends in and results of development assistance during the 1960s and 1970s. Both offer an understanding of the basis for the massive famine that swept the Sahelian zone of Africa in 1972—74.

In West Africa two externally assisted development projects helped prepare the way for the famine of the early 1970s. In the 1950s and 1960s a series of wells were sunk in the Sahel to be used by pastoral people and their cattle. In addition to the altruistic desire to provide permanent water supplies, governments and donors had other motivations. It was hoped to settle nomads in a fixed area and subject them to regular government control. In the new scheme the pastoral people were expected to sell their cattle to meet the demands for meat in urban centres of West Africa and in Europe. Finally, it was expected that settled livestock-holding people would open up land that previously had been used only occasionally because of its marginal nature. All these things happened . . . and more. The permanent water supplies did attract the pastoralists, but overgrazing around the wells occurred so that cattle and people had to search far beyond the wells for sufficient grazing. Soil cover, which had regenerated under normal nomadic use, was now lost.

When the rains and grass failed in the late 1960s and early 1970s the vulnerability of the pastoralists became acute. The nomads and their animals migrated south in search of new grass. However, hundreds of thousands of cattle died, as did an estimated quarter-million people.

Ironically, the drought facilitated meat exports, as the nomads sold their animals rather than lose them altogether. The cash helped some people to buy grain to survive. But concurrently with water development and pastoral settlement in the 1960s, the growth of export crop production in the Sahel limited the ability of people to purchase food. French private companies and assistance from France, the Common Market and the World Bank stimulated cotton and peanut production in new areas. Far fewer resources went into food crop production. Again, ironically, as the Sahel suffered drought and famine from 1968 to 1973−74, the region continued to export those crops which were sought overseas and which earned foreign exchange (used, in part, to import food).[4] In fact, one Sahel government was negotiating with the World Bank at the time of the famine for a $20 million loan for the expansion of a peanut production project. It is interesting to note that during the life of that project (1974−78) the government extracted over $12 million in revenue from farmers by offering low prices and by imposing export taxes. Farmers increasingly turned to private traders to sell peanuts at higher prices and chose to increase corn production (for which prices were better) rather than grow peanuts. Also, the project increased social differentiation in several ways: subsidies were given to a relatively small number of large farmers who enjoyed a far higher income from peanut production than the majority of small-scale farmers; women producers were largely ignored; and smaller-scale farmers faced indebtedness following the 1973−74 drought which forced them to continue to grow cash crops in order to redeem their debts.[5] As one observer noted:

> even before the 1973 drought struck, poor farmers were almost at the end of their defenses. They had eaten their seed reserves and depended on 'friends' for gifts or loans of seed; they had no more livestock to sell, as all animals had already died or been sold. . . . For many of the poor the only resource left by mid-1973 that they could pledge or sell was their land.[6]

The process of growing inequalities which we have noted so often continued to play itself out in the food crises of the 1970s and 1980s.

The second case study comes from Ethiopia and also involves water, in this instance for irrigation of commercial crops. Until the 1950s the Awash river valley of central Ethiopia was considered of little importance by the central government. However, at about that time the government sought to develop the flood plain in the valley for cash crop production. A feasibility study in 1965 recommended large-scale cotton and sugar cane cultivation, and several large dams were built with World Bank funding. The farmers and pastoralists of the area were displaced by larger, commercialized holdings by the early 1970s. The government made little effort to resettle those people who lost land or whose previous way of life was disrupted by the flooding and by commercial agriculture. The displaced people remained in the area but were greatly impoverished, forced to maintain a living on marginal parcels of land and overgrazed pastures. Local food supplies were limited, as food was either imported for the agricultural labourers on the large estates or raised in small amounts on the margins of the commercial holdings. When rains failed between 1971 and 1973 in the highlands of central Ethiopia, massive in-migration of refugees to the Awash Valley pushed the former valley inhabitants into famine conditions as well. Development had occurred around them, at the expense of their land and food producing systems. But those impoverished people were not excluded from the impact of development; over 50,000 people died in the 1973–74 famine in Ethiopia.[7]

The politics of famine

The famines in Africa in this century have been man-made. They have been the result of decisions to organize national economies in specific ways. The processes which determined those decisions originated early in the colonial era and were strongly reinforced at the time of independence. Those political decisions on the distribution of resources have resulted in the steady extraction of value from African labour in order to enrich industries overseas and African governments and national elites.

The Sahel famines of 1973–74 and 1983–85 were precipitated by prolonged drought. In earlier centuries drought also occurred, but the recent famines have their underlying causes in decisions which altered the ways of life and agricultural production of the majority of rural peoples. Unfortunately, those decisions have not significantly improved rural life. Rather, hundreds of thousands of people have died and tens of millions have faced severe hardship and disruption of their lives.

The present anguish within Africa results from choices made to view and use African resources — and the producers of those resources — in certain ways. Those choices have accumulated over time, creating structures within an international economy in which African states now operate. Those structures of the global economy support a large international and domestic bureaucracy and a large and/or influential urban-based elite in African nations.

Few African countries have sought, let alone been able, to dilute the influence of these elite groups in order to direct more resources toward the rural poor and agricultural self-sufficiency. Even the more progressive states in Africa have developed an urban-based civil service which dominates the direction of state policies and resource distribution. The decisions to create large, central bureaucracies and quasi-governmental agencies have, in turn, handed great power to such elite organizations. Naturally, they are self-serving. Wealthy people seek cheap food and adequate housing, paved streets for their cars, comfortable offices, servants, imported luxury foods and drink. Even in this time of financial hardship for many African countries, it is common to find larger stores stocked with Scotch whisky, colour television sets and video cassette recorders. The privileges of the elite mean that others get less. It is impossible (without very heavy government subsidies) to offer high producer prices for food crops and low consumer prices for finished food products. Every imported car or bottle of wine costs foreign exchange which is earned, in most African countries, by exporting minerals or crops like coffee, cotton or peanuts. Within the structures of African decision-making, choices are made to use foreign exchange to purchase a car rather than basic drugs for a rural health centre. It is one of the ironies of Africa's 'development' history that food crises coincide with the continued production of surpluses of agricultural commodities for export.

Table 1
Agricultural exports and imports (in $ millions)

	1978	1979	1980	1981
Ethiopia				
exports	293.8	397.6	392.7	343.7
imports	65.7	78.6	113.5	84.7
net exports	228.1	319.0	279.2	259.0
Mali				
exports	118.7	163.4	220.7	203.2
imports	46.7	36.4	68.1	65.5
net exports	74.0	127.0	152.6	137.7
Sudan				
exports	477.7	570.5	551.6	472.3
imports	168.1	174.5	389.8	335.2
net exports	309.6	396.5	161.7	137.1
Tanzania				
exports	398.9	385.1	392.1	428.9
imports	91.1	60.8	167.6	128.0
net exports	307.8	324.3	224.5	300.9

Source: FAO, *Trade Yearbook 1982.*

Urban dwellers and international commodity pushers

In addition to choosing to keep producer prices and urban food prices low, urban elites have made decisions which entail looking to overseas farmers and manufacturers to meet many of their food tastes. Those tastes were often created by food aid, which encompasses not only relief in times of severe food shortages, but the export of U.S. and European crop surpluses in order to solve their own production problems. Food aid has been designed to create increased demand for Western crops and stimulate new markets. Food aid has been so successful a marketing tool that African nations now import from the U.S. at commercial rates three to four times the amount of food that they receive as 'aid'.[8]

I have heard ... that people may become dependent on us for food. I know that was not supposed to be good news. To me, that was good news, because before people can do anything they have got to eat. And if you are looking for a way to get people to lean on you and to be dependent on you, in terms of their cooperation with you, it seems to me that food dependence would be terrific.
— Senator Hubert Humphrey, on the U.S. Food for Peace programme, 1957.

Food is a weapon but the way to use that is to tie countries to us. That way they'll be far more reluctant to upset us.
— John Brock, during confirmation hearings as Secretary of Agriculture, 1980.

The clearest example of changing food tastes in Africa, resulting in part from the pattern of food aid over the past 15 years, has been the rapid expansion of wheat imports to satisfy urban desires for bread. In many African cities bread is now considered a staple; at independence it was consumed by but a small minority of urban dwellers. Few countries grow more than a small percentage of the total wheat they require. Substantial foreign exchange is now spent to import wheat from the U.S., Canada and the European Economic Community countries. While commercial imports of wheat are substantial, wheat continues to enter African countries as food aid. Statistics from the Food and Agriculture Organization of the United Nations indicated that wheat was a major 'food aid' request among some of the 24 countries in Africa listed as affected by the 1982—85 drought. Yet, bread remains a predominantly urban food, with the implication that urban desires (important in political stability considerations) are a key part of the complex relations of food aid.[9]

In many African countries, food imports have become a necessity if not a preference. Internationally adopted criteria are used to justify the need for such imports. But the rationale may incorporate only a limited view of internal food needs and demand. The decisions to seek food externally have less to do with the failure of the internal food production system — although this cannot be denied in certain crisis situations — than with a political and bureaucratic unease about interacting with local producers. Those producers are often thousands of small-scale farmers, who are meeting their own food needs as well as producing for the market. Fluctuations occur from year to year, from region to region in the amount farmers are willing to place on the market. Rural marketing is both difficult and costly, from the perspective of urban-based development planners. Price is also a consideration in this decision-making process. Food aid or partially subsidized food imports can relieve pressure on national budgets while payments to local producers can be costly, this especially being the case in the 1980s as governments faced pressure from international donors to increase food supplies by offering producers higher prices. Thus, food imports are justified not only on the basis of urban-determined need which is said not to be met by rural producers, but by a view that farmers are unable to supply either the quantities or variety of foods expected by urban consumers. It is at this point, of decisions within African countries to minimize the contributions of rural producers to meet food security requirements and of policies within the U.S. and the European Community to export at subsidized rates their agricultural surpluses, that the rationale develops to speak of Africa's food crisis and to justify policies that retain African countries' orientation toward external markets.[10]

Perhaps by meeting urban food demands through imports more food will be left for consumption in the rural areas. The argument has some validity, especially in times of severe food shortages. There is some contradictory evidence, however. Urban food preferences may be for crops normally not grown, consumed or available in rural areas — such as bread or imported canned goods or rice, as in some West African countries. Several observers have noted that in some countries food shortages are defined by urban groups who normally have been among those who are well-fed. A disruption in their normal consumption pattern results in talk of 'food shortages'. Further, it is noted that peasants have in some instances chosen not to sell food to marketing boards or traders, keeping it for themselves or trading it through informal channels which are not recorded in official marketing figures, which may create urban shortages but leave rural food supplies in fairly good shape.

Finally, urban food tastes have already created hardships in rural areas. Agricultural development projects and commodity pricing policies have been designed to produce foods generally in demand in urban areas (and for export). Zambia, for example, has launched at least three large rice growing projects with external assistance. Rice is overwhelmingly for urban consumption. Meanwhile, pricing policies and research have neglected major rural crops such as cassava, sorghum and millet. The urban bias that runs through so many African agricultural policies is a major factor in the prolonged agricultural crisis affecting the continent.

The politics of famine relief

The response to famine is not based entirely on meeting the food needs of the hungry. Rather, the response is based as much on decisions about evidence of hunger, the perceptions of governments involved and relations between rural and urban people. The nature of the response to famine is very political, as it relates to choices of when to act, in what form, for whom and by whom and with what quantities of assistance. For example, during the famine in Sudan in 1984–85, the central government initially refused to acknowledge it and thus refused to cooperate with local government officials and relief organizations.[11] A similar situation had occurred in Ethiopia in the early 1970s. There, when the extent of famine in the northern part of the country could no longer be hidden and denied, popular disgust at the emperor led to his overthrow.

The choices that influence relief response occur within a wider economic and political context. As we have argued, Africa continues to expand agricultural exports while efforts to define development in international, rather than local and national, terms alienates rural producers. The ties that bound the continent to external forces for hundreds of years continued to operate during the 1980s and extend into the 1990s. Western powers and their development agencies offered Africa little choice. Planners and decision-makers in Africa itself have been a part of those choices or found minimal opportunity to restructure their countries' economies against the powerful external and internal opposition. Debts incurred in the 1960s and 1970s by chasing the false promises of growth can only be repaid with foreign exchange earned by exports. The debt constraints faced by many African countries have given Western lending agencies new leverage in seeking to direct African policies toward a free market and export orientation. In Mali, food aid is tied to that government's satis-factory performance in instituting policy changes which major lending agencies deem correct. 'Satisfactory', in turn, is defined by agencies which include the World Bank and USAID. Yet the flaws in making these linkages between policy changes and food aid only threaten low-income people. When Mali faced severe food shortages in 1984—85, USAID and other food aid agencies were so unprepared to assess and target need that estimates were up to 100 per cent off. In the following year, local production rapidly recovered, but food aid was still flowing into the country and undermining prices and markets available to Malian farmers.[12] For the majority of rural people well-being, if not survival, became more dependent on the interaction between national elite and international financiers, policy-makers and development planners. In neighbouring Niger, the government was required by its chief donors to sell off its major grain reserves (maintained against possible shortages) in order to repay its debts to French banks.

In the case of the Ethiopian famine of 1982—85, international response was long delayed by disagreements within United Nations and U.S. agencies about the severity of the food crisis. It is now well documented that the Ethiopian Relief and Rehabilitation Commission (RRC), charged with famine relief within the country, had identified for the international community the need for food assistance as early as 1982. It was only two years later that the renewed assessments of RRC were generally accepted by FAO and the U.S. Even when the severity of the crisis in northern Ethiopia was recognized and a supplementary appropriation for famine relief was being considered by the United States Congress in 1984, the Reagan administration attached as a condition for such monies Congressional approval of an increase in military assistance to the anti-government Contra forces fighting Nicaragua. It was only when overwhelming popular support in the U.S. forced Congress and the Reagan administration to address the Ethiopian famine that money was made available without the Contra strings. But even then, U.S. food aid was given with the expectation that it would wean the Ethiopian government away from its alliance with the Soviet Union. Now, while the U.S. claims credit for saving thousands of lives in 1985 and 1986 in Ethiopia, it ignores its complicity in allowing the famine to reach major proportions and delaying relief when people were already starving.

Nor can the operations of famine relief avoid political implications. Private voluntary organizations (PVOs) — generally known as non-governmental organizations (NGOs) outside the U.S. — blatantly exploited the hungry and starving people of Ethiopia in their publicity designed to raise funds. A study of European media and NGO coverage of the famine produced similar results. Not only did some of the money given by a generous public in donations and mega-events go to expand the staffs of PVOs, but it also was used to create the obscene publicity and one-dimensional reports that contributed to the racist stereotypes of African people as being dependent, passive and needy recipients of outside aid, incapable of confronting their own problems. At least as important as the narrow images projected of African people, was the absence of analysis underlying the famine.

Newspapers and television ignored the open warfare that existed in northern Ethiopia and Chad, yet these wars severely limited agricultural activity and distribution of food to critical areas. Nor did journalists give background to the famine by reviewing the structural violence aimed at the majority of rural people in much of Africa. To their credit, a number of NGOs in Europe and Africa did respond to the famines with solid analysis designed to better inform their constituents and to urge long-term responses to events in Africa.[13]

In these conditions [of general scarcity] the depletion of village food reserves caused by the bad season [saw] the development of new circuits for commercialization of cereal crops. It is the peasants themselves who have taken the initiative to create these circuits: they are, all at the same time, producers, sellers and buyers.
— *Construire Ensemble*, CESAO, 1984.

Finally, famine response from Northern countries is often conducted in general ignorance of African conditions, social structures and organizations. In one of the most insightful and provocative books to assess recent famine conditions and responses, Alexander De Waal raises a number of critical issues. His conclusion is simple: in Darfur, western Sudan, where famine struck in 1984–85, people adopted a variety of coping strategies, including going hungry in order to preserve some assets that could be used to resume socially acceptable life when rains returned and crops were restored — as they did in 1985–86. He argues: 'people's principal aim during the famine was to preserve the basis of an acceptable future way of life, which involves not only material wellbeing but also social cohesion'.[14]

Food aid, the logical (and conditioned) response of Northern citizens and governments to African famines, is also value-laden. Yet, De Waal found that susceptibility to disease was of greater significance than food deprivation in the life and death struggle for survival. He suggests of U.S. and European food aid to Darfur that 'there is little evidence that the food relief had any impact on mortality'.[15] Improved water supplies, health and sanitation facilities and immunization programmes probably would have been more appropriate responses to the Darfur famine.

Other studies point to similar conclusions. Relief camps in Ethiopia in 1983–85 were deadly places, primarily because the closely packed people were exposed to numerous illnesses. Relief distribution methods to Ugandan refugees in southern Sudan in the early 1980s undermined their initiative and social cohesion.[16] The prime lessons to be learned from these studies of famine is that to solve the problems of hunger the initiatives and social frameworks of African people themselves, especially people most susceptible to hunger and those involved in food production, are of critical importance in defining famine, relief and development.

Famine, then, can be triggered by natural disaster, but it is caused by longer-term political and economic decisions. Famine is also political because it affects some groups far more than others. There have been no reports of massive famine in the capitals of African nations although shortages of food have occurred and steep price rises have left many people hungry. Likewise, traders, businessmen, civil servants and political leaders are not among those found in relief camps. Famine is very much a class issue and those classes affected by famine have been determined by the course of history. Those most affected are predominantly rural poor, pastoralists, small farmers, and agricultural labourers who have lost the ability to raise or purchase food. People who are already poor are (and have been) those most likely to have inadequate resources to respond to further hardships. Their positions are already so marginal, their edge of survival already so narrow, that drought, civil war, loss of land to 'development' projects, adverse government policies and declining world commodity prices all can precipitate famine.

The famine is upon us. We have no millet, maize, or beans. Our cattle, sheep, and goats are dead, so are our chickens. The women and children are hungry. Therefore we have decided to set up our homes in this unoccupied place. O nurturing Earth, we offer thee this chicken; accept it we beseech thee, and in exchange give us bountiful harvest, numerous herds and flocks, and many children. Keep us free from sickness, epidemics and all evils.
— Prayer of the Lobi, Ivory Coast.

Notes

1. World Bank, *Rural Development Sector Policy Paper* (Washington, DC, 1975), pp. 3, 16.
2. On the EEC, see Philip Raikes, *Modernizing Hunger: Famine, Food Surplus & Farm Policy in the EEC & Africa* (Catholic Institute for International Relations, London, 1988); on FAO's agribusiness ties, see Frances Moore Lappe and

Joseph Collins, *Food First*, revised edition (Ballantine Books, New York, 1978), pp. 74–75.

3. Robert Chambers, *Rural Development: Putting the Last First* (Longman, London and New York, 1983).

4. Richard W. Franke and Barbara H. Casin, *Seeds of Famine* (Allanheld, Osmun Publishers, Montclair, New Jersey, 1980); Michael Watts, *Silent Violence* (University of California Press, Berkeley, 1983).

5. World Bank, *Project Performance Audit Report: Mali — Integrated Rural Development Project (Credit 491–MLI)* (Washington, DC, 1980).

6. G. Jan Van Apeldoorn, *Perspectives on Drought and Famine in Nigeria* (Allen & Unwin, London, 1981).

7. Helmut Kloos, 'Development, drought, and famine in the Awash Valley of Ethiopia,' *African Studies Review*, Vol. 25, No. 4 (December 1982, pp. 21–48).

8. *How U.S. Food Aid Programs Help American Agricultural Exports* (International Trade and Development Education Foundation, Washington, DC, 1988). A concise, uninhibited statement of how food aid promotes agricultural exports.

9. Gunilla Andrea and Bjorn Beckman, *The Wheat Trap: Bread and Underdevelopment in Nigeria* (Zed Books, London, 1987).

10. Phillip Raikes, *op. cit.* In Guinea Bissau an internationally backed economic reform programme has as a goal an increase in rice production and marketing by improving producer prices. The programme also entails reducing consumer subsidies on rice. While production has increased, many low-income urban dwellers are unable to afford the higher prices.

11. Alexander De Waal, *Famine that Kills: Darfur, Sudan, 1984–1985* (Clarendon Press, Oxford, 1989), pp. 205–206.

12. AID, *Evaluation of the African Emergency Food Assistance Program, 1984–85* (Washington, DC, 1986).

13. *The Image of Africa*, report from the international exchange on communication and development between Africa and Europe (Rome, 1988).

14. De Waal, *op. cit.*, p. 227.

15. *Ibid.*, p. 208.

16. B. E. Harrell-Bond, *Imposing Aid: Emergency Assistance to Refugees* (Oxford University Press, Oxford, 1986).

7 Established World Order: Destructive Engagement

In the 1980s Africa was the focus of world attention due to massive famines and the violent reactions of the South African government and military forces to the end of white domination. Our analysis suggests solid historical and global reasons for these crises that took the lives of millions of people and exposed millions of others to declining living standards. In essence, people's livelihoods had been undermined by decades of exploitation, particularly the extraction of wealth, which in recent years has been carried out under the guise of programmes of 'development', enforced by multiple webs of political and military control at both national and international levels. The mid-1980s brought together in Africa many threads of internal and external change. This chapter provides a summary of several of those key issues and sets the grounds for examining Northern and African responses.

Terms of trade

The international market for African agricultural and mineral commodities has long been unstable. The mid-1960s saw a general boom for many commodities, and production increased. Governments expanded their revenue base by taxing commodity sales and exports. Revenues were invested to meet the demand for social services and infrastructural development. Some expensive, massive, but inappropriate projects were undertaken by combining governments' resources with external funding and advice. State bureaucracies also expanded to service the growing involvement of the public sector in national affairs.

Toward the end of the 1960s, the expanded production of commodities began to saturate world markets while Northern economies reacted to the instability of the U.S. economy in the wake of the Vietnam war. Prices declined or fluctuated widely. Concurrently, inflation spurred by U.S. financing of the Vietnam war increased the prices of many manufactured goods which Africa regularly imported. Oil prices climbed in the 1970s, helping several African countries but hurting numerous others. Especially during the decade following the mid-1970s, Africa experienced a dramatic change in its terms of trade. Its exports commanded lower prices; its imports were more expensive. In the 1980s the situation worsened. The real value of Africa's exports declined from $58 billion in 1980 to $36 billion in 1983, rising only slightly to $38 billion in 1985. The terms of trade declined by 25 per cent between 1977 and 1985. In 1986 alone terms of trade plummeted by 32 per cent, costing African countries $19 billion in lost income.[1]

Figure 1
Africa's terms of trade (Index 1980 − 100)

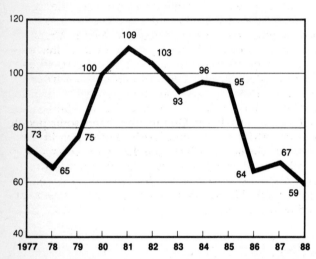

Source: UNCTAD, *Handbook of International Trade and Development Statistics*, 1988.

Such a decline in the relative value of exports meant that African countries had to export 30 per cent more in 1987 in order to simply purchase the same amount of goods as in 1977. In some countries the change is far more dramatic. Zambia, one of the most affected countries, had to export three times the value of goods in 1982 to gain the value equivalent to 1970 exports; Liberia and Zaire had to double their mineral and agricultural exports. Some countries increased the volume of exports in order to maintain revenue levels, but the changes in world prices rarely compensated African efforts adequately. Industrial and agricultural programmes that used imported components were disrupted and output declined; factories often closed for extended periods of time when foreign exchange was unavailable; farmers' fields sat idle or were planted late when fertilizers were not available. The declining purchasing power of African goods was exacerbated by individual countries' dependence on one or two major commodities. For example, Zambia earns over 95 per cent of its foreign exchange from copper exports and Burundi 93 per cent from coffee. Twenty-seven sub-Saharan African countries depend on agricultural exports for 50 per cent or more of their foreign exchange.[2]

Thus, Africa has not done well through its recent interaction with the world economy. Conforming to the economic modes created during the colonial era and subsequently urged by the major development agencies, African states have been subject to trends and forces determined by other countries and regions. Within Africa, the economic contractions caused by declining revenues have impacted most harshly on low-income people. During the 1980s already strained social services deteriorated and/or became more expensive, food prices increased and official corruption and oppression became more pervasive. Malnutrition increased in many areas after having declined in the 1960s and early 1970s. On the other hand, some people have benefited from Africa's economic crisis. Lower world commodity prices benefit businesses which purchase the commodities and consumers who may eventually use the finished products. African oil producers experienced a 50 per cent drop in export earnings in the early 1980s. Meanwhile U.S. drivers were paying 50 per cent less for gasoline at the pump.

Debt and the IMF

The second structural feature of Africa's interaction with the world economy is the impact of debt. The issue has two significant features: the size of the debt, and the imposition of restraints on African governments' economic, financial and social policies by the International Monetary Fund (IMF), the World Bank and most other financial contributing agencies.

The IMF programme has been with us for close to 12 years now and we began to see nothing but a contraction of the economy, contracting, contracting. In the end, we were living to pay the IMF, nothing else!
— Kenneth Kaunda, President of Zambia, 1987.

Most African governments hoped that the fall in commodity prices in the late 1970s and early 1980s was temporary. There was every expectation among international economists that the decline in terms of trade was a feature of the cyclical pattern of the capitalist world economy. It was anticipated that a revival in commodity prices and external earnings would occur as the cycle played out. The experts guessed wrong. The reason is not hard to find. Growing competition among Third World countries for export markets in the North has tended to depress commodity prices. That competition has been exacerbated by (1) trade restrictions imposed by industrial countries to protect their home production and (2) the intense pressure to service huge debts incurred in the 1970s under the illusion of rapid development. The competition has been fostered by the 'logic' of comparative advantage — countries that can produce goods (because of factors such as geography, access to natural resources, wage rates and technological sophistication) at prices appealing to a world market ought to do so; countries that lack that ability ought not to seek to produce such goods but import them and concentrate on producing items where they have an advantage over other producers. The World Bank has been a prime proponent of comparative advantage economics for Third World countries, but has also lent major sums for national programmes to develop commodities of which there is a surplus on global markets. Thus, the Bank recommended coffee production in Zambia and has provided sizeable loans for the development of a coffee plantation sector. However, Zambia does not have a large domestic market for coffee and other East and West African countries have much larger and more extensive coffee export programmes. Zambia, in fact, does not meet the World Bank's own criteria of comparative advantage for coffee production, but the country was offered and took on sizeable debt nevertheless. The extra coffee (or copper, or cocoa) on the global market will tend to push down prices.

Sub-Saharan Africa's external debt grew from $16.2 billion in 1975 to $130 billion at the end of 1987. In 1975 the sub-Saharan African debt totalled two-thirds of its annual exports; by 1987 debt stood at over three times the value of annual exports.[3] African countries accumulated these debts by borrowing from the IMF and the World Bank, bilateral lenders, commercial banks and suppliers of imports. By the mid-1980s it was clear that the debt burden of many African states not only was a significant drain on economic recovery and development planning, but resulted in serious cutbacks in human welfare programmes. Moreover, Africa's future was mortgaged to the Northern lending community.

The IMF plays the role of an international monetary policeman. Its job is to urge or coerce countries out of step with the capitalist norm to take internal measures to conform. These 'deviant' countries are assisted with one- to three-year loans to cover foreign exchange shortfalls. In order to bring national economies into greater balance with world market forces, the IMF attaches conditions to these loans. These conditions often include: reductions in government expenditures through cuts in the civil service, public investment and subsidies; expansion of foreign exchange earnings through both devaluation of national currencies and incentives to companies and farmers to increase exports; and reduced imports. While ostensibly monetary policies, these conditions have carried important political implications which African governments quickly recognized. Too little is known about the conditions associated with the secret agreements. Citizens in Africa, however, have felt the impact of the conditions attached to the IMF loans. Food subsidies have been reduced, occasioning dramatic price increases in basic supplies. One of the ostensible reasons for the popular overthrow of President Nimeiri of the Sudan in 1985 was his seeming acquiescence to demands by the IMF and U.S. to reduce food subsidies. In other countries, farmer credit programmes have been cut and workers' wage increases carefully kept in check. For example, in Zambia, subject to five IMF loan agreements in the 1970s and 1980s, real wages for manual workers fell by 13 per cent between 1980 and 1987.

There are other, longer-term impacts associated with IMF loans. Declining government support for social services had led to the deterioration of health, education, transportation and marketing services. In Africa as a whole, the average share of education and health expenditures by governments fell from 25 per cent in 1986 to 19 per cent in 1988.[4] In order to make up for reduced public support, user fees have been introduced for some services which previously had been free. The rural and urban poor majority have suffered the most as a result of these changes. Malnutrition rates among young children have increased. In Ghana, malnutrition among pre-school children increased from 35 per cent of all such children to over 50 per cent between 1980 and 1984.[5] After several decades of improvements, infant mortality rates increased in Ghana in the early and mid-1980s. For a decade beginning in the late 1970s, Zambia was subject to IMF loan conditions. The health results have been devastating for low-income groups. During the mid-1980s, when Zambia was under intense pressure to conform to IMF, World Bank and other lenders' reform programmes, nearly half of lower-income people in Zambia's capital, Lusaka, cut back on food purchases or food consumption. From at least the early 1980s, infant and child mortality rates have risen in response to increased malnutrition.[6] Public investment has declined, affecting employment opportunities, and inflation has seriously eroded incomes.[7] These changes also are associated with a greater concentration of wealth in the hands of the elite. Further, rather than accepting the decaying public facilities, national elites have created a demand for private services which only they can afford. Increased unemployment, high prices for basic goods, and fewer and more costly social services have all met with popular discontent. In many instances the official reaction has been to repress dissent, whether it takes place in the streets or in political involvement and debate.

... I am tired of being told that Tanzania's present condition arises out of our own mistakes of policy, our own inefficiency and our own over-ambition. I am tired too of being told that Africa's present condition is the result of African incompetence, venality or general inferiority in capacity. I am even more tired of being told that the solution of our problems is an agreement with the IMF or any pursuit of private investment — local and foreign — and the encouragement of 'personal initiatives' without regard to its social consequences.
— Julius Nyerere, former President of Tanzania, 1985.

Finally, the conditions for economic reforms which the IMF attaches to each of its loans undermines national sovereignty. The situation of Zambia offers a glimpse into that process. By 1977 Zambia's economy had experienced three years of falling copper prices. The government turned to the IMF for support. Among the conditions set by the IMF for its loan was that Zambia was to buy equipment for its copper and other industries from the cheapest source. On the surface this seemed a logical and economically efficient demand; however, it carried dire political consequences. As the IMF well knew, South Africa was the cheapest source for much of Zambia's industrial equipment needs. During the prior decade, Zambia had made concerted efforts to reduce its dependence on South Africa, a dependence inherited from the colonial era. Trade relations had dramatically declined and new transportation routes avoiding South Africa were established. Obviously, the IMF was not alone in urging cheaper sources of goods for Zambia. Zambian businessmen and multinational companies were simultaneously urging the government to grant greater imports from South Africa. Thus, both internal and external pressures from elite groups challenged Zambia's courageous policy of economic disengagement. The circumstances changed following the agreement with the IMF. The percentage of Zambia's trade with South Africa now exceeds what it was in 1970 and the nation's dependence on South Africa's transportation system and trade credits has been re-established.[8]

Militarization and intervention

The third facet of the world order which has been so destructive for Africa has been the militarization of the continent. Spending on military equipment and standing armies has rapidly expanded in the past 15 years and the military has become centrally involved in national politics. Concurrently, Africa has again been subjected to external military intervention, often under the guise of 'aid' and surrogate armies. In both cases, militarization has curtailed the ability of African people to guide their own futures and has more closely tied a number of African states to external influence. More than any other immediate factor, wars have caused famine in Africa in recent years.

External violence against Africa is centuries old, encompassing 350 years of European and American slave trading, the European imperialist expansion into Africa — often by military means — and the European colonization of the continent. Weapons have continued to enter Africa since the 1960s. The United States, the Soviet Union and NATO countries all have made major contributions to Africa's military build-up. The Soviets supply 50 per cent of Africa's weapons, primarily to Ethiopia, Libya and Angola. Several European countries supply about 30 per cent of Africa's arms. The U.S. is a much smaller supplier, accounting for 4 per cent of Africa's arms imports. But the U.S. provides weapons, training or other military assistance to 40 African states, up from 14 countries in 1980. In 1985 the U.S. provided about $200 million in military aid and credits to African governments, an amount nearly half that given for development assistance. More worrisome has been the steady build-up of U.S. military support to select African governments since 1980, an increase of 40 per cent in dollar terms between 1981 and 1985.[9]

African governments argue that their arms purchases and growing armies are necessary for national security. The argument has some validity, especially in southern Africa, as all of the independent African countries, known as the 'Frontline states', have been attacked or invaded by South Africa in recent years. Mozambique and Angola have faced the brunt of these wars, especially since 1980. South Africa trains, supplies and directs the rebel groups in Mozambique and Angola. The costs of South Africa's wars have been high. The independent states of southern Africa estimate that South Africa's military and economic destabilization campaign against them has resulted in 1.5 million deaths — 900,000 of which were of children — and damages and lost productivity exceeding $60 billion between 1980 and 1988.[10] The steady message from these countries is that their development is impeded and distorted as long as South Africa seeks to dominate the political and economic direction of the region. The independence of Angola and Mozambique in 1975 and Zimbabwe in 1980 was followed by an intensification of external violence by South

Africa. South Africa's goal has been to gain the acquiescence of the independent states to apartheid and resist the creation, through the Southern African Development Coordination Conference (SADCC), of a viable alternative regional economic structure.

In other nations, the military build-up also is justified in defence terms, but the effect of the militarization of the state has been to suppress internal dissent and provide a cover for greater Northern involvement. For example, an attempted overthrow of the government of Togo in October 1986 was quickly followed by the arrival of 400 French troops to support the regime. Kenya and Somalia, which border the Indian Ocean and are near the shipping routes for Middle Eastern oil, have military agreements with the U.S. In both countries, the U.S. has strengthened airfields and ports for possible use by the Rapid Deployment Force which is designed to strike into the Middle East at short notice to protect Northern oil interests. These two countries received the second and third largest amounts of U.S. military aid to Africa in the 1980s. There are no significant threats to the external security of these countries. In fact, the military aid strengthens the state against internal dissent. In Kenya, for example, that dissent comes from the growing number of impoverished rural and urban people who have seen a small minority of politicians, business people and civil servants consolidate their hold over half the nation's resources. The government of Somalia, isolated from popular concerns, used its military forces, largely equipped with U.S. weapons, in 1988 and 1989 in a devastating war against dissenting groups. An estimated 40,000 people died as the government bombed civilian centres and attacked refugees.[11]

Liberia's recent history offers another example of external intervention to prop up an unpopular, repressive and corrupt government. In 1980 a coup brought a new military government into power. Almost immediately, U.S. military aid increased, to over $13 million in 1985, and to a total of $66 million between 1980 and 1986. There is no external threat to Liberia, but there has been strong opposition to the military government since the mid-1980s. That opposition is due not only to the government's anti-democratic character and actions, but to its systematic draining of the national economy to the point where lower level civil servants go without pay for several months at a time. The U.S. has also provided substantial funds for imports. In return, the U.S. has constructed a transmitting station for communication with its own naval traffic in the South Atlantic and has maintained its Voice of America transmitter in Liberia.[12] To the north, the United States has developed a strong relationship with Senegal. Security and development aid dramatically increased during the 1980s. In turn, the U.S. has access to military facilities in Senegal and there have been suggestions that the U.S. is seeking to open a military airbase in the country.[13]

In 1977 the Soviet Union took over from the U.S. as the major arms supplier to Ethiopia. Arms imports there have been substantial and sustained. Imported weapons have been used to repulse an invasion by Somalia, against the liberation movement in Eritrea and against internal resistance to the regime, as in Tigray. These wars have been extremely costly: tens of thousands of lives have been lost as a result of the fighting. The wars exacerbated the famine conditions in 1983—86, in 1987—88 and again in 1989—90 and have caused hundreds of thousands of Ethiopians to flee their country as refugees. Currently, Ethiopia spends over 40 per cent of its annual budget on its military, a figure far greater than is spent on health and agricultural services.

The so-called wars of national liberation are putting into jeopardy our ability to influence world events . . . and to assure access to raw materials.
— Alexander Haig, U.S. Secretary of State, 1981.

Sexist stereotyping

The fourth facet of a world order detrimental to Africa is the imposition of Northern sex-role and labour division stereotypes. These stereotypical and Euro-centred assumptions have particularly undermined women's roles as food producers. Historically, Africa was self-sufficient in food. Now it is not. Now, as in the past, women have been responsible for nearly all food raised for family consumption. To understand the impediments to its production, one must look at the colonial legacy for African women.

Two of the major concepts which underlaid colonial agricultural policies in Africa were that men farmed while women took care of the household and children, and that men were responsible for their childrens' and families' needs and expenses. These were idealized concepts among male colonial officials who tended to come out of the upper middle class in Europe, but they were not true for African society. Labour and other production responsibilities *were* traditionally divided by gender, but not along the same lines as in Europe. Women grew food and were responsible for feeding themselves, their husbands and their children, and for taking care of families' daily needs through the exchange of surplus food crops. Men provided housing and tools, and helped their wives with heavy agricultural work such as clearing land and construction of granaries. But these were not hard-and-fast divisions and it was not uncommon for women and men to share the work of food production, especially during peaks in the demand for labour in the fields.

With little or no comprehension of African family and agricultural systems, European colonial rulers took three actions that were particularly disruptive, and which still adversely affect agriculture. First, they imposed taxes which had to be paid in currency; second, they expected or forced households to grow agricultural commodities to be exported for the colonial rulers' profits and to build the roads and other infrastructure necessary for profitable exporting; and third, they assigned communal land — newly designated for export crops — to presumed male heads of households. These actions assumed that men were responsible for farming and that, as household heads, it was the men who would work to earn cash. These assumptions were carried over into the post-colonial era. The African male elite looked to white-collar employment for income and status while arguing that the privileged male role in agriculture was 'traditional' and 'culturally' sacrosanct. Most international development agencies maintained the male, middle-class tradition of the colonial period and focused their agricultural programmes, credit schemes and extension advice on those people they assumed were the responsible farmers — men.[14]

For women, the repercussions of the transformation to cash cropping and a cash economy have been particularly devastating. Women have less and less land to cultivate because when land is scarce and revenue is needed, women's land for food crops is often taken by male leaders or husbands and re-assigned to men. Women's traditional land rights and agricultural independence have been reduced because they must devote more time to working on the cash crops whose revenues are controlled by their husbands. Consequently, women have less revenue, for they no longer have as much surplus from their food crops to sell for their own income. Their work loads also have increased, for women are expected to do the sowing and weeding tasks on land used for cash crops, as well as all agricultural labour on their own food crops. Often they are not even able to grow enough food for family consumption. The 20 to 50 per cent of women who head households in various parts of Africa may be less controlled by male direction, but generally have fewer rights to good land and alone must meet their families' cash and food needs. It has been found that the size of harvest is often dependent not on what the land will produce but on how much work in the fields women can squeeze into their already busy days. Finally, because national policies focus on training and furnishing inputs to the men who are doing cash cropping, little research has been done on improving cultivation of food crops, developing labour-saving technologies for women, or providing women with the training and organizational support which are likely to assist their tremendous contribution to African well-being and economic growth.

The end result has been a vulnerability among rural women and children to circumstances which may affect their precarious food and living conditions. Those circumstances can be as subtle as seasonal changes in food availability and disease fluctuations. Often, new 'development' projects either alienate women or require of them expanded work loads.[15] The ever expanding pressures on rural women to perform a multitude of tasks for survival have not been rewarded by any serious efforts to promote women's needs. The general economic crisis throughout Africa, both as described by official development agencies and as experienced by the people themselves, derives in large part from the neglect and mistreatment of women.

Thus, the 1980s have brought to a head the Northern exploitation of Africa. The economic and social exploitation of Africa has intensified, often undermining the achievements of earlier decades. For most of us in the North, exposure to these changes has meant glimpses of starving children and regular stories about additional food aid needs. Yet, the crises not only reflect these images, but incorporate major structural wrenching of African states and people, and a continued transfer of resources out of Africa to serve Northern interests.

Notes

1. World Bank, *World Development Report 1985* (Washington, DC, 1985); United Nations, *Africa: One Year Later* (New York, 1987).
2. Stephen Commins, *Africa's Food Crisis: Which Way Out?* (Africa Faith and Justice Network, Washington, DC, 1984).
3. Carol Lancaster and John Williams, *African Debt and Financing* (Institute for International Economics, Washington, DC, 1986), pp. 30−46; Tony Killick and Matthew Martin, 'African debt: the search for solutions', *Briefing Paper* of the UN Africa Recovery Programme, No. 1 (June 1989).
4. Africa Recovery News Feature, 'An alternative necessitated by unremitting decline', 26 June 1989.
5. Giovanni Andrea Cornia, 'Economic decline and human welfare in the first half of the 1980s', in Giovanni Andrea Cornia, *et al.* (eds.), *Adjustment with a Human Face*, Vol. 1 (Clarendon Press, Oxford, 1987), p. 25.
6. Dorothy Muntemba, 'The impact of IMF−World Bank programmes on women and children in Zambia', in Bade Onimode (ed.), *The IMF, the World Bank and the African Debt: Vol. 2, The Social and Political Impact* (Institute for African Alternatives and Zed Books, London, 1989), pp. 122−123.
7. See the essays on Senegal and Nigeria in Onimode (ed.), *op. cit*.
8. Bill Rau, 'Conditions for disaster: the IMF and Zambia', unpublished paper for Interfaith Action for Economic Justice, Washington, DC, 1983; Economic Commission for Africa, *South African Destabilization: the Economic Cost of Frontline Resistance to Apartheid* (UN, New York, 1989), pp. 32−33.

9. J. G. Donders, *War and Rumours of War*, Spearhead No. 94 (Gaba Publications, Eldoret, Kenya, 1987).

10. Economic Commission for Africa, *op. cit.*, p. 6.

11. The estimate of casualties comes from *Africa Watch*. See also United States General Accounting Office, *Somalia: Observations Regarding the Northern Conflict and Resulting Conditions* (UN, Washington, DC, 1989).

12. Larry James, 'A seven-cornered solution?', *Africa Report* (November–December 1986), pp. 31–33; U.S. General Accounting Office, *Liberia: Need to Improve Accountability and Control over U.S. Assistance* (Washington, DC, July 1987).

13. Abdoulaye Bathily, 'Senegal's structural adjustment programme and its economic and social effects: the political economy of regression', in Onimode (ed.), *op. cit.*, p. 137.

14. A good treatment of these ideas is found in *Feeding the Nation — Women of Cameroon* (Match International Centre, Ottawa, nd.).

15. Jennie Dey, 'Gambian women: unequal partners in Rive development projects', *Journal of Development Studies*, Vol. 17 (1981), pp. 109–122; the entire issue of *IDS Bulletin*, Vol. 17, No. 3 (July 1986) is devoted to the theme of 'Seasonality and Poverty'.

Part II

The Official Cures
for Africa

8 Strangers of Disorder: Northern Answers for Africa

For hundreds and thousands of years, African societies managed their affairs in such a way as to grow, prosper, become and remain self-sufficient in food production, and to develop elaborate cultural, ritual and political systems. Values of sharing, cooperation and respect for the forces that remain unseen but central to peace, harmony and well-being have guided social relations. Complex economic relations — ranging from long distance trade across the Sahara to daily labour management — evolved in ways that provided most people with the necessities of life. And life was usually accepted as good by most people. To be sure, there were wars (although not on the scale to which we have become accustomed today), disease, hardships due to drought and pests. Slavery existed in various societies and at various times and further divided Africans into separate groups. There were periods of food shortages and of famine. Yet, throughout the centuries, the skills, knowledge and organization existed in most African societies that enabled them to retain balanced systems that promoted stability and effective change and, usually, food self-sufficiency.

The intrusion of the world economy, with power concentrated in the Northern nations, began to alter the conditions Africans had created for themselves. The slave trade, followed by the era of colonial rule and now the period of national independence, in turn progressively integrated Africa into the world economy. Indigenous skills and knowledge of crops, soils, environment, manufacturing, labour relations and religion have been challenged and widely discredited as Africa has become further incorporated into a global political economy. Narrow concepts of development have replaced African concepts of well-being; Northern technical expertise has come to be seen as more legitimate than African scientific experimentation and observation. Internal management of social relations for the social good often has been subsumed to the control of political power by national elites who maintain links with international capital. And although Africa retains the ability to produce food to meet the needs of its people, policies which favour food production and agricultural growth for broader economic expansion, as largely existed 100 years

97

ago, have been replaced by policies that promote production of agricultural crops for export.

It is against this background of colonial and neo-colonial intrusion, and African responses, that we can assess the common prescriptions for dealing with Africa's problems and measure the success of popular attempts to redefine development.

As the world's citizens responded to the human suffering of famine in Ethiopia and Sudan late in 1984, there began to emerge in the public mind the belief that Africa as a whole was close to collapse. The repeated scenes of starving people on television and in the literature of relief agencies reinforced these impressions. The public in Europe and North America was led to believe that all Africans were helpless and in need of assistance. In turn, the search to identify the causes of 'Africa's crisis' became more intense among Northern-based financial and technical agencies involved in 'development'.[1] The causal factors most often cited include: overpopulation, desertification, failed national government policies, and, in the case of Ethiopia, Mozambique and Angola, Marxism. However, these alleged problems were not derived from a careful analysis of the past nor of actual conditions within African countries and communities themselves. Rather, the reasons most often cited in many Northern development circles for Africa's problems were simply a rehash of development views long held in the North, and which have served Northern interests for fifty years. Often prognoses were made on the basis of superficial symptoms and intended outcomes, rather than in-depth assessment of popular needs and interests. Processes of planning were devised that encompassed Northern economic experiences and these were splinted onto Africa's emerging planning ministries. Inevitably, the programmes put forward assumed a high degree of Northern intervention in African affairs. In this chapter we review some of the opinions emanating from major institutions in Northern countries.

... [T]he present structures of development and assistance continue to be based on the principle of developing the communities by competent outside developers as if they could not develop themselves. This infantilization of the deprived populations, added to an ideology of development which tends to consider them as objects of wider national plans rather than the living subjects of their destiny, is the primary reason why development activities do not take root in the life of the communities.

— Majid Rahnema, United Nations Development Programme, 1984.

The World Bank

There were many precedents for the prescriptions offered to treat 'Africa's crisis', but a major source has been the writings of the World Bank in the 1980s. The World Bank is the largest multinational lending and technical agency involved with Third World development issues. The World Bank uses an annual administrative budget of nearly $900 million, two thirds of which goes for the salaries of its 6,000 plus employees. It has an annual lending authority of over $20 billion and, as a commercial lender, regularly makes annual profits of over $1 billion. The Bank commands a powerful place in the development establishment with its views, programmes and financial resources. And behind the Bank itself, its membership (and voting authority) is dominated by the United States, Japan and the Western European countries. The Bank has used its position and resources both to interpret the causes of Africa's food and development crises and to offer a series of major solutions.

In both its analysis and prescriptions, the World Bank begins with a series of working assumptions. Among those assumptions, the following tend to be at the forefront of the Bank's writings on Africa:

• the need for nations to export goods and commodities in which they have a comparative advantage in the international market place;
• the value of biotechnology in promoting any form of agricultural growth;
• the importance of economic growth over other social development programmes and the need to express social programmes within the context of their contribution to economic growth;
• the need for technocratic bureaucracies to direct and control economic growth; and
• the need to maintain national economic systems in line with the dominant structure of the world economy.

The World Bank's view of the world is primarily that of macro-economists of a capitalist tradition; other perspectives are far less important. Most of the staff economists are trained in or are from Northern countries with a long history of capitalist economic growth. Not surprisingly then, the World Bank's views of Africa encompass the cultural and economic heritage of Western Europe and the United States, with both its positive and negative values.

Probably the most influential public document which the World Bank has produced on African development is *Accelerated Development in Sub-Saharan Africa*, also known as the 'Berg Report' after its principal author.[2] Published in 1981, the report still incorporates and reflects the Bank's basic position on Africa, and more recent sub-regional and national Bank strategies have all been based on that position. The Berg Report sought to address the severe economic and developmental problems in Africa which were becoming increasingly obvious to

Africans and outside observers in the late 1970s. Later described by World Bank officials as a contribution to the dialogue on Africa's economic future, the report nevertheless is written as an authoritative piece, offering little room for compromise, dissent or popular alteration. In essence, it is a polemic that describes the continent in crisis terms and prescribes solutions which conform only to Northern and World Bank realities, not those within Africa itself. Not surprisingly, any African input into the World Bank's diagnosis was from technocrats whose ideas were in line with those of the Bank itself.

Key to the Berg Report is its direct attack on African governments for their failures to design effective policies for economic growth and to manage their economies in sound ways. It is a theme which has acquired wide popularity in development circles in the North. While peripherally acknowledging that African states 'inherited unevenly developed economies with rudimentary infrastructure' at independence, the Report is far more concerned with the inadequacy of policy support to non-public sectors of the economy. Thus the World Bank's assessment underplays the historical constraints on development faced by all African states, arising out of their colonial experience. As we have argued in earlier chapters, the distorting and extractive impact of colonialism severely curtailed Africa's independent ability to quickly or effectively pursue policies of broad economic and social development. Further, the advice which many African governments were given by the World Bank and other donors in the 1960s and 1970s directly contributed to 'Africa's crisis' in the 1980s.

In Tanzania, for example, the World Bank helped design and finance an industrial policy divorced from the agricultural base on which almost all Tanzanians gained their livelihood. Also, the World Bank provided substantial loans for Tanzania's village consolidation process. Later, the Bank roundly criticized the latter programme without mentioning its own earlier advice and lending. Distortions in Zambia's economy also were perpetuated by the World Bank. Following independence, Zambia remained very dependent upon a small number of commercial farmers, most of them former white colonials. Among the first projects funded by the World Bank in Zambia were two designed to assure the continuity of this minority segment of the farming community in the Zambian economy, although fully 95 per cent of the rural people were small-scale farmers.[3] These two examples typify the Bank's continued focus on large-scale and commercial projects which have ignored and thereby undermined food security, especially that of African women who are responsible for raising nearly all the food eaten by their families.

The crisis which African states faced in the late 1970s and into the 1980s was, to a significant degree, the result of development policies and projects imposed by outside contributors who had used money and their experts' mystique to gain government compliance. The overwhelming majority of the projects supported by outside contributors failed. Many failed to achieve their own objectives, many could not be sustained once external funding ended, and others could not be replicated.[4] Isolated instances of increased rural incomes, of greater agricultural output, of on-going health and nutrition programmes are often cited by World Bank staff and companies attached to the Bank through operating contracts as examples of the Bank's achievements. Privately, and increasingly publicly, both large and small foreign contributors are saying that their work in Africa has not brought about sustained growth, nor equitable development, nor greater structural stability. The Berg Report reflected these frustrations, but rather than carefully searching out the range of reasons for such massive developmental failures, the World Bank — and others — blamed Africans themselves for being poor managers and planners. The crisis, in the view of the World Bank, was very much 'Africa's crisis'.

Despite commanding the largest group of development technocrats in the world, the Bank's analysis is frequently subject to technical and ideological flaws. In seeking to garner support for its Structural Adjustment Loans (SAL) and policy reform packages to African countries, the Bank produced a report in 1989 arguing that countries undertaking reforms showed better economic performance than countries which had not. The Economic Commission for Africa, a UN agency, but representative of the views of African states, convincingly countered by showing that the Bank's analysis was based on faulty use of the Bank's own data and only limited consideration of all available evidence.[5] More specifically, an examination of the World Bank's review of Nigerian agriculture found that the data describing differentiation between groups of farmers, their farming methods and the crop outputs were unrealistic. Further, the Bank's favourite method of assessing project feasibility, cost-benefit analysis, has relied in Nigeria on unreliable surveys and incomplete use of available data — such as the impacts of subsidies on agricultural inputs.[6] What is clear is that the World Bank is quite capable of both making mistakes and engaging in cover-ups and lying to pursue its ideological mandate.[7] World Bank public documents often are deceitful in their choice of certain examples and the emphasis given to others. Late in 1989, the World Bank produced yet another prescriptive piece for Africa.[8] In its 300 pages, this report repeats the ahistorical approach of the Berg Report. In a chapter given over to 'Sustainable Growth with Equity', the latter issue receives about one page of attention and then in the context of increasing the productivity of poor people and checking elite corruption. Structural adjustment programmes are suggested as examples of promoting greater equity, but the Bank fails to mention its central interaction with African governments during the 'economic crisis of the early 1980s [which] diverted attention from basic needs programmes'. In admitting that this diversion was a mistake, the World Bank seems to have forgotten that it and other policy and lending agencies were instrumental in requiring cutbacks in governmental social welfare spending programmes.

Given its ideological mission, the World Bank's proposals for African governments to remove themselves from their own entanglements fit a pattern reflective of the 'free market' economic climate prevailing in the United States, Great Britain and other Northern countries in the 1980s. Three issues are central to the Bank's arguments: increased exports and greater openness to external investments; greater attention to agriculture; and a reduction in the role of government in the economy.

Export economies

The issue of increasing exports is related to a series of recommendations affecting trade relations. The core of what the World Bank suggests is that African countries must export more of their commodities in order to earn foreign exchange. The foreign exchange will be used to purchase goods and services on the world market. In theory such purchases will contribute to internal growth, both agricultural and manufacturing. The Bank was concerned that the volume of agricultural exports from Africa had declined during the 1970s. The value of most mineral exports had also declined during the same period, leaving many African countries with a diminished economic base from which to support social and other programmes.

The Bank's recommendation to increase exports of both agricultural and mineral commodities, however, contains several flaws. First, Africa has been exporting its human and natural resources for over 350 years and this has greatly distorted the structure of national economies. Africa's national economies are already export-oriented, with policies and resources programmed to support the production of select agricultural goods for which official markets exist. Roads, markets, credit schemes, massive irrigation projects and land clearing have been features of these programmes to facilitate production and marketing of cash crops. However, to expand export production at this time, as the Bank and like-minded agencies suggest, can only place greater strains on the survival of rural people. Food needs of the poor rural and urban majority will be sacrificed. Women in particular, who often head households, will be pressed even harder to meet both the food and cash requirements of their families.

Second, the more important question for African states is not simply whether to export but at what value to themselves and their producers. The value of many agricultural and mineral commodities has declined on the world market since the middle of the 1970s. In

1986 alone, the total value of Africa's commodity exports collapsed by $20 billion on world markets; consumers outside of Africa, in turn, paid $20 billion less for coffee, cocoa, oil and other commodities. In 1987, the prices Africa received for its exports improved slightly, but declined to the lowest level of the decade in 1988. However, the prices Africa must pay for imported manufactured goods and oil dramatically increased. The issue, then, is not so much one of expanding exports, but of getting a fair return for those items exported. On this issue, Africans have sought to influence world trading structures through negotiations, but with little impact. The Bank itself notes the discrepancy between export and import prices, but refuses to become involved in effective negotiations to alter the world trading system. Instead, the burden remains on African states and producers to take up the slack and adjust to the international market system.

Third, the export prescriptions of the World Bank perpetuate many of the imbalances in internal social relations. As development policies and resources are funnelled into export production, those groups of people least able to deal with the level of production required of exports are ignored and pushed to the side. Women who once controlled access to land for their own use lose out to men who engage in export-oriented production; poor households which are unable or unwilling to buy into the export sector are expected to become the hired labourers of those who can; national infrastructure becomes designed to facilitate exports rather than respond to local needs, thus reinforcing the structures created by colonial regimes that discriminated against peasant farmers.

Agricultural performance

The second emphasis of the World Bank, said to be a key to Africa's future, is the need of governments to revise policies so as to improve agricultural performance. On the surface, most people would have little objection to this position. The Bank blames the poor performance of agriculture on the lack of sufficient price incentives for producers, on costly subsidies used to keep food prices low for urban consumers, and on mismanaged and heavily subsidized marketing boards. All are, indeed, factors in agricultural performance. But other factors, essentially more critical, are ignored by the Bank. Such factors include differential access to production resources by rural people, massive poverty which requires many people to enter the market at a disadvantage and popular interest in maintaining food security before catering to external benefits from production.[9]

As others have also argued, farmers are unlikely to produce for the market if they are denied a reasonable return for their efforts. This, apparently, is what has been occurring in many places in Africa. But what also seems to be happening is that as people sell less through official marketing channels, they are turning to 'unofficial' channels for the bulk of their sales — markets they themselves or private traders have created.[10] A main measurement of agricultural performance is through sales. Official figures indicate decreases in sales of many commodities, but no attempt is made to account for the ever increasing levels of 'informal' sales that are not reflected in official statistics. Thus, it is not possible to assess levels of agricultural production effectively from the commonly used data, nor to claim a spreading crisis of declining food availability. Unfortunately, the Bank and its member governments are less concerned with the who and why of production and marketing than with gaining greater control over producers and the marketing of their produce. The assessments of declining agricultural production have 'logically' led to solutions that involve greater integration of rural areas and people into the global economy.

One effective method of control over producers is the insistence of donors that production packages of hybrid seed, chemical fertilizers, pesticides, extension advice and marketing be used by farmers for most efficient results. Expanding irrigation systems is often added as a component of these packages. The African experience has shown this 'green revolution' approach to productivity increases to be especially risky for all but the most established and largest farmers. The risks include the high costs of acquiring hybrid seed, fertilizer and pesticides; the vulnerability of the seed to drought and local storage; the increased labour needed for weeding; the questionable advice of research and extension departments whose orientation is often biased toward the largest, most productive farmers; and reliance on a marketing system that must operate efficiently to make investment in the package worthwhile. These risks entail increased costs of production which are likely to be passed on to consumers either in the form of higher food prices or higher public subsidies. Governments have indeed sought to keep food costs down, often paying low prices for marketed goods. But they have also had to seek a balance between producers and consumers, as well as deriving some economic benefits for the state from the marketing of agricultural products.

Thus, the issue is more complex than it is often presented. Simply to increase producer prices will not alone deal adequately with the food crisis of many African states and may increase the crisis for the poor who will have to pay higher prices. Further, farmers have demonstrated that the 'green revolution' methods and implications advocated by the World Bank do not meet their needs. Farmers have demonstrated that viable alternatives exist, but these require alternative approaches to development by many African governments and contributing agencies.

Public policies and investment
The third issue raised by the Berg Report is that of government

involvement in national economic concerns. The Bank argues that a high level of state ownership and investment in industry, agriculture, commerce and transport has resulted in the misuse of scarce resources. Also, the Bank feels that the commitment that many governments have made to providing social services to the population as a whole has severely reduced the amount of capital available for 'productive' investment. Again, the Bank's views have some validity. Bureaucracies did expand dramatically following the independence of most states, with the ambiguous intention of offering public services neglected by colonial governments while extending the authority of the state. The need of the state — and the national elites — has been to assert control over production in order to acquire wealth and assert a policy of national unity. Those goals are not always compatible, and in many countries the national elites have expanded their positions at the expense of the nation.

The fault with the World Bank's argument, however, is the assumption that public investment is non-productive. At independence, the private sector in many African countries was too weak or small to offer even basic consumer goods to a portion of the population. Foreign investors controlled many of the large industries or companies and profits were regularly transferred out of African countries rather than reinvested internally. The choice for governments was to invest public funds in what were felt to be important industries; the alternative was to remain dependent upon foreign-owned businesses. For example, Mozambique's housing policy incorporates construction methods that include using locally produced materials, an approach that seeks to encourage local industry and low-cost housing while reversing the colonial pattern of dependence on similar imported materials. Most states opted for a mixed approach, investing in needed industry, buying out companies which were considered essential to national security and development while maintaining a flexible relationship with other foreign investors. This, in fact, has been the advice long given by the World Bank, but which it now rebuts. The reality is that public involvement in the economy, in planning and investment, is vital for African growth and well-being. What is at issue is how the state is involved in economic and development activities, and from whom the state takes its direction for defining change. To date, the views of the World Bank and other contributing agencies have played a key role in contributing to the choices governments have made in defining their developmental policies. After a careful review of the social impact of policy changes undertaken by Mozambique in the late 1980s, one researcher concludes:

> One of the most troubling dimensions [of these changes] was Mozambique's dramatic dependency on the donor community. Control has shifted out of African hands in an alarming fashion. Economic policy

has come to rest very much with the IMF/World Bank, with bilateral donors lining up behind it. UNICEF is more and more taking the leading role in social policy. The emergency situation [caused by war and drought] has resulted in a large amount of control passing into the hands of a multiplicity of NGOs and bilateral donors.[11]

In Mozambique, in Nigeria, in Tanzania and across the African continent, the World Bank has contributed to what it calls 'Africa's crisis' more than it knows or at least more than it acknowledges. In essence, the World Bank has been the lead public agency in disrupting African agricultural production and undermining African sovereignty.

'Free markets' and USAID

Following in the path of the World Bank, USAID outlined an 'Assistance Strategy' for Africa in the mid-1980s. Like the European Economic Community's development programme and many other bilateral financial and policy contributors, USAID places most of the blame for structural deficiencies on African countries themselves. Not surprisingly, the policies of the United States in creating and sustaining those deficiencies are not noted. Assistance to Africa from the United States is based on two major assumptions: first, African developmental interests are secondary to protecting and strengthening U.S. security and business interests; and second, the U.S. model of 'free enterprise' and 'individual initiative' overrides local realities and indigenous choices.

The realities of the politics of a major international power like the U.S. mean that national self-interest is and will remain the most significant factor in foreign policy formulation. Even the U.S. response to famine in Ethiopia was determined by such considerations. U.S. officials knew in 1983 of the plight of rural people in Ethiopia yet postponed any response in part because of U.S. disagreement with Ethiopia's politics. As we have seen, when the U.S. Congress proposed emergency aid to the famine victims in 1984, proponents had to beat back a Reagan Administration attempt to tie famine relief to increased military aid for the Contras in Central America. In 1985 food aid was eventually given to Ethiopia — grudgingly by the Reagan Administration — with the explicit hope that it could also be used to force Ethiopia to realign its strategic ties, away from the Soviet Union and toward the United States.[12]

The use of U.S. aid to combat communist influence in Africa reflects a belief that all political and economic events can be reduced to a conflict between the United States and the Soviet Union. The fact that Africans do not agree with this East-West mentality does not change the United States' approach to African affairs. The superpower mentality which underlies U.S. involvement in Africa resulted in the mid-1980s in the U.S. joining with South Africa in providing major military and intelligence assistance to anti-government forces in Angola. This assistance affected the children of Angola by causing one of the highest infant mortality rates of any country in the world. Even in the wake of growing detente between the U.S. and the Soviet Union at the end of the 1980s, the U.S. expanded its military assistance to the UNITA forces. Another outcome of U.S. military relations with Africa has been the contribution to increased militarization in Kenya, Somalia and Senegal where the U.S. now has military landing rights for its Rapid Deployment Force — rights it protects with large amounts of military and other security aid to those countries.

Corporate capitalism

Under the Reagan Administration, U.S. foreign aid more fully and blatantly expressed the ideology of private enterprise. The Reagan interpretation of private enterprise applies primarily to the corporate level, as many private farmers and low-income people in the U.S. discovered to their sorrow throughout the 1980s. But this ideology of U.S. corporate capitalism ignores the reality that the vast majority of rural people in Africa already work as private farmers and that most trade already flows through private channels. U.S. aid would seek to displace these people in favour of corporate agribusiness and construction, manufacturing and mining companies. The private sector rhetoric also ignores the reality that many governments which the U.S. supports regularly expropriate the private capital of their citizens.[13] In Zaire, Kenya, the Sudan and Liberia, government leaders utilize their treasuries and ties to the 'private sector' for self-enrichment. Of the 48 sub-Saharan countries and regional programmes receiving U.S. foreign aid, these four countries receive nearly 60 per cent of all U.S. military aid to sub-Saharan Africa and 23 per cent of all development aid. U.S. military and security assistance to Africa rapidly escalated at the beginning of the Reagan Administration, topping out at over $560 million in 1985.[14] Budget constraints in the United States were a factor in causing a reduction from that level in the late 1980s. A probably even more important factor was the subtle but real shift in U.S. thinking that recognized the vulnerability of African governments to external financial and policy controls. Essentially, the destabilization fashioned by military and security aid opened the way for more subtle but no less insidious intervention by financial agents representing U.S. and European corporate interests. Policy reform became the instrument of power from the mid-1980s. USAID proudly boasts: 'America is only the fifth largest donor in Africa. . . . But America's impact on policy reform in Africa is greater than this would imply.'[15] 'Policy dialogue' and reliance on the open market pressures being exerted by the World Bank and the IMF became the follow-up to security aid to ensure African compliance with U.S. global needs for security-related minerals, markets and investment opportunities, and isolation of countries seeking substantive economic transformation, such as Angola and Mozambique.

The quality of the multinationals' soap is not always better than the local products, but it's publicised and packaged as though the good life depends on it. All part of a 'taste-transfer' process that is turning Kenya into a Western-style consumer society.

The multinational soap merchants in Kenya run up an annual advertising bill of some $1,500,000. This is over one-and-a-half times the money the government allocated for a five-year programme to build rural health centres.
— Revd Henry Okullu, Anglican Bishop of Maseno South, Kenya, 1978.

USAID's private enterprise ideology emphasizes 'individual initiative', a concept used by a narrow elite of financially well-off people who have the resources and power to ignore the collective contributions which have gone into creating their positions and wealth. Within the African context, the U.S. ideology of individual initiative seeks to create or stabilize elite groups which are ideologically and politically tied to global capital. In rural areas this has entailed supporting agricultural production projects with credit, subsidized inputs and close managerial attention. The risks connected with such projects normally discourage poor people from taking part, leaving the way open for farmers with greater initial resources who regularly and inevitably receive the most attention and support from such projects. Following an extensive review of a USAID-assisted livestock programme in Niger, a senior research scientist concluded that the politicized and narrow nature of USAID's private sector actions may render 'smallholders less and less able to pursue satisfactory lives in their own countries and on their own lands'.[16]

The ideology of individual initiative seeks to substitute American values of competition and consumerism for African values of collective gain and well-being for the community. Advocates of the private sector fail to address the extreme disparities in wealth which have resulted from corporate control over the economy. Within Africa, most states experienced similar inequalities during the colonial era and, at least at the level of national ideology, have voiced a commitment to rectify past and potential class divisions.

The European Community and food security

The colonial history of Africa places Western European countries in a special position toward the continent. Clearly, Africa would not now be where it is without intimate involvement with European states over the past three hundred and fifty years. Food security in African states is an official concern for the European Community for humanitarian reasons and, as during colonial times, to assure internal stability and movement of raw materials out of African countries. Starving people are not good producers of goods. Thus, the aid and trade programmes that have grown up between Africa and the EEC reflect both the advantages and disadvantages of those historical connections. At the same time, the aid programme of the EEC reflects close collaboration with other major Northern actors, notably the World Bank.

The food shortages in Africa in the early 1980s coincided with an internal review by the EEC of its development policies toward Africa. Large-scale infrastructure projects and supply-driven food aid had been the EEC norm. 'Food strategies' became the new model for EEC aid and food aid was de-linked from internal surplus pressures of the Community. The approach was attractive for several reasons. First, food and project aid would be integrated with the food policies of African states, giving more focus and support to sustained food security efforts. Second, the EEC's programme was initially limited to four countries: Mali, Rwanda, Kenya and Zambia. These 'pilot' efforts would allow closer supervision and dialogue with national governments. Third, the emphasis on food strategies suggested practical and more sensitive relations with African countries, in contrast to the heavy-handed policy reform focus being pursued by the World Bank at the same time. Fourth, the EEC food strategies programme, like other donor initiatives in the 1980s, called for donor coordination as a means of improving the efficiency of aid packages.[17]

In seeking to develop a food strategies approach for its aid programme, EEC thinking reflected a strong disillusionment among development practitioners following the collapse of many large-scale projects. Those projects had been designed in the wake of the 1973–74 food shortages and famines in the Sahel. Aid agencies sought to transform the African countryside with ambitious and costly irrigation, livestock and agricultural projects. However, those projects failed on several counts. The costs of maintaining such extensive infrastructure — both the personnel and the technology — were beyond the capacity of most African governments. The needs and experiences of local people were regularly ignored in the contributors' rush to prevent further famines. Intended beneficiaries were, in fact, subordinated to managements' needs for regulated systems that conformed to paper plans rather than to local economic, social and political realities. By the late 1970s and early 1980s, many of the costly projects were operating at reduced levels or had collapsed due to their poor design and rejection by local people.

Yet the EEC food strategies approach of the mid-1980s contained some of the same flaws as the earlier 'development' decade and other flaws particular to the 1980s themselves. First, the food strategies model, despite its name, was concerned with promotion of agricultural production for export purposes, whether to overseas or national urban markets. The focus was not on the food security needs of rural people who were most vulnerable to hunger and poverty. From the point of view of European planners — and manufacturers and consumers — maintaining the flow of tropical products to European markets was as logical and needed as were regular and reasonably priced food supplies for urban consumers in the view of African planners and politicians. Thus, among the EEC-funded projects in Africa in the early 1980s, projects that were explicitly designed to produce export crops were three times as common as those designed to produce food crops.[18]

Second, the EEC approach was in terms of national food security: an adequacy of food from production and imports to meet an aggregate national demand. Determining national demand is easily skewed by inadequate data on population size and dietary needs, and by vocal urban demand. But even more crucial in terms of real food security is the way in which national food security easily obscures the specific needs of particular groups of people. For example, in 1988 the Sudan on a national basis produced a substantial surplus of food, yet at least 1.5 million people, displaced from their homes due to war and having taken refuge around the capital, did not have adequate food. The aggregate national figures which most international aid and lending agencies rely upon in designing agricultural projects fail to differentiate between well-to-do urban consumers, poor women who are heads of households and pastoralists whose herds may have been decimated by lack of fodder or water. The result is that projects and EEC policy retain a bias toward national, aggregate figures and are designed to address assumed average needs and conditions rather than the special needs of lower-income people.

Mali's agricultural reform programme, begun in 1982, typifies the situation. Under pressure from the IMF in the late 1970s, Mali was forced to adopt a series of measures designed to reduce state spending. EEC, U.S. and World Bank assistance in the early 1980s became linked to the expansion of opportunities for private grain traders and intensified efforts to increase grain production. Both the EEC and the U.S. tied food aid shipments to effective implementation by the government of a programme of reform. The food aid could be sold by the Malian government to cover operating deficits of its agencies associated with the reforms.

Grain production did, on average, increase during the 1980s, but in the two most productive years favourable weather conditions rather than improved prices for farmers are credited with the increased output. But these national averages obscure significant differential impacts on various population groups. It was assumed that almost all rural households sold grain and would benefit from increases in producer prices. The first part of the assumption was correct, but not the latter. The vast majority of low-income rural people did make grain sales on the market because they needed cash for other purchases. In many cases, these low-income households sold small amounts, on average just over 100 kilograms of grain; but they also purchased grain on the market, on average over 250 kilograms. Nearly 50 per cent of the households in the dryer, less productive northern part of the country depended upon purchased grain for their food supply. Thus, any advantages gained by low-income farmer households from improved grain prices were offset by higher expenditures on purchases of grain they needed to survive.[19] In a country where vulnerability to hunger is a recurrent threat, the types of agricultural reforms undertaken with external direction have the potential for increasing the problems of marginal and poor households.

Finally, while clearly a semblance of coordination and efficiency in contributors' programmes is needed, the EEC food strategy approach overlaps with and plays along with the structural adjustment programmes being pursued by the World Bank. As we noted above, these programmes are designed to promote export production and greater opportunities for external investment and to correct internal policy and management problems that are said to inhibit effective development. The World Bank and other lenders and aid contributors have been able to exert coordinated pressure on countries to enforce adherence to the structural adjustment and reform packages. African countries are faced with an all-or-nothing approach from external agencies, leaving them little choice but to accept the reform conditions set down by the lenders' coalition in order to acquire the hard currency used to buy goods and service existing debts.

EEC involvement in the structural adjustment programmes has been slightly moderated by strong African resistance, but the added pressure from the IMF and the World Bank has limited such resistance. Thus, the EEC is a party to the attack on African sovereignty. In this case sovereignty means the right and responsibility of countries to draw upon their history and social relations to define the political and economic systems that meet people's needs. There is plenty of room for criticism of the misuse of that responsibility by African rulers. But it remains essential to the African experience that those contradictions be worked out from within, not through external intervention, no matter how subtly or benevolently applied. However, as we have argued, the history of external intervention in Africa is anything but subtle; the impacts of the structural adjustment reforms carry similar forms of direct and indirect violence against peasants, women, children, low-income and unemployed urban workers and refugees as occurred under colonialism.

Thus, the EEC development assistance programme offers little that can provide leverage for African countries to transform the unequal international and national relations that have characterized European-African interaction over the past century. The EEC programme is somewhat less ideological than USAID's, which harps so much on privatization, and less powerful than the financial and technical impositions of the World Bank. But in the main, the EEC programme replicates and often overlaps with the involvement of the World Bank and USAID in Africa. In the end, European interests, not African, form the essence of EEC involvement on the continent.

PVOs/NGOs

The 'private' sector also has outlined its recommendations for Africa in a number of documents. We will look at one of the most conspicuous ones from the United States, the *Compact for African Development*.[20] The private sector refers to PVOs, also called NGOs, and sometimes to the for-profit corporations and consulting firms also involved in international development work. Even the terms PVO or NGO convey more of an ideal than the current reality of most development groups in this category. Many PVOs have close ideological and financial ties to official, governmental aid and most do not actually operate as volunteer agencies. In fact, the salaries paid by PVOs for so-called professional staff and consultants are often in excess of $40,000 per year. It is estimated that it costs between $100,000 and $200,000 to place a U.S. or UN 'development worker' in the field for one year. This cost rapidly distorts any meaningful grassroots planning and control, a role which PVOs hold up as one of their most significant in the development process. It is not uncommon for some PVOs to obtain 75 per cent of their funding from government sources. The U.S. government and some PVOs themselves regularly contract with for-profit corporations to carry out development projects. In fact, a significant proportion of the members of the committee which produced the *Compact for African Development* worked at for-profit corporations doing business in the Third World.

PVOs/NGOs often provide structural alternatives to the large, bureaucratic and politically guided donors, like the World Bank and USAID. The PVO sector does tend to work on a smaller scale, through less elaborate bureaucratic layers and occasionally closer to indigenous people's groups. There are some instances where PVOs/NGOs are working in collaboration with local African NGOs, sometimes even taking a subordinate role. Gradually, the experiences of PVOs

are receiving more recognition from major contributors, although
there are few examples of the adoption of NGO methods and lessons
by official government funders.[21] Finally, the PVO/NGO sector is not
homogeneous — it is diverse in attitudes, methods of work, sensitivity
to development issues, funding sources, and field experiences. Some
NGOs accept no government funding and conduct successful collaborative programmes; others are overtly corrupt and self-serving.

'Perpetual chaos'

The 'private' sector documents on Africa are a response to the
1984–85 famines. As such they seek to clarify the causes of the
development and food crises in Africa and to offer solutions. The
situation they describe in Africa is bleak. They report that 'Entire
communities may perish', and present images of 'perpetual chaos ...
natural disasters, political upheaval ... [and] financial ruin'.[22] When
seeking to clarify the causes of such problems, the *Compact for African
Development* looks no further back than 30 years ago. The impact of
colonialism on African development structures is ignored; rather, the
themes of internal mismanagement, weak policies and corruption are
stressed without reference to the debilitating structural linkages
dictated by Africa's position within the world economic system. To its
credit, the *Compact* also critiques 'well-intentioned outsiders' for
contributing to Africa's development and financial problems.

The contrasts between the document's explanations of internal and
external contributions to Africa's problems are striking. Financial
and technical contributors are 'well-intentioned', Africans are
'unwise' and 'wasteful.' Corruption among national elites has drained
national resources, but contributors merely 'have jumped from one
fad to another to justify development expenditures'.[23] The implication
in these descriptions is that the errors of Northern 'development'
agencies are less severe than those of African countries and while
there is a sharing of responsibility, the 'well-intentioned' outsiders
have only to become less faddish in order to deal with Africa's
problems.

This latter point is central to appreciating the limitations of the
'liberal' agenda outlined by the private sector. The missing elements in
the *Compact* are an analysis of the underlying causes of Africa's crises,
and an analysis of the *contribution* of national and international elites to
the resource drain experienced by Africa. As it stands, the document
is just a list of symptoms. Finally, the role of the great majority of
African people in redefining the meaning, processes, and structures
for alternative actions is ignored. The result is that the *Compact*
proceeds to offer a series of recommendations for U.S. action which
either perpetuate in slightly changed form old attitudes and programmes or urge incomplete responses. Thus, it is perhaps under-
standable that the first two recommendations, written in 1985, deal

with food aid. In the light of the generally good year in African food production in 1985–86 and the long history of very mixed results from food aid, it was unfortunate that food aid was presented as a solution rather than merely as a possible tool for covering temporary shortfalls. Ironically, in the context of Africa's food crisis, food aid has become a vital component for the maintenance of stability by governments, not for saving lives. The type of food aid most commonly given to Africa is not that provided in emergency situations, as in Ethiopia in 1983–84, but regular food aid programmes of the U.S., the EEC and the World Food Programme. From the supply side, these programmes were designed to rid 'donor' countries of surpluses and to create markets for commercial sales. From the demand side, food aid offers governments a financially inexpensive way to meet internal demands for select commodities. A study of Sierra Leone argues that food aid, while meeting urban demands for rice, deflects government commitment to providing the means for increased internal production. The official approach in Sierra Leone, and many other African countries, to dealing with the 'food crisis', which becomes defined in terms of urban demand, is to import the food that non-nationals have produced. Local farmers are then by-passed and government is able to postpone dealing with the numerous constraints to production for peasant farmers which would provide them with a reasonable return for their efforts.[24]

Other solutions presented in the *Compact* entail greater U.S. financial commitments to the World Bank and to USAID, part of which will be passed on to PVOs, for projects in Africa relating to population control, 'green revolution' technology and small-scale agriculture. A total of $3 billion per year in U.S. aid to Africa is suggested, with some provisions for debt relief and trade modifications.

How feasible is all this?

Can such an approach work? It is unlikely. On the one hand, the U.S. has not shown a willingness to enter into a financial 'compact' with African states which would involve substantial increases in assistance. The reverse position is the reality of U.S. 'aid'. The plan to increase financial support for Africa lacks political credibility in the U.S. On the other hand, the amount of money is largely irrelevant when the structures which have contributed to Africa's crises are not first addressed. Additional unqualified funding from the World Bank will exacerbate existing development problems. Also, most farmers in Africa are unwilling to adopt the technological packages as presented to them. There are few indicators in the *Compact* and other PVO documents which confront the reality of national and international elite control over definitions and processes of development. Indeed, the *Compact* praises the elite position within Africa:

The new attitude among . . . government officials, military officers, and the small but influential middle class is that the economic and political management of their nations must improve. . . .[25]

The crises facing African national leaders combined with strong pressures on them by external contributors may promote some reforms in economic management. But Africa's problems are far less managerial than structural. And many of these structural problems arise from the forms of external relations that the framers of the *Compact* would seek to perpetuate.

In a sense, we're talking about a kind of recolonisation — about sending smart white boys in to tell them how to run their countries.
— a northern aid official quoted in the London *Financial Times* (3 April 1985).

The U.S. has taken the exceptional step of establishing what amounts to a shadow economic cabinet in Liberia, dispatching 17 financial advisers to Monrovia [the capital] to take over the operation of the country's debt-ridden economy.
— news item in *Africa Report*, May–June 1987.

Collective irrelevance

The analyses offered by the World Bank, USAID and much of the PVO/NGO community assume that Northern organizations know what is best for Africa. However, the analyses are often both interventionist and racist. Despite the power of the institutions described here, their prescriptions lack the relevance of reality as it exists within Africa. Their analyses are contradicted by events and actions in Africa. The *Compact*, like almost all other Northern prescriptions for African development, fails by ignoring the struggle of the vast majority of African people to create new systems within which effective development will occur. Hope lies within the innovative organizations and structures which rural and urban Africans have created to define and solve their own problems; it is not to be found in the paternalistic solutions of the exploiters.

The analyses of many organizations that relate to Africa do not seek to interpret the assessments which Africans themselves have made of their food and development crises for U.S. or European audiences. They do not involve a careful evaluation of the development community's failures. Rather, each of these Northern statements is moulded by the internal views and interests of the organization concerned. The prescriptions offered for Africa are based on predetermined assumptions — widely shared in each of the four cases we cited — about what development ought to be, not what it has been nor what popular action in Africa suggests it is and can be. Each document assumes continued and increased U.S., European and multinational involvement in Africa and thus greater — not less — participation by the respective agencies in Africa. Absent from these views is a recognition of the strong and increasing doubts among many Africans about external involvement in their affairs and their determination to define their own solutions with their own resources. The attitude of many U.S. development workers was succinctly put by one high-ranking representative of a coalition of U.S. PVOs at the United Nations Special Session on Africa in 1986. After hearing African PVO leaders describe their programmes and future plans, he said incredulously, 'My God, they want to do it themselves!'

Whose problem?

There is no doubt that Africa is in crisis. It is not simply 'Africa's crisis', as many experts and institutions will have us believe, but a crisis that extends well beyond Africa into the Northern world. It is a crisis of development thinking and strategies, represented by such broad failures of programmes and projects that tens of thousands of lives have been lost as a result. While Northern contributors offer little that is new or creative to the shared crisis, they do apply their power and economic resources to control African decision making.

In the next chapter we look at the responses of African organizations to the development crisis. These responses offer a more comprehensive and realistic assessment of the causes and potential solutions to the crisis than those posed by the West. However, approaches designed and carried out at the grassroots and working class levels of societies are missing — deliberately missing — from both national and international development strategies.

Notes

1. Terminology presents a real problem in dealing with foreign lending and aid agencies. First, there is a great diversity in such agencies, from very small to enormous, and from the types of programmes and conditions attached to financial loans and grants to forms of technical assistance given. Second, the usual terms for foreign and development assistance — aid — and agencies — lenders, donors — are misleading and distort a heavily biased process designed to achieve economic and foreign policy goals of the 'donors'. It is interesting to note that the original use of the term 'aid' in medieval English described payments by subordinates to superiors. Third, in the case of Africa, the trend in recent years has been a reverse flow of money, as African states are repaying larger amounts of cash than they receive in financial assistance. Further, financial flows toward the North are even more intense given unfavourable terms of trade experienced by Africa. Thus, the term 'donor' to describe Northern foreign aid programmes is a misnomer; African countries are and remain the donors both of money and commodities in their relationship with Northern countries. We will use the word 'contributor' to describe Northern development, financial, military and food assistance programmes, recognizing that contributions can be both positive and negative.
2. *Accelerated Development in Sub-Saharan Africa: An Agenda for Action* (World Bank, Washington, DC, 1981).
3. Cheryl Payer, 'Tanzania and the World Bank,' DERAP Working Papers, No. A285. The CHR Michelsen Institute, Department of Social Science and Development, Fantoft, Norway, 1982; World Bank, *Project Performance Audit Report: Zambia Integrated Family Farming Project* (Washington, DC, 1981).
4. The trend continues, despite years of alternative learning that is available to the World Bank. In April 1987 the author visited a World Bank-financed agricultural extension project in eastern Zambia. Project staff readily admitted that the government would be unable to sustain the level of financial, infrastructural and training support for the field extension workers once the project's subsidy ended. There were even doubts expressed about the applicability of the extension approach to the realities of most rural Zambians. Efforts by project staff to bring these issues to the attention of World Bank managers in Washington had met with silence, I was told.
5. Economic Commmission for Africa, *African Alternative Framework to Structural Adjustment Programmes for Socio-Economic Recovery and Transformation* (UN, Addis Ababa, 1989).
6. Gavin Williams, 'The World Bank in rural Nigeria, revisited: a review of the World Bank's Nigeria: Agricultural Sector Review 1987', *Review of African Political Economy*, No. 43 (1988), pp. 42—67.
7. On the continued ideological character of World Bank policies, see H.W. Singer, 'The World Bank: human face or facelift? Some comments in the light of the World Bank's annual report', *World Development*, Vol. 17, No. 8 (August 1989), pp. 1313—16.
8. World Bank, *Sub-Saharan Africa: From Crisis to Sustainable Growth* (Washington, DC, 1989).
9. In pursuit of its policies, the World Bank often demonstrates an amazing

lack of vision toward the real world. Mozambique is a clear case in point. In recommending policy changes, including increasing prices paid to farmers for their produce, the Bank's analysis completely ignores the impact on production of the war waged by South Africa and its surrogate forces against Mozambique. The Bank, instead, cites government policies at fault for declining delivery of crops. The critical result has been the form that World Bank/IMF demands (called 'negotiations' by the international agencies) take in granting loans to Mozambique. A loosening in price controls and food subsidies caused prices to skyrocket, placing the cost of food out of reach of most wage earners. The latter have turned to a variety of other strategies to increase household income, but for the poorest people food insecurity has increased as a result of these changes. See Judith Marshall, 'Structural adjustment in Mozambique — the human dimension', unpublished paper prepared for Canadian International Development Agency, 1989.

10. This so-called 'informal sector' is estimated to account for about 20 per cent of total output and employment in many African countries. This seems to be a conservative estimate, for both rural and urban areas, in the late 1980s. The estimate is made by the Economic Commission for Africa, *op. cit.*, p. 3.

11. Marshall, *op. cit.*, p. 19.

12. Peter Gill, *A Year in the Death of Africa: Politics, Bureaucracy and the Famine* (Paladin, London, 1986).

13. Ernest J. Wilson III, 'The public-private debate', *Africa Report* (July–August 1986), pp. 93–95; Michael Maren, 'Hear no evil', *Africa Report* (November–December 1986), pp. 67–71. An excellent overview of the privatization issue is Kevin Danaher, *Can the 'Free Market' Solve Africa's Food Crisis?* (International Union of Food and Allied Workers' Associations, Petit-Lancy, Switzerland, 1987).

14. These trends are summarized in *Security Assistance: Update of Programs and Related Activities*, GAO/NSIAD-89-78FS (Government Accounting Office, Washington, DC, 1989).

15. *USAID Highlights*, Vol. 6, No. 3 (Summer 1989).

16. Michael M. Horowitz, 'Ideology, policy and praxis in pastoral livestock development', in Michael M. Horowitz and Thomas M. Painter (eds), *Anthropology and Rural Development in West Africa* (Westview Press, Boulder, CO, 1986), p. 272.

17. For a summary of the European Economic Community involvement in African development issues, see Philip Raikes, *Modernizing Hunger* (CIIR, London, 1988), pp. 195–197 and Chapter 9.

18. *Ibid.*, p. 211.

19. John M. Staatz, *et al.*, 'Cereals market liberalization in Mali', *World Development*, Vol. 17, No. 5 (May 1989), pp. 703–718; Mike Speirs, 'From food aid to food strategy — the case of Mali', *C.A.P. Briefing*, No. 3 (October 1987), pp. 12–17.

20. *Compact for African Development: Report of the Committee on African Development Strategies* (Council on Foreign Relations and Overseas Development Council, New York and Washington, DC, 1985).

21. A useful summary of the difficulties of working within the system to reform World Bank policies and operations comes from a group of Third

World, European and North American NGOs which have been engaged in dialogue with the Bank for a decade. See the 'Position Paper' of the NGO Working Group on the World Bank, (ICVA, Geneva, 1989).

22. *Ibid.*, p. 4.
23. *Ibid.*, pp. 9–10.
24. Isabella Ayodele Johnston, 'Food energy and debt crisis in relation to women', unpublished paper presented at the Africa Regional Meeting of Development Alternatives for Women in the New Era (DAWN), 1988.
25. *Ibid.*, p. 11.

9 Africa's Official Response: The View from Above

African ideas are missing from Northern development prescriptions for Africa. One basic assumption is common to most of the writing on Africa produced in the North: little or no African initiative has been made in the attempts to solve the development riddle and to offer alternatives to the continent's underdevelopment. The Northern assertion of policy mismanagement conveniently negates the Africans' credibility in analyzing the development problems and defining solutions. However, Africans have offered insightful analyses and produced alternatives to their current crises at several levels: the very existence of such alternatives is the strongest indictment of the arrogance of the Northern assumptions that such thinking does not exist. This chapter will discuss an indicative range of the inter-African, regional, church and intellectual proposals, programmes and initiatives designed by Africans to define and deal with their own problems. It will conclude with a review of the internal and external constraints which arise out of elite control and which affect progressive change in Africa.

The *Lagos Plan of Action*

The *Lagos Plan of Action* (*LPA*), like many Northern documents which have described Africa's problems, arose out of the development crisis on the continent. It incorporates the collective views of African political leaders. The analysis in the *LPA* begins with different assumptions than those which underlie the World Bank's several reports or those of USAID. Four assumptions are featured in the *LPA*, which was issued in 1980.

First, the global strategies outlined by major Northern contributors have failed to improve Africa's economy. If anything, the successive strategies which the developed nations have set out to explain the nature and processes of development have directly contributed to Africa's stagnant economy and made the continent more susceptible to economic and social crises which periodically occur in industrial nations. This criticism of 'global strategies' is never addressed by contributing agencies, like the World Bank and the EEC; at best, contributors speak about their uncoordinated approaches to development financing and faddish approaches to development planning. The African critique, as outlined below, is far more central to identifying the structural causes of sustained poverty.

Second, the document argues that Africa was exploited during the colonial era and remains so. The exploitation has been directed from the outside by 'forces which seek to influence the economic policies and directions of African states.'[1] Those external forces are not elaborated upon. For people who have lived through the harshness of colonialism and who have experienced the subtle as well as the obvious overtures and involvement of donor and major power representatives, detailed explanations are unnecessary. However, for outsiders who do not have such experiences and who have believed in the altruistic nature of their development assistance, some explicit description of external influence on African economic policies would have been useful in the text of the *LPA*. The point is also important in terms of defining future strategies. By not explicitly outlining the inappropriate external influences on national and regional policies, the signatories of the *LPA* lose much of the effectiveness of their arguments. They seem to assume that the external institutions which they criticize can be moderately reformed to support African interests. However, as suggested in the previous chapter, contributors have sought reforms in African institutions, not their own.

The third assumption is that the continent is overly dependent on the export of basic raw materials and minerals. This is totally at odds with the World Bank and USAID positions which seek to promote greater exports from Africa. The difference in the two sides is crucial, for this is where African and contributor policies most often conflict. The *LPA* is not suggesting that isolation is a preferred way. However, national leaders argue that their countries have had a particularly unfair relationship with the world economy. Expanding exports of raw materials without significant changes in prices received for those commodities will only perpetuate the decades of dependency. The African leaders argue that their nations' resources must be applied to meet the needs of their people, not primarily to benefit external consumers. The importance of the argument has been demonstrated in the reluctance of many African countries to accept IMF loans which are given conditional to promotion of exports.

The fourth assumption is one of hope, that Africa can pull itself out of its current troubles. Based upon their abilities to survive and end colonialism, the African leaders argue that the effective mobilization of all human and material resources on the continent can free Africa from the exploitation associated with dependency. Again, the *LPA* signatories do not reject external assistance, but suggest that such aid and support can only supplement Africa's own efforts toward economic and political liberation.

After setting out this framework of analysis, the *LPA* briefly examines the policies connected to effective change. Policies range from the environment to industry, from science and technology to promoting the position of women. The first issue discussed is food and agriculture. By focusing attention here on that section of the publication, we shall illustrate both the strengths and limitations of the *LPA*.

Like many Northern documents, the *LPA* begins by linking rapid population and urban growth with declining per capita food production and consumption. It suggests that the shortfalls in food production are exacerbated by post-harvest losses and periodic shortages. Dependence on food imports has resulted, placing a severe strain on available foreign exchange.

> At the root of the food problems in Africa, is the fact that Member States have not usually accorded the necessary priority to agriculture, both in the allocation of resources and in giving sufficient attention to policies for the promotion of productivity and improvement of rural life.[2]

This critique of their own agricultural policies should discredit the widely held assumption that Africans are unconcerned about or unwilling to address policy questions unless forced to or guided by outside contributors. In fact, both before and since the publication of the *LPA* in 1980, African governments have been reforming agricultural policies. The pressures by contributors to promote internal changes may have stimulated some policy reform considerations. This pressure, however, may also have inhibited changes as national elites resisted external pressures or responded only verbally but not in substance.[3]

The official position

Is the analysis in the *LPA* for change of agricultural policies correct? And where does the motivation for change come from? It seems quite clear that the creators of the *LPA* took their analysis of Africa's food situation from mainstream development thinking. There is a general sharing of data about food and agricultural production between the *LPA* and the World Bank reports, for example. Although the 'Preamble' of the *LPA* speaks about dependence on exports, failed development strategies and the impact of colonialism, that analysis does not carry over into the core of the report. Thus, African states assume full responsibility for failed policies although they have been regularly advised on those policies for several decades by the World Bank, the UN system, USAID and other technical and financial contributors. Also, no distinction is made between the food needs of rural and urban people, nor between agricultural production for export and the promotion of internal manufacturing needs. Post-harvest loss is a trendy subject for UN agencies like the FAO and is also presented as a priority problem by the *LPA*, but the issue is only significant in large-scale storage sites, rarely in on-farm or local community storage. Irrigation is urged for cereal production, but Africa's experiences with irrigated production have been miserable and extremely costly.

The main problem with the *LPA* description of food and agriculture is that it assumes that Africa's agricultural production has declined over the past two decades. However, this decline may not be nearly as severe as suggested. In the aftermath of massive famines across the continent in the period 1984—86, a suggestion that food production figures may not be as bad as widely asserted may seem strange. However, there is emerging evidence that neither governments nor outside agencies have a definite understanding of food production figures, and that the existing data are incomplete if not gravely distorted.[4] Statistics about food production are particularly weak, as are figures about food and agricultural marketing outside of official channels. What is clear is that there have been per capita declines in officially marketed produce and that food imports, primarily for urban consumers, have dramatically increased in recent years. But this is very different to declaring that all agricultural production is declining. Scattered evidence indicates that in fact farmers have increasingly decided to sell more of their produce through private markets, many of which they themselves have organized. Clearly, far more research is needed on actual food production levels — particularly in the light of the evidence presented in subsequent chapters about popular initiatives. In the interim, scepticism about the dire warnings of Africa's imminent agricultural collapse and about policies that are built on suspect data is warranted.

What runs through the *LPA* food section is the leaders' dilemma of looking at many failed programmes, inspired and directed both by themselves and by outside agencies, and recognizing that their own legitimacy is at stake. The *LPA* is a collective statement of concern about the failure to deliver on the promises of independence. In many ways it is a document of self-interest, or self-survival, by Africa's leaders. This is not to suggest that Africa's national leaders are all wrong or only self-interested, but rather that their perspective is very definitely from the top down, that of an elite group. As such, control over agricultural production is a serious goal, not only because of the expected economic benefits but also because of the desire for political control over producers. The types of programmes urged by the *LPA* to increase food production include improvement of nomads' livestock routes, the promotion of the 'intensive use of improved input packages', and an increased number of irrigation schemes. A suggestion is made, but not elaborated upon, that increased research attention is needed on the many food crops important to rural people but usually neglected by scientists. Services to meet the needs of small farmers are urged. Yet these latter actions do not represent a significant new policy orientation. Lip service by external aid agencies and governments alike has been given to improving the conditions for smallholder food production for many years without any major shift in resource allocations to back up the rhetoric nor any real transfer of authority to villages, cooperatives or collective groups to determine production and consumption priorities. The *LPA*, like the documents of most contributors, does not draw out the many values of the human base from which African agriculture and food production arise. Thus, while the African elite argue for their own independence, they too, like their international counterparts, ignore the tremendous energy, talent and resources of peasant farmers and workers.

The breeze of change

How successful has the *LPA* been to date? At one level, that of international negotiations, the *LPA* has given African leaders a framework for outlining their programmes with donors. The document has also been refined and adapted to a limited extent by some countries in order to prepare their own national reform plans. The self-critical approach of African states has continued, reinforced by near unanimous international criticism of national policies and programmes. If anything, African governments have been too accepting of the international consensus. They have judged their own economic efforts too harshly; but so long as they measure development in terms largely defined by Northern experiences, lifestyles and expectations, a more introspective view that gives credit and legitimacy to the attributes and energy of Africa's people will be lacking.

... [W]hether we, the leaders, want it or not, the people carry on their own trade. I was amused, recently, to hear of a case where Ugandan women were smuggling vehicles from Botswana to Uganda. That is their own pan-Africanism. They see the viability of Africa. I think, eventually, governments will follow the people's example.
— President Yoweri Museveni of Uganda, 1987.

Many countries have begun or continued reform programmes since the publication of the *LPA* in 1980. The impetus for change has two sources. The first has been the tremendous popular pressures felt by governments to deliver services and programmes. Where performance has failed, people have exerted strong pressures in two ways. Formal demands by peasant and workers' associations for greater governmental commitment have occurred in almost all African countries.[5] Official responses to these demands have been limited. Simultaneously, popular pressures on governments occurred as workers and farmers have withdrawn their labour and produce from the official economy in order to define their own legitimate and effective means of change. They have not reverted to some pre-modern economy, but in many instances have created new structures for providing for their welfare. Subsequent chapters describe some of these alternatives. The second source of pressure on African governments has been external: the IMF, the World Bank and other lenders. Over the long term, these external pressures are probably less influential than internal ones, but they have been conspicuous and remain important.

The reason for the influence of contributors in Africa is simple: money. The signatories of the *LPA* felt that their commitments to reform should be supported by wealthy world agencies. The money has not been forthcoming in the amounts African states feel they need for sustained growth. Money that has been offered has carried strong demands for reforms as determined by the various external contributors. However, African arguments for reforms have not been supported by the international community. These reforms include: a change in the way commodity prices are determined; greater utilization of each country's own agricultural and mineral resources for industrial growth; development of national and regional technological and training programmes; and greater intra-regional trade. So long as African states maintain development programmes tied to Northern funding, they remain tied to the criteria of the funders. This is a situation acknowledged by the *LPA* but one which governments have insufficiently addressed and lack the power to correct. As a result, African states are unable to pursue internal reforms at the rate envisioned in 1980 nor with the degree of self-direction and control suggested by the *LPA*. In the process, many African countries have bowed to the power of the international contributors and have adopted parts of the latters' reform packages rather than those agreed to by African leaders themselves.

Regional groupings

A constant theme of the *LPA* is the need for African states to create and support regional organizations. Trade, food security, industry and training all can be promoted through collective relations. This has been one area where some progress has been made in recent years.

The most notable example is the Southern African Development Coordination Conference (SADCC), made up of the ten independent states of southern Africa (Namibia became the most recent member in April 1990). Founded shortly after Zimbabwe's independence in 1980, SADCC's goal is to promote the security and development of the member states through collective arrangements. This will reduce their vulnerability and dependence on South Africa's economic, political and military domination. Each of the nine member states is responsible for developing priorities and plans for specific sectors. For example, Mozambique is responsible for regional transportation and communication projects, Zimbabwe for food security projects, and Zambia for mining projects which will have a regional impact. The initial priority has been to revive regional transportation networks which will immediately reduce the area's reliance on South Africa's rail   and   port   systems   which   could   be   —   and have been in the past — closed or curtailed at any time.

By the middle of 1985 SADCC had approved nearly 400 of 500 projects that had been proposed by member governments for consideration. Over half of the projects were at various stages of implementation, with a secured funding base of $1.1 billion and another $1.2 billion under active negotiation. Among the projects implemented were emergency repairs to the railway from the Mozambique port of Beira to Zimbabwe, the establishment of satellite communication networks between the ten countries, the beginning of a 25-year agricultural research programme on drought- and pest-resistant strains of sorghum and millet, and the creation of early warning systems in all countries in order to provide weather and crop data for use in assessing potential food problems.[6]

The goals of SADCC's food security programmes are to satisfy the basic food needs of the whole population of the region, to achieve national self-sufficiency in food supplies, and to eliminate occasional food crises, as may be caused by drought or warfare. SADCC also argues that national and regional food security are preconditions for reducing dependence on international grain markets (including those of South Africa) and removing the constraints of underdevelopment.[7]

This regional approach of the southern African countries has received warm international praise. One reason for SADCC's success has been the sense of positive alternatives it has created among the 'Frontline' states which have been attacked, intimidated and economically disrupted by South Africa. Another reason has been its structure. The organization has only a small secretariat, in contrast to the bureaucracies of other regional bodies in Africa and elsewhere. SADCC members are expected to utilize their existing national civil services and planning agencies to identify and prepare projects appropriate to the region.

SADCC has not enjoyed unbroken success nor external support.

South Africa, of course, is strongly opposed to the economic independence of its neighbours and has attacked SADCC's integrity and the sovereignty of its member states.[8] For example, rebels in Mozambique have regularly disrupted traffic between that country's ports and Zimbabwe, Zambia and Malawi and they have threatened to attack the revived Beira railway which returned to operation early in 1987. The costly effect of this and other South Africa-instigated wars and destabilization campaigns has been to place SADCC countries in a far greater degree of dependence on external agencies for project support than had been anticipated. This is of acute concern to SADCC members themselves and has long-term implications for the viability of the organization. However, as SADCC, the *LPA* and individual African countries have long argued, as long as they do not receive fair and reasonable prices for their exports, they will not have the resource base to carry out the large infrastructure projects which will more completely join the region together. Neither the SADCC countries nor Africa as a whole are powerful enough to press for changes in commodity prices set by industrial countries. Nor are the industrial countries likely to make changes voluntarily, as they have the most to gain from the present operations of the international economy.

SADCC's opposition to South Africa and its own non-bureaucratic structure have been attractions for contributors, but not to the degree that SADCC's priorities will always be respected. For example, in 1986 Zimbabwe proposed a triangular trade agreement with the United States and Mozambique. Zimbabwe would purchase U.S. wheat and pay for it by shipping part of its surplus corn to Mozambique; Mozambique was scheduled to receive U.S. food aid in the form of yellow corn. Only one-tenth of Mozambique's food aid was met in this way, however. A USAID official argued against the larger deal because it would harm the U.S. goal 'to make the people of southern Africa change their preference from white maize to yellow maize in order to create a market for U.S. yellow maize'.[9]

SADCC projects are meant to supplement the programmes and priorities of the individual states. The SADCC projects will offer services, such as agricultural research findings and transportation plans, that should strengthen national development efforts through regional support and collaboration. The member countries are seeking to expand their limited economic and infrastructural resources through collective action. The goal is a commendable and important one, but it is built upon the assumption that national leadership has the best interests of its citizenry in mind and best understands how to achieve the sectoral goals. Although the leaders of the SADCC countries have been decent, hard-working and concerned, some of their decisions about national priorities have had adverse impacts on groups of their citizens. For example, the Zambian government is responsible for SADCC's mining sector because it has the largest mining industry of all the member states. However, it has regularly been in conflict with mine workers over issues of wages and local control. As a result, mine workers' leaders have been subject to human rights abuses over the past fifteen years as they have sought to protect the workers' position against government action. Also, although the Zambian government has given lip service for nearly two decades to diversifying its economy away from copper mining and to supporting small-scale farming, such structural changes have been minimal.

Furthermore, by appointing Angola, whose major industry is oil production, responsible for SADCC's energy sector, the SADCC leadership seems to be giving greater priority to energy sources related to large-scale industry. However, the major source of energy for the region's people is firewood and charcoal. Industrial and household energy are both important, but will they receive equal attention? Are SADCC's best interests served in this way? Will the trickle-down framework that SADCC member states have created lead to improved living conditions and human rights for the countries' poor and disenfranchised people?

These are crucial questions if SADCC and other African nations are going to redefine the nature of development, as suggested by the *LPA*. SADCC's ideals incorporate the element of collective self-reliance. However, much work remains to be done to devise and institute ways which will incorporate popular action in the plans and programmes of the region.[10]

ECOWAS

Another programme of regional cooperation is seen in ECOWAS, the Economic Community of West African States. Founded in 1975 and including sixteen West African countries, ECOWAS has an ambitious programme, the goal of which is greater economic integration and greater economic development among member states. The Community seeks to achieve its goal through the promotion of free trade within the region, primarily through the creation of a customs union, jointly developed transportation and communications facilities, and the creation of mutual monetary and economic policies. Trade liberalization within the region has been the most ambitious part of the programme and in the period 1978−84 intra-regional imports more than doubled and exports nearly doubled over those in the period 1968−76. However, there were wide differences between countries and four 'more developed' countries — Nigeria, Senegal, Ghana and Cote d'Ivoire — dominated the intra-regional trade (Nigeria alone accounts for about 60 per cent of the region's GDP), thereby offering little benefit for the smaller economies in the region. The constraints on regional economic development through expanded trade include the production of similar products, thus limiting the basis for trade, problems related to convertibility of currencies, and the existence of other regional organizations that sometimes undercut ECOWAS's efficiency.[11]

If these constraints to success were not enough, the model of economic integration used by the ECOWAS countries offers little likelihood of regional (and national) structural independence from the dominant economies of Europe. Although there is meant to be a 'harmonization' of agricultural and industrial policies over time, the mechanisms for achieving this internal base for production are not identified. Yet for the region to achieve the economic power to offer individual states goods and markets now largely attained in trade with Europe, an integration of production using the region's rich raw materials (mineral and agricultural) and a more balanced distribution of production facilities is needed. Free trade, where 'There is simply very little to trade', does not hold favourable prospects for ECOWAS.[12] The economic constraints on all of West Africa in the 1980s have further reduced the ability of individual states to support collective efforts, whether for free trade or multi-member production.

While important as an attempt at regional cooperation around trade issues, ECOWAS has not been able to fulfil its objectives effectively. Part of the problem has been the model of economic integration, based on internal free trade with common external tariffs, which contributed to already skewed economic strength in the region. Further, the idea of free trade offers national political leaders a symbol of achievement without commitment to either supporting the idea or engaging in substantive redistribution of resources in order to expand regional agricultural and industrial production. A strong West African regional community will be achieved through both a programme of mutually beneficial trade and an enhancement of the productive base. There is little indication that policies are in place giving sustained and direct support to the productive efforts of farmers, small-scale traders, workers and artisans. Only with such policies can a regional framework exist.

Intellectual critics

There is a long tradition of criticism and action by African intellectuals against the inequities of colonial and post-colonial rule and social systems. These critiques, however, are regularly ignored by Northern media and development agencies and regularly suppressed by African governments. The reasons are clear: most of the critiques of post-colonial development place responsibility for the continent's food and development crises on the policies and programmes arrived at by an alliance between international agencies and national leaders.

The centre of much intellectual thinking is the university. Students have regularly challenged their governments' policies and decisions and nearly as regularly have seen their classrooms closed around them. Governments have, in turn, blamed university teachers for inciting students and have threatened, fired, expelled and intimidated university faculty. Many progressive African intellectuals are now in exile from their countries, barred from teaching and conducting research at home.

A solid core of progressive critique is built upon an analysis derived from a Marxist perspective of economic relations and power and has been put forward in the context of the dependency theory of development. In brief, dependency theory holds that the form and direction of economic relations in the Third World is largely determined by the power of the Northern, industrial countries to extract commodities and labour for their exclusive benefit. The Third World is dependent upon the intensity and economic direction of the capitalist world, and unable to explore alternatives or exploit its own wealth for internal growth. Dependency is maintained by alliances between Northern capitalist agents and Third World elites, often those holding the reigns of political power.

The dependency theory has been assailed by other thinkers as too narrow in its analysis of national — as opposed to international — economic and political relations, ahistorical and unable to account for a wide range of exceptions. A number of thinkers have abandoned their initial support for the dependency theory, but it does still have a following among some Africans who have refined the theory with more in-depth study of the internal conditions within African countries. In fact, some of the strongest and most effective critiques of national economic and development policies come from people who retain elements of dependency theory in their overall analysis.

De-linking

One of the leading proponents of the dependency theory is Samir Amin. Egyptian by birth, Amin in the early 1960s directed the preparation of a five year development plan with the newly independent government of Mali. The goal was to help create a socialist model of economic and political development. The effort was thwarted in Mali by international resistance to the progressive regime and the limitations of the state structure in implementing and experimenting with the five year plan. During the 1970s and 1980s Amin has worked out of Dakar, Senegal, writing extensively on the philosophy of Third World development. In recent years, Amin has refined the dependency approach to analyse the effects of structural adjustment on development, an issue of crucial importance to African countries and peoples.

An important concept developed by Amin is that of 'de-linking', a means by which the Third World can break out of the domination and exploitation of the North. De-linking is not an isolationist position, but does require 'the subordination of external relations to internal demands for popular transformation and development, as against the bourgeois strategy of adjustment of internal growth to the constraints of the worldwide expansion of capital'.[13] De-linking, according to Amin, is the means for popular forces — workers, peasants, landless labourers, pastoralists — to create both a political and an economic environment in which the gross income inequalities and repression of past decades can be transformed along lines that meet people's needs and interests before those of a national elite and international capital. Amin argues that inequality in income distribution has worsened for Third World people over the past century and that events of the past twenty years have intensified the process. The post-colonial attempt by some African states — such as Egypt, Mali, Tanzania, Mozambique — to seek changes that broke with colonial exploitation was often thwarted by military action or coups. But there were also internal constraints on the changes being sought. Amin argues that these, and other reforming African governments, sought the *support* of the people with various reform and social welfare programmes, but only went a part of the way toward ensuring popular *control* of the political and economic processes of change. Amin speaks about the failure of national bourgeois governments to reverse the tide of inequalities, thus losing their democratic political support and reverting to various forms of repression. In many instances, the ruling elite have adopted the 'logic of capitalism'. As put forward by the IMF and the World Bank, this logic requires the implementation of internal strategies of adjustment in order to better fit national economies within the external requirements of global capitalism. In the late 1980s, some thirty African countries were wedded to adjustment programmes which have been shown to increase both income inequalities and poverty, and decrease local control over national resources, local markets, financial institutions and technology. The World Bank, of course, argues that such pain is only temporary and that adjustment will eventually lead to new opportunities for economic growth. Amin and others argue that quite the opposite is the case, that so long as people and countries are tied to the dominant forces of the capitalist North, political and economic transformation by and for popular movements will be increasingly constrained.

Assessing Africa's development crisis

Progressive intellectuals are clear that the 'crisis affecting Africa ... has its profound roots in the integration of African economies into the world capitalist system', a system over which Africa has 'absolutely no control'.[14] During the struggle for political independence, African leaders were able to harness mass support to confront the colonial powers. However, after the achievement of independence, that reliance on popular power gave way to the consolidation of economic privilege for the ruling class through their control of state and public property. Despite rhetoric to the contrary, the wealthy and powerful were ready to make alliances with international capitalist interests — often through 'aid' agencies — to assure their continued access to wealth. One of the most influencial critics of contemporary Africa argues:

> Like the colonial state, the post-colonial state is a repressive mechanism in charge of an export-oriented economy that serves primarily those who manage it and their trading and other business partners in the developed countries, at the expense of the welfare of ordinary people.[15]

Indeed, African researchers, writers and teachers have sought to provide both an analytical framework and careful evidence on the processes of neglect of ordinary people. The intellectuals are the most consistent and articulate critics of national and international policies which have fostered inequities and of the repressive reactions of governments to those who demonstrate dissatisfaction in writing or in practice. The position and role of the state is crucial in much of this writing, for it is the state that links domestic policy and repression with international interests in the continued extraction of Africa's wealth. The state is the political arena in which substantive transformation will occur, setting the ground for the promotion of popular social and economic development.[16]

African progressive intellectuals are among the most outspoken critics of 'development' as it is normally practised in Africa, and elsewhere in the Third World. Development as it has unfolded in Africa has amounted to little more than improvements in infrastructure and management capabilities which can facilitate the further imposition of the state and international interests upon rural areas and the extraction of agricultural and mineral commodities for international markets. Onimode argues that famines, staggering debt burdens, slow economic growth and widespread poverty are manifestations of Africa's crisis of underdevelopment, symptoms of the continent's structural and historical position within a capitalist world system. The capitalist system promotes inequalities. The inequalities of colonialism were not ended at independence, but continued in the form of neo-colonialism in which Northern, industrial powers used transnational corporations, 'aid', and collaboration with indigenous leaders to sustain their exploitation of Africa's wealth. It is the process of Northern economic domination in alliance with the internal African ruling class that distinguished neo-colonialism from colonialism, which was overwhelmingly a product of external control.[17]

The most common alternative to dependency and exploitation for Africa that is offered by African intellectuals follows from Amin's concept of de-linking. De-linking offers, according to proponents, the means to create and effectively use autonomous space to foster, build and promote popular alliances of workers and peasants that will work toward achievement of social, as opposed to private, property. Not all intellectuals agree, however, with the approach. Turok, for example, does not feel that de-linking is necessary to complete the struggle for full national liberation. He argues:

> Looking at political life in most post-independence states in Africa, who could deny that ... the political conditions for a new level of consciousness are more advanced than under colonialism and that there is a new capacity among the masses to relate to more advanced ideas in a way inconceivable before.
>
> The call for the completion of national liberation is capable of creating a popular united front composed of the vast majority who do not benefit from neocolonialism.[18]

African intellectuals have used a persuasive set of analytical tools and arguments to view the continent's crises and assess the changes that are occurring. In general, they do not feel that the current set of African rulers will promote processes of transformation in economic and political relations. They argue that the repressive, anti-democratic pressures have stymied the momentum for change that was generated by the nationalist movements. Reformist approaches to change only perpetuate the poverty of African people and the domination of Northern capitalist structures over the wealth of Africa. Consequently, a sustained alliance between workers, peasants and intellectuals is crucial for mobilizing to achieve the major changes that will allow African people to control and build upon their wealth. African progressives argue that similar alliances are needed in the North, alliances that will place environmental, worker, and poverty issues in an international context that will challenge the power of the ruling classes in the North. Among some intellectuals there is the implication that popular change in Africa is dependent upon prior or concurrent changes in the North. Not enough credit is given to the continual internal struggles for change devised and undertaken within Africa itself, particularly at a local level.

The church and development

African religious institutions — whether those of Christianity, Islam, traditional beliefs or some combination — have provided dramatic structures and support systems for change. In the mid-nineteenth century, Islamic revival movements swept across the Sahel and bordering regions, contributing to new political formations. Christian missionaries played a significant role in creating and sustaining the European colonization of Africa at the end of the nineteenth century and through the first half of the twentieth. African-led religious movements, especially those that combined elements of Christian or Muslim and local beliefs, have regularly appeared in this century as a form of protest against the oppressive character of the colonial and post-colonial states.[19]

Within the dynamics of post-colonial development, the church in Africa has emerged as an important factor. The church carries the same historical legacy as do other post-colonial institutions: it is strongly influenced by external powers; it is struggling to define an African character for itself; it is dependent upon external financing for on-going work and upon external personnel who may be less than willing to relinquish authority to their African colleagues. Also, the church hierarchy has been formed by the same elite biases as have government and other political institutions. Yet the church also works through and with its grassroots members to a greater degree than do most government bureaucracies. In some ways it may be possible to speak of some elements of the church as embodying the 'middle ground' between grassroots communities and national and international development programmes.

Churches and the community

The work of the Evangelical Church of the Republic of Niger (EERN) is representative of many of these features of the Christian church in Africa. A small church, composed of a high proportion of highly educated people who hold positions in the civil service of a country that is 99 per cent Muslim, EERN members have concentrated on working with peasant communities to promote development, focusing their work on activities that the government cannot undertake. Small-scale irrigation schemes have been created which enable villagers to produce two crops a year.

In eastern Zaire, the Catholic church has played both a supporting and coordinating role among people regularly exploited by the state's power structure and multinational corporations. The church has provided credit for cooperatives and legal defence against arbitrary laws and enforcement. Networks of locally controlled schools and health centres have sprung up with church support.[20] These are not substitute services filling a void left by government neglect, but positive efforts by people to create alternative programmes to those of an extractive and repressive government whose authority is not, however, all pervasive.

Church work in development at the grassroots has the potential of energizing not only base communities but also the church hierarchy itself. The base communities are small groups of locally organized believers, usually united not only by religion but by a sense of alternative development. In western Kenya, for example, the training of village health workers under the direction of the hospital was initially a failure. Subsequently local people took greater control of the programme and brought it to fruition by linking community responsibility with the spiritual symbolism of caring inherent in the local Catholic parish and the medical insights of staff at the hospital. An evaluation showed strong community support, although the programme was not without on-going problems.[21]

The progressive elements of the church hierarchy respond to and facilitate the development process among their communities and parishioners. The church participates in institution building and, in turn, is built as an institution. This is most clear in South Africa. Grassroots demonstrations and well-organized African initiatives in the areas of labour relations, community services, and political rights have motivated the Christian churches to take a far more assertive and creative role in sustaining the African drive to majority rule and economic transformation. Desmond Tutu, Frank Chikane and hundreds of other church leaders have linked the spiritual with the political. Where others have been prevented from speaking out, many church leaders have provided a forum for expressing people's anger and determination and the church communities have offered a base for organizing. *The Kairos Document*,[22] issued by a broad range of South African church leaders in 1985, illustrates the growth of the church as an institution of social justice and equity. The document strongly condemns the violence being carried out by the state against the African people in the name of Christianity. 'The situation we are dealing with here is one of oppression,' argue the 150 religious leaders from all of South Africa's major denominations. They have committed themselves to side 'with the Oppressed' and to struggle for a just society. A year later, the Dutch Reformed Church which had provided the theological and moral justification for Afrikaner people to openly enslave and abuse Africans for 300 years, acknowledged that a Biblical basis did not exist for asserting the inferiority of African people. The DRC continues to be a bastion of apartheid belief, but this theological shift is another indication of the institutional changes occurring within all of South Africa.

We need to confess that traditionally, the churches have paid more attention to helping people adjust to existing systems than to questioning those systems. . . . Our charity approach has not gone beyond legitimizing the political systems.

The primary task of the church will be to participate in the rebellion of the poor against domination and dehumanisation. Our primary objective as a church must be to struggle alongside

the disempowered, to gain a new sense of dignity and power, not only as individuals but as communities of faith.
— Revd Peter Kodjo of the Presbyterian Church of Ghana, 1987.

The CDAA

Both inter-African and global analyses of Africa's developmental crisis are reflected in the report of the Churches' Development Action on Africa (formerly Churches' Drought Action in Africa) — CDAA.[23] The study was sponsored by several international Christian associations and carried out by nine teams of African researchers. Their mandate was to examine the causes of the food crisis in Africa and to suggest ways that African churches can address solutions. The final report is insightful and critical of many development beliefs sacred to both African and international elites. Not surprisingly, there have been tensions between African and some outside church groups in the interpretation and use of the CDAA study.

The report looks at the root causes of hunger by examining several areas of Africa, including Zimbabwe, Sierra Leone, Tanzania, Rwanda, Burundi, Zaire, the Sahel region and the Muthara community in Kenya. The problem of hunger and food insufficiency is defined as one of poverty, arising out of decades of external exploitation and continued misuse of human and natural resources. A serious disequilibrium between people and their environment has resulted from this process of underdevelopment. As underdevelopment became more intense, people placed greater pressure on their environment causing losses of soil fertility, erosion and clearing of marginal land. These conditions were the result not of ignorance or poor farming practices, but of the tremendous outside pressures exerted on communities to produce crops for external markets while also seeking to maintain some level of household food production. Since independence, governments have not altered these patterns, but exacerbated them with their own policies and alliances with international development agencies and multinational corporations. The dependence of African churches on external financial support and their recent entry into developmental questions are two other features which reflect the theme of underdevelopment raised by the report.

The document's policy recommendations begin with an appeal that African churches assume the initiative for control over their affairs by more fully engaging in developmental thought and action. Other recommendations speak to the need and desire for more practical involvement in the development process by African churches, the need for local-level cooperation among various churches and groups, the questions of financial autonomy and a reduction in the role of multinational corporations in Africa. Although not explicitly stated in the report, the absence of popular political and economic democracy is recognized as a central cause of Africa's crises. In its recommendations, the report speaks of the need for critical debates — written and verbal — on development issues as one element among several which will contribute to the empowerment of people at the grassroots level.

At other times, also, the church has been particularly vocal on the issue of democracy. A report from an All African Council of Churches meeting on development in 1983 underscores the theme:

> For many nations the building of a stable political system which protects basic rights and maximizes the opportunities for participation in the political process has been ignored. In many places undemocratic systems have hindered the transformation of society in a progressive and participatory manner, creating or reinforcing social systems of subjugation and exclusion from the process of decision making. We note the tendency of governments in Africa to concentrate the power entrusted in the hands of State.... It has become clear that the state often uses development projects to create social institutions that act as channels for social and economic control.

As with other African-defined plans and initiatives at the regional and continental levels, the CDAA report represents the opinion of an elite group — albeit more progressive in its analysis than many of the official statements issuing from African governments which we have noted here. The group shares a common body of assumptions about development. Those assumptions illustrate a preoccupation with global economic concerns and global players; the emphasis on the 'external forces' without clear and specific statements about the 'forces within' and the connections which bind both external and internal groups. The emphasis coincides with international interests in that, for the most part, it neglects to address, in specific terms, the needs and potential of the rural and urban poor who can make meaningful change in their political and economic conditions. The CDAA report, like the *LPA* and SADCC's programmes, looks for its legitimacy to peers rather than to the people who will provide the sweat, blood, knowledge and commitment to development.

Continuing constraints on official programmes

Clearly, there is an important and thoughtful body of African thinking and action about the development crisis facing the continent. This thinking counters the false assumptions woven into many Northern-produced prescriptions for Africa that external direction, guidance and prompting are needed for the continent's recovery. Those Northern views contain an arrogance reminiscent of the attitudes expressed to justify the slave trade and colonialism. Such views are

used now to justify new ways to exploit Africa as Northern governments, aid agencies and creditors ignore and scorn Africa's own
efforts to push forward. Not surprisingly, Northern agencies distort
and obscure the analyses of African people and groups that reflect the
contemporary realities of their conditions, their hopes and the
negative impacts of international capitalism.[24] It is to the body of
critique, knowledge and action which Africans themselves have
developed that Northern citizens must look for initial analysis and
direction.

However, much of the African analysis and action cited in this
chapter is representative of only a part of all African initiatives. The
priority programmes of regional groups like SADCC have been
created by the existing power elite without the involvement of
grassroots representation or a reflection of grassroots abilities. The
LPA and subsequent pan-African statements have been written by and
for ruling classes who perceive their positions and legitimacy
threatened by the food and development crises occurring around
them. Thus, it is not surprising to find that the *LPA* begins with a
different analysis than does the World Bank, but ends with similar
conclusions which call for further squeezing of workers and peasant
farmers. While criticizing the development strategies which have
contributed to the development crisis, most African governments
have not devised and implemented effective alternatives. No African
country has reoriented its political and economic structures as
proposed by the *LPA*.

Two reasons seem particularly relevant for understanding this
situation. The first is that any effective developmental process must
arise from and integrally involve and be directed by the actions of the
great majority of African people — small-scale farmers, the landless,
pastoralists and urban workers. It is within these groups that production and productivity is concentrated; it is to these groups that the
rewards of growth and development must accrue. To date, African
leaders have given little support and legitimacy to most farmers and
workers. Instead, the pattern of African development has been to
expand state control over political and economic affairs wherever
possible in order to assure a power base and financial security. Several
countries — such as Tanzania and Zambia — which have paid lip
service to decentralization have not matched rhetoric with real
transfers of power to sub-national groups. Centralized decision-
making and financial disbursements remain firmly in place.
Bureaucratic, political and business elites have monopolized the
economic resources and power in most countries.

Elite alliances

Added to these centralizing and controlling tendencies of the
national elite has been the response of international monetary and

technical contributors. The statements about African mismanagement and policy failures discussed in the many documents, conferences and meetings of the Northern states and 'aid' agencies indicate a deep frustration with the multiple and widespread failure of their projects and programmes and a gut recognition that the potential exists for radical change spurred by popular discontent — expressed at various times in Northern jargon as the 'communist threat', 'civil disturbance', 'instability' or other such terms that convey a fear of fully effective democracy and popular development. There is a widespread sense that the billions of dollars loaned, granted and otherwise invested in Africa have gone down a bottomless hole — and that African governments are to blame. With the exception of some progressive NGOs/PVOs and to a certain extent the Scandinavian aid agencies, the response of contributors in recent years has been to blame Africans and to seek to influence internal African affairs more broadly than at any time during the past two decades. A major goal of the IMF, the World Bank, the EEC and bilateral lending agencies has been to impose the views of these agencies upon the management of African states. In return, the African governments receive foreign exchange or manufactured goods, both of which are in short supply. The dire fiscal and economic conditions of many African countries and the prolonged collapse in prices of commodities Africa usually sells on the international market give those countries little leverage in resisting the pressures exerted by donors.

The elites which control African states have, in some cases, accepted the 'wisdom' of the North and have attained favoured client status: Zaire, Morocco, Senegal and Malawi are examples. Not surprisingly, the reforms which have been negotiated at the instigation of the North have resulted in a greater concentration of power in the hands of the wealthy, at the expense of the poor. Senegal, which has bought into the Northern prescription for reform, has imposed user fees on its health services. Malawi, guided by the World Bank, has seen an acceleration of an earlier trend to concentrate land and resources in elite-owned estates. At the same time, many children suffer from chronic malnutrition. Zambia, subject to six IMF loan agreements and to World Bank donor coordination, has imposed school fees and abandoned subsidies on basic foods, greatly discriminating against the poor. Also, doctors have abandoned their posts in the free government health system to cater to patients who can afford the rapidly growing private consulting practices.

These three trends — the centralization of power and legitimacy in the national elites, growing inequalities between classes, and greater external influence over national policies — are complementary. The attention and money provided by aid contributors give continued credibility to national elites. Together, aid programmes and elite-defined policies exert greater pressure on peasants and workers, intensifying inequalities while demanding greater productivity in order to earn foreign exchange. Pressures from below for change are regularly resisted, although we shall point out exceptions below. Externally imposed reforms are followed with handouts of foreign exchange for the import of the luxury goods demanded by the national elite and the payment of interest on loans. Politicians, while acceding to these reforms and passing them along to the people, can for public consumption proclaim their hard bargaining and resistance to the harshest set of reforms. No IMF agreement or new World Bank structural adjustment loan goes by without governments announcing that tough times are ahead but that improved conditions will soon emerge. Countries which have sought either to retain control over the decision-making process for national development policies or to give greater legitimacy to the voices of all of their people have not fared well against the Northern assault on Africa's alleged failures. When a coup in Burkina brought in a government that has sought to decentralize development authority, U.S. aid declined. Zimbabwe has closely guarded its right to speak out on its regional security concerns; U.S. aid has been totally cut off.

Who is in control?

A common assertion among many people in the North is that governments as institutions are the cause of the problems within Africa. If our analysis is correct, it is clear that governments are not the problem. Rather, it is the ruling groups which control government and their alliances with external sources of aid, policy and material aggrandizement. Quite simply, it is not a problem of governments *per se*, but of class interests and class conflicts, of an elite control over the instruments of government and the economy. In many — but by no means all — cases in Africa, national elites have worked with international counterparts to expand control over the extraction of wealth from the vast majority of producers and workers in society. That wealth (capital) is needed for public investment, but much of it has gone overseas — for luxury imports, debt repayments, expatriate contracts — and into individuals' own accounts. Despite the rhetoric of the *LPA*, few African leaders have created a functional ideological base which legitimizes the extraordinary skills and contributions of rural people and urban workers. Nor have leaders implemented programmes which involve the reinvestment of public capital into programmes that strengthen the class base from which that capital is originally drawn. Nor is it in their interests to pursue such policies.

The forces are strong and prevent substantive change by excluding grassroots initiatives and redefining the direction of development only in elite terms. However, we argue in the next two chapters that there is much cause for hope within Africa. People there are drawing upon their own knowledge and skills, and creating and adapting their own organizations to pursue effective problem-solving. These initiatives demonstrate the incomplete nature of much of the analysis of the national and international elite. This is not to suggest that the power and influence of the elites are irrelevant, for they are extremely relevant. It is obvious that effective analysis and creative and sustained problem-solving have been a feature of life in Africa. These popular initiatives demonstrate the inadequacy of the elite models of development. Thus the challenge for the future remains the struggle to transform these popular initiatives into broad national and international movements.

Notes

1. Organization of African Unity, *Lagos Plan of Action for the Economic Development of Africa, 1980—2000* (International Labour Office, Institute for Labour Studies, Geneva, 1981), p. 7.
2. *Ibid.*, p. 11.
3. Paul Mosley, 'The politics of economic liberalization: USAID and the World Bank in Kenya, 1980—84', *African Affairs*, Vol. 85, No. 338 (January 1986), pp. 107—119.
4. Philip Raikes, *Modernizing Hunger: Famine, Food Surplus & Farm Policy in the EEC & Africa* (Catholic Institute for International Relations, London, 1988), Part 1; Sara S. Berry, 'The food crisis and agrarian change in Africa: a review essay', *African Studies Review*, Vol. 27, No. 2 (June 1984), pp. 61-64; Sayre P. Shatz, 'African food imports and food production: an erroneous interpretation', *Journal of Modern African Studies*, Vol. 24, No. 1 (1986), pp. 177-78.
5. For examples, see the articles in *Review of African Political Economy*, No. 39 (September 1987).
6. 'Simbarashe Makoni', interview in *Africa Report* (July—August 1986), pp. 35—41.
7. Southern African Development Coordination Conference, 'Food and agriculture', report prepared for the January 1983 annual meeting, pp. 3—4.
8. On South African destabilization see Joseph Hanlon, *Apartheid's Second Front* (Penguin Books, New York, 1986); Phyllis Johnson and David Martin, *Destructive Engagement* (Zimbabwe Publishing House, Harare, 1986).
9. Cited in Carol B. Thompson, 'SADCC's struggle for economic liberation', *Africa Report* (July—August 1986), p. 63.
10. 'An Agenda for action', in *Another Development for SADCC* (Foundation for Education with Production, Gaborone, 1987), pp. 159—182.
11. Wolfgang Zehender, *Regional Cooperation through Trade and Industry? The Prospects for Regional Economic Communities in West and Central Africa* (German Development Institute, Berlin, 1987).
12. Akinola Owosekun, 'Gains from integration and the growing disillusionment in ECOWAS', in Akinola A. Owosekun (ed.), *Towards an African Economic*

Community: Lessons of Experience from ECOWAS (Nigerian Institute of Social and Economic Research, Ibadan, 1986), p. 366. Also on ECOWAS, see John P. Renninger, *Multinational Cooperation for Development in West Africa* (Pergamon Press, New York, 1979). I have also used Julius Emeka Okolo, 'Intra-ECOWAS trade liberalization: an assessment', paper presented at the International Studies Association, Washington, DC, 1987.

13. Samir Amin, 'Democracy and national strategy in the periphery', *Third World Quarterly*, Vol. 9, No. 4 (October 1987), p. 1148. For a fuller discussion of de-linking, see Amin's *La Deconnexion* (La Decouverte, Paris, 1986).

14. Mohamed Lamine Gakou, *The Crisis in African Agriculture* (Zed Books and United Nations University, London, 1987), p. 1.

15. Nzongola-Ntalaja, *Revolution and Counter-Revolution in Africa* (Zed Books and Institute for African Alternatives, London, 1987), p. 78.

16. See, for example, Thandika Mkandawire and Naceur Bourenane (eds), *The State and Agriculture in Africa*, (Codesria, London, 1987).

17. Bade Onimode, *A Political Economy of the African Crisis* (Institute for African Alternatives and Zed Books, London, 1988).

18. Ben Turok, *Africa: What Can Be Done?* (Zed Books, London, 1987).

19. T. O. Ranger, 'Connexions between primary resistance movements and modern mass nationalism in East and Central Africa', *Journal of African History*, Vol. 9, No. 4 (1968), pp. 437–453.

20. Catharine Newbury, 'Survival strategies in rural Zaire: realities of coping with crisis', in Nzongola-Ntalaja (ed.), *The Crisis in Zaire* (Africa World Press, Trenton, NJ, 1986), pp. 99–112.

21. 'Base Christian communities and health: Nangina CBHC project', *Contact*, No. 110 (August 1989).

22. *The Challenge to the Church* [The Kairos Document] (The Kairos Theologicans, Braamfontein, South Africa, 1985).

23. Churches' Drought Action in Africa, *Report on the Root Causes of Hunger and Food Insufficiency in Africa* (Geneva, 1985).

24. Late in 1989, the United States was the only country to vote against and veto a proposal before the United Nations to adopt a plan of economic recovery developed by the Economic Commission of Africa, on behalf of African states. The U.S. position was that the adjustment programmes arranged by the World Bank and the IMF were more suitable for country-by-country negotiations.

Part III

The Popular Alternative
for Development

10 People's Knowledge: Foundations for Change

For many decades, rural and urban Africans have struggled to assert their interests and creatively utilize their talents for their own security and national development. However, colonial and post-colonial administrations and international development agencies have systematically sought to shape the lives of the poor majority of people to conform to a narrow image of development. Locally defined problems and solutions have been largely ignored or discredited because they did not easily fit into the framework of the self-serving economic plans prepared by the national elites and their cohorts in international agencies.

An example of such narrow and rigid thinking is expressed in a story related by a friend. He tells of a Zambian in the 1950s who built a bicycle entirely from wood. When the man went to the office of the colonial government to purchase the required registration certificate, the colonial officer ordered the bike destroyed because it did not conform to the specifications dictated for standard bicycles. As destructive to creative initiative as this example was, it was replicated three decades later, in the 1980s, in the same area. Zambian extension agents working within a World Bank-financed project repeated the colonial example when they spoke contemptuously of small-scale farmers as 'ignorant peasants, too lazy to farm'.

Against this background of elitism, it is little wonder that official development approaches have created, rather than prevented, precarious living conditions for the vast majority of people. However, Africa's rural and urban people do not conform to the popular Northern stereotype of passive and dependent victims. Instead, they have utilized knowledge, skills and structures which their societies have effectively developed over decades and centuries in order to assert control and direction over their lives and safeguard their social structures. It remains for us to listen and learn from these examples.

In Part I of this book we examined the forces that have worked against food security. In this and the next chapter we have the opportunity to listen and to discover the strong and viable countervailing pattern at the village and community levels as people have applied their knowledge, skills and resources to attain food security. Peasant farmers, artisans and pastoral people have struggled for over a century to retain the integrity of their lives against external forces that have threatened their well-being. That struggle has been at great odds and cost, but the challenge made by common people to survive and develop integral social and economic systems is a powerful alternative to the exploitative agricultural and rural development programmes of governments and external 'aid' agencies.

Africa has the human and natural resources for dramatic and sustained popular development. This chapter describes but a few instances of the innovative character which African people have shown in promoting their own futures. The emphasis is on agriculture and food security, but examples are also given from other areas.

Peasants teaching scientists

One of the great unasked questions regarding African agriculture is: In the wake of all the news about declining food production and famines, how have people managed to produce adequate food for themselves for centuries, including in recent years?

If this question is not addressed, the tremendous accomplishments of food producers themselves are largely ignored. In fact, for centuries Africans have generally provided well for themselves, drawing upon and adapting a body of agricultural and environmental knowledge which many observers acknowledge has been and remains relevant to local conditions and which is capable of providing food for all, except in extreme conditions. It has been obvious to sensitive outsiders for over a century that African agriculture has been highly productive. Travelling in eastern Zambia and central Malawi in the 1880s, one European explorer exclaimed:

> Village after village surrounded by wavering cornfields, and green plains dotted with herds of cattle, stretched away in the distance. Never before in any of my African wanderings had I seen such an extent of land under cultivation; the cornfields seemed unending, and the size and number of the villages fairly astonished me. . . .

Thirty years later, in northern Nigeria, an early colonial officer wrote,

> There is little we can teach the Kano [Nigerian] farmer . . . they have acquired the necessary precise knowledge as to the time to prepare the land for sowing; when and how to sow; how long to let the land be fallow; what soils suit certain crops; what varieties of the same crop will succeed in some localities and what varieties in others . . . how to ensure rotation; when to arrange with Fulani herdsmen to pasture their cattle upon the land.

In colonies as dispersed as Sierra Leone and Zambia, the few European agricultural officials who carried out comparative experiments between indigenous and imported agricultural production methods generally found the indigenous methods more productive, reliable and risk-reducing. They were impressed with people's knowledge of the factors which influenced their well-being. For instance, this comment from the 1950s illustrates these findings:

> [T]he pastoralists know their grasslands. They are, one might say, authorities on grasses.... They recognize ecological associations ... and can assess their value and stock-carrying capacity at different times of year. Masai herdsmen in Kenya and Tanganyika [now Tanzania] pointed out ... various species and associations that they regarded as good for supplying mineral deficiencies, for conditioning animals, for improving the potency of bulls, and for making milk and beef.

Finally, writing in 1985, Paul Richards, a geographer, records that 80 per cent of all farm land in West Africa is intercropped. In addition to the sound ecological and agricultural knowledge on which inter-cropping is based, peasants are continually experimenting with their farm systems. Of this planting of a mixture of crops in the same field, Richards says:

> [I]t is also a theme upon which small-scale farmers have quietly elaborated many new and interesting variations in recent years. Quite rightly, the topic of intercropping has now begun to attract the scientific attention its regional preponderance so clearly demands.[1]

Richards' comment about intercropping confirms what many observers are 'discovering' about African agriculture. Far from being primitive and a drag on growth, African agricultural knowledge offers the strongest hope for igniting and promoting sustained development throughout the continent. Intercropping is a clear example. Used by African peasant farmers to reduce the risk of single crop failures and to provide a regular supply of food over the year, intercropping has been criticized by Northern agricultural 'experts' as unsightly and low yielding. But intercropped fields offer a mix of grains and vegetables whose abundance protects the soil from erosion and physical break-down while providing symbiotic nutrients between plants. The various crops mature at different times, thus offering a sequential supply of food. Most agricultural projects have ignored these lessons known to farmers, promoting instead stands of single crops of rice or maize, for example.

But peasants regularly reject the conniving and threatening pro-grammes of planners. For example, unwilling to accept the project recommendations for rice production, farmers of the Uboma Rural Development Project in central Nigeria have experimented with an innovative intercropping system of planting rice in furrows, and cassava and cocoyams on the adjacent ridges. The experimentation tried by Nigerian farmers is now widespread. Senegalese farmers within an irrigation project devised their own water management

system and found that their rice and tomato crops could be successfully grown with less water than recommended by the project's
'experts'.[2] A recent study in Niger found a dynamic, experimenting,
innovative and deeply knowledgeable peasantry, regularly experimenting with and adapting cultivation techniques, seeds and advice to their
own conditions. It is worth quoting from one of the case examples:

> About 20 years ago, villagers began to notice increasing wind erosion on
> their fields. The fierce, gusting winds of the Sahel were sweeping away the
> sandy soil, leaving bare the sterile hardpan underneath, 'Where nothing can
> grow.'
>
> Until this time, villagers had always prepared fields for planting by
> burning off all standing stover. But they began to rethink this practice,
> hypothesizing that if they left the stalks in place 'This would keep the wind
> from blowing away all the earth.'
>
> Their reasoning was simple. 'We saw that, so long as some sand was left
> around the base of the plants, they would live. But if all the sand had blown
> away, the stand would die.' So a conscious change in land preparation (and
> soil conservation) techniques was made. When queried about the source of
> this then-new idea, informants shrugged that 'We saw this for ourselves.'[3]

Peasants are well ahead of agricultural researchers in understanding the conditions which influence crop growth while reducing the
risks inherent in all agriculture. Detailed knowledge about the
specific characteristics of seeds and soils is commonplace. In parts
of West Africa, peasants use ten to twenty different varieties of rice
which respond to different soil and weather conditions and which
have varying maturing rates. Dey points to the 'enormous range of
skills and knowledge that women have about rice cultivation
conditions and practices which have essentially been passed on from
mother to daughter'. These women farmers command detailed knowledge about soil types and salinity conditions; about problems of water
control and the changing responses of plants to water variations over
the growing season; and about methods to minimize weed growth and
erosion and to maintain soil fertility.[4] Farmers in Niger are well aware
of the official recommendations for fertilizer use, but few follow them.
Instead, they have adapted their own fertilizing patterns which take
advantage of the specific benefits of chemical fertilizers, the
results of which offer more efficient operations on the farm.

In northern Zambia and southern Zaire, peasants judge soil quality
by the types of wild plants growing on it. Their farming method — a
form of slash and burn agriculture — incorporates a detailed
knowledge of fertilization, weed control, crop rotations and fallow
periods, all factors regularly cited by scientists and agricultural
extension agents as fundamental to productive farming. However,
despite the parallels with the research recommendations, the slash
and burn farming method has been regularly criticized as inefficient
and destructive to the forest lands. Both the colonial and independent

governments of Zambia officially banned the practice on several occasions. Nevertheless, peasants there continue to follow and adapt their own tested methods. Some changes have occurred as a result of the pressures on rural households caused by male out-migration to urban areas. A more intensive cutting of trees and a shortening of the fallow periods have occurred as households adapted to the lack of farm labour in the absence of men. Also, new, less labour-intensive crops which do not require the slash and burn methods have been adopted, such as cassava and maize. What has not occurred in Zambia is an innovative spirit among agricultural officers which parallels that of peasants. If anything, there has been official disdain of the knowledge and methods of small-scale cultivators who are referred to derogatorily as 'peasants' as opposed to 'farmers', the latter characterized as growers who use chemical fertilizers and produce crops for the official market.

The storage of crops is carefully practised by farmers. Ash mixed with mud produces an insecticide along the walls of granaries. Mixing stored grain with the leaves of certain plants provides a repellent against pests. Studies have found that local granaries are far more efficient in reducing grain losses than large storage depots, most of the latter designed to serve urban areas as well. Also, local varieties of grain store longer, with less insect loss, than hybrid varieties.[5]

Health and nutrition advice predicated on Western mores and resources is another example of how traditional practices are misunderstood, and therefore undermined. Many ethnic groups instruct pregnant women to eat little and to avoid protein-rich foods such as eggs. Where obstetrical services are not available, it is safer for women to deliver smaller babies, and food taboos make good sense. Further, the value of communal membership is central to African societies; food is used as a way to teach those values and the sharing of the communal pot is an essential method. As nutritionist Gill Gordon points out, rigorous nutritional monitoring, often imposed in feeding programmes, is not compatible with what families need to teach their children about sharing food. She quotes a Ghanaian woman: 'You can't teach sharing if you insist that everyone sticks to their own bowl.'[6]

One of the major constraints imposed on farming households in the past decades has been insufficient labour to complete all agricultural functions, including land clearing, planting, weeding, crop protection, harvesting, storage and handling and food processing. Female-headed households, which represent at least 20 per cent and in some cases 50 per cent of all rural households, face major problems in food production. Such households lead the way in adopting cropping methods which are less reliant on the labour normally available to jointly headed households. In high rainfall areas of Sierra Leone and Liberia, what agricultural scientists have come to call 'minimum tillage agriculture' has assumed a marked prominence. This farming method involves relatively limited land clearing and minimal disruption of the soil and weeding. It is less labour intensive than other methods and carries less risk of soil erosion. The method has been criticized by the agricultural research establishment as unproductive and inefficient as agricultural crops compete with wild growth. It is also said to be 'unsightly'. However, in recent years as environmental and social factors have come to play a more significant role in determining the course of African agriculture, the scientists have 'discovered' minimum tillage as a worthy research subject for the very reasons that peasants have used it over the years.[7]

It is clear that peasant farmers have a much deeper and firmer knowledge of the conditions which influence crop and livestock production in their immediate areas than many research scientists and extension agents. Furthermore, these farmers are often more aware of wider economic factors than scientists who usually work from a centralized research station or the nation's capital. However, farmers are often cited by scientists, agricultural extension workers and politicians for their conservatism, laziness and ignorance! Yet it is the elite research and bureaucratic groups that are insulated by their own methods and attitudes.

Peasants teaching economists

Because of their knowledge of crop and livestock production, peasants are often more aware than 'expert' economists of the economic factors influencing and resulting from their work, and are more able to calculate and plan for realistic economic returns.

In the late 1970s, the Botswana government began to subsidize the purchase of draft animals and modern farming equipment for small-scale landholders. The government hoped small-scale farmers would increase their herds and the amount of land cultivated, emulating the favoured position of the wealthiest 5 per cent of Botswana farmers. But smallholders have not used the subsidies. Their reasons were both rational and indicative of a more equitable development policy than that followed by the government. Small-scale farmers know that animals used for ploughing grow more slowly, need more veterinary services, and reproduce less, thus giving low economic returns. Farmers also know that fields ploughed as widely and extensively as possible have more chance of catching sufficient rainfall than smaller fields, even if the latter are better prepared. And it is more economically feasible to plough widely with traditional equipment than with expensive mechanized equipment. Finally, rural people recognized the government policies as part of a trend toward consolidating commercial land in the hands of the wealthiest people, leaving the rural poor landless.[8]

After studying two multi-million dollar agricultural 'development' projects in Liberia, an evaluator commented that 'Farmers have done their own 'project redesign' work in order to bring financial risks into line with likely benefits as they perceive them.' As we have argued, the plans of national and international development elites have often exacerbated the problems of the majority of people in Africa. This is especially true in their desire to control peasant agricultural production, which has been suspect for its 'independence' from official markets and influence. However, rather than accept the many impractical and potentially risky aspects of projects and schemes, project participants have often sought to alter recommendations handed down to them to fit their needs, abilities and constraints. The peasants in the Liberian projects, for example, have

> experimented with the amount of fertilizer, adjusted the balance between traditional and newly introduced [seed] varieties, grown alternative crops such as cassava, and broadcast swamp rice seeds rather than transplanting them ... mostly to save on labor costs.[9]

In short, they have been active and creative experimenters.

After the experience that some people had where their soils had become completely useless because of all the fertilizer they had used we have decided to ban the use of chemical fertilizer on our fields. We are also sure that in this way we might save our soils, and produce food that will cost us less because we won't have had to take out loans for chemical fertilizer.
— Zimbabwean peasant farmer, 1984.

In Senegal, peasants have taken the initiative to re-order projects which do not conform to their priorities. An irrigated rice project was redesigned by participants who began irrigating maize and sorghum, their food crops. 'Their stated objective was to investigate the likelihood of higher returns from these cropping alternatives'.[10] In a similar way, peasants discounted the project's recommendations for a uniform application of fertilizer, and they adapted the application rate to the types of soil they encountered. In a significant victory for farmers' knowledge and initiatives, the government and project officials now permit cultivators to select the crop and cropping patterns which maximize returns under local conditions.

Again in Botswana, in 1981, several dozen women and a few men formed a vegetable production group in the town of Molepolole, close to the border with South Africa. The group now supplies more than a quarter of the town's vegetables, and provides the only cash income for most of its members, who once were forced out of grain farming by drought and economic constraints and who are now 'proud to be back in agriculture'.[11] What makes their success surprising to economists is that a national horticulture survey had deemed southeastern Botswana unable to compete with produce grown in South Africa and transported easily across the border, thereby undercutting local producers and increasing Botswana's dependence on the apartheid regime. But the survey failed to take into account the high demand for locally produced vegetables, and the large supply of efficient labour provided by poor women, factors which the gardeners themselves understood and set out to use.

The adaptation of crops for sale and consumption has been a feature of African farmers for centuries. An exciting but almost totally unreported example of economic innovation is soybean production and processing by Nigerian women. Soybeans were initially introduced to Nigeria early in the twentieth century as an export crop. Much later, the crop was incorporated by women into their fields, usually intercropped with sorghum and maize, and women regularly shared with one another seed and advice on the growing and processing of soybeans — an informal extension service of their own. In central Nigeria, almost a quarter of the land is now devoted to soybeans and because of its profitability men have begun to adopt the crop. Women have used soybeans to make *daddawa*, a protein-rich seasoning for soups and stews, substituting the new soy product for one previously made from locust beans. The locust bean *daddawa* took longer to process and required women to pay men for harvesting rights from the locust bean trees. The soybean-based mixture provides women with greater control over the entire production and marketing process, including the sale of *daddawa* in local markets and through trade networks in Nigeria and other parts of West Africa.[12]

The artisans who sell equipment to farmers have often shown the same kind of knowledge of economic return. A 1980 study of blacksmiths in Tanzania found that they did not need improved techniques, tools or training to turn out efficient products. Their manufacturing methods were quite adequate, as can be confirmed by a casual visit to nearly any African marketplace. Tanzanian bureaucrats, however, refused to accept this judgment and insisted upon a training project for blacksmiths in order to improve their methods and techniques. Not surprisingly, the blacksmiths rejected the presumption of their ignorance and inability, and the project failed.[13] On the positive side, resourcefulness in developing appropriate technological methods to fit a changing environment characterized the response of Ghanaian women when confronted with the disappearance of small herring from West African coastal waters, and the proliferation of a leathery bad-tasting fish that traditional processing methods could not transform into a saleable product. Refusing to give up and thereby abandon their livelihood, the women persisted and eventually

> developed a quick-gutting process and an effective brining system for rapid and total penetration of the salt. They learned how to easily remove the leathery skin, how to pack the preserved fish for storage and transport, and how to use their highly-developed marketing system to sell consumers on this new, inexpensive, nutritious product.[14]

The crisis engendered by ecological change beyond their control stimulated the women to work together to create a new technology now being adopted by people in neighbouring countries who are faced with the same problem.

The widespread failure of agricultural and rural development projects in Africa is largely due to the failure of planners to work with and reflect the complexity and diversity of rural and urban realities. The dreams and myths of development 'experts' have been repeatedly altered or rejected by peasants, artisans and the urban poor because the projects were irrelevant, impractical or directly threatening to their well-being. Not only are these people acting rationally in an economic sense, but their resistance to and rejection of inappropriate projects is one of the most articulate means by which poor people can deal with the mounting threat to local and national autonomy posed by the development models and programmes widely propounded by the Northern 'aid' agencies. The grassroots leadership provided by peasant farmers, artisans and small-scale traders in questioning the development models of the 'experts' remains to be fully taken up by responsible national and regional leadership. Instead, many national leaders have failed to heed the popular warnings, aligning themselves with the elite of international donor organizations.

Peasant resistance

In some instances, adaptation of projects or non-participation in national policies has been insufficient to counter the threats posed to people's security and well-being. In parts of Zambia, many poor farmers who have tried the 'Green revolution' agricultural packages propounded by the government have been badly hurt when inputs were not delivered on time or produce was not picked up, leaving the farmers stranded with rotting grain and heavy debts. The rural disaffection with government policies and advice was incorporated into protest songs and a search for security in the ritual authority of local chiefs whose powers had been by-passed for years.[15] In other countries, instances of sabotage and organized and coordinated resistance have occurred as people have opposed external efforts to impose programmes upon them and extract wealth from them. For example, in a rice-growing scheme in Mali, the 'autocratic management style encourages smallholders to take an anarchic approach to resolving their problems — for example, by destroying sections of dikes. . . .'[16] Although much studied within the context of the colonial era, instances of recent rural resistance to oppression have not received much attention from researchers. However, the existing examples suggest that active resistance has remained a significant form of popular initiative and the theme warrants much closer attention.

Nigeria's dependence upon wheat and other food imports has encouraged the country's rulers since the late 1960s to look to large-scale irrigation and mechanization projects to grow crops otherwise purchased abroad. The oil boom of the 1970s offered the financial means to ignore rural realities and peasant needs and to hire multinational firms to plan and develop those projects. In the Bakalori area, south of Kano in northern Nigeria, farm families lost their land and farm improvements to a new lake created behind a dam built for irrigation of wheat and other crops. Other farmers were prevented from using their land for two to three years as infrastructural 'improvements', such as roads, irrigation channels, land levelling and buildings, were made. Neither the project nor the federal government was prepared to offer adequate compensation to peasants who were regularly voicing their discontent and concerns about the project and the methods by which it was being established.

Eventually, farmers began to organize to press their claims and to seek to alter the cropping proposals being made by the project staff. When no adequate response was forthcoming, farmers began to blockade access to the project's headquarters and halted construction on the dam. The protest and blockade went on for a year, until in 1980 the government intervened with its mobile police. In a ruthless sweep against the farmers, police are said to have killed several hundred people. Overt resistance ended, and despite the embarrassment of having attacked its own people, the Nigerian government ordered construction to continue. Yet, despite the harshness of the government action, peasant resistance did achieve some changes within the project: compensation payments were speeded up; cropping recommendations were altered to reflect more adequately the food and cash needs of growers; and most importantly, the peasants retained control over how their labour would be used. The project abandoned plans to rely upon contract labour and was forced to provide subsidies for inputs which were made available to the independent producers. These achievements were significant, if costly to attain, but the fundamental conflicts between peasants and a government which seeks to control all aspects of production remain.[17]

On a smaller scale, women cassava growers and sellers in eastern

Zaire organized a protest against official corruption and unjust taxation. In order to reach the market from surrounding villages, women were required to pay, in produce, three tolls along the road. Over many months, they understood more and more clearly that these tolls, rather than being used to repair the road and bridge as was claimed by the tax collectors, were confiscated for personal use by local officials. Confronting these officials as a group was an extraordinary achievement, not only because women's status is badly compromised by male elites, but, also because of the pervasive violence and repression emanating from the political and economic corruption throughout Zaire. Even more extraordinary was the women's success in carrying their protest to higher administrative authorities in the region, and in organizing to elect sympathetic candidates in the next local elections. Once elected, those candidates abolished the market tax and bridge tolls. As one woman expressed it, 'It was as if we were sleeping, and we woke up.'[18] A similar occurrence was the 'Ondo Women's War' in southwestern Nigeria in late 1985. Following an effort by the state government to increase tax revenues from the market sales of women, ten days of increasingly complex protest occurred. The market was initially shut down by the women in protest against the tax. This was followed by a march in which tens of thousands of women protested the government action. The march became a rallying point to protest the losses suffered by common people from economic austerity measures imposed by the federal and state governments: increases in school and health fees and mandatory contributions to the 'Ondo State Development Fund'. As the confrontation escalated, ritual symbols were used to threaten the life of the governor. Prudently, he arranged a compromise agreement that protected lower-income women from some of the economic threats they regularly faced.[19]

The first cooperatives in southern Mali were set up in the mid-1970s because local farmers refused to continue being cheated by the parastatal Malian Cotton Company, whose employees misweighed and misrecorded the cotton which producers presented for sale. When farmers threatened to stop producing cotton, the Company finally agreed to allow them to manage the weighing and sale of their crops in order to assure continued production. The cooperatives trained young people from their villages to take over these tasks, and created a pricing structure that deposited into savings accounts the small profits between what the Company paid the cooperatives, and the cooperatives paid the producers. 'It is noteworthy and significant', wrote one observer, 'that every single village decided to use its money collectively, rather than to rebate it directly to the individual families.' Cooperative associations used the pooled money to buy the equipment they needed to market their own cotton, build storage facilities, purchase spare parts, and grant loans to peasants who did not own oxen and had not yet been able to increase their cotton production. This effort to reduce the inequalities among village families stemmed from, and in turn reinforced, traditional communal values that were not promoted by the national Cotton Company, whose concern was enhancing export and foreign exchange earnings. The farmers' initial resistance moved their villages toward more independence within the economy and, as villagers set themselves the tasks of becoming literate and proficient in accounting in order to handle their new marketing role, they were able to demand and receive the education and services they needed. Five years after the start of the cooperatives, there had been 'an extraordinary multiplication of development activities at the local level'.[20]

In eastern Senegal, the Federation of Sarakolle Villages — a peasant group — has successfully resisted efforts by the state agricultural agency to impose irrigation systems, cropping patterns, uniform pricing policies and marketing restrictions. Senegal, dependent upon peanuts for 60 per cent of its foreign exchange and upon massive amounts of imported rice to feed its urban population, has placed great emphasis on the production of both crops. Rural producers have responded to these national priorities with mixed feelings. They desire the cash earned from marketable crops, but are frustrated by the low prices offered for their crops and fearful of engaging too deeply in cash crop production while neglecting their own food and environmental security needs. The Sarakolle villagers have an astute perception of the dilemmas they and their nation face:

> The young people should stay here to work, but there's no way of paying the tax; we have to let them go so that they can send money for taxes and food. Now they're having trouble. . . . We old men are here in the village, powerless; we let the young men go, to get something to live on, but they can't manage now. We have nothing. The village will die. The country will die.[21]

The peasants' federation began in the 1960s as a way to provide villagers, young and old, with opportunities for equitable development through collective action and work. Crop production was primarily for food, secondarily for surplus distribution within the villages and only lastly for sales. However, as the government and its agricultural agency sought to promote rice production via large-scale irrigation schemes and centralized control over producers, the different interests of the two sides quickly became apparent, exacerbated by a decision of USAID to provide substantial assistance to the national scheme to support rice production. The differences revolved around the issue of control: whether peasants could organize to pursue development as they defined it; or whether they would have to conform to the production requirements of the agricultural agency (with the initials SAED), government itself and international interests. In 1976 the chairman of the peasant association argued:

Up to now, all of us, men and women, are determined to work independently. I think we have the heart for it. If this peasant development continues, it will be good for the people of the [Senegal] River. If there's too much SAED development, it will be bad for us; we'll have to give up. We're not against SAED. But we've seen how SAED tells peasants nothing, and gets them into debt.[22]

Resistance by the Federation to national and international pressures has continued over the past decade. The alternative vision of peasant-defined development has sustained the Federation. To some extent, the Federation's persistence has forced changes in SAED's approach in other areas where it operates. The Federation thus continues, offering a hopeful light for other rural peoples in Senegal and eastern Mali who now face — as have peasants in Nigeria — internationally financed schemes to construct large dams along the region's rivers and thereby promote capital-intensive irrigation of export and cash crops.

Although rarely organized on a regional basis, women farmers across Africa have resisted substituting production of food crops with capital-intensive cash crops. There has been strong resistance by women to spending ever-increasing time and labour in their husbands' cash crop fields. Studies of women in Zambia and Cameroon have shown that women without husbands worked harder than did women with men present. The latter know that proceeds of cash crops accrue almost always to the men, whether or not the crop was grown on the husband's or the wife's land, and that these profits are unlikely to be spent on family needs. Women have recognized that the modern agricultural implements and other technology made available to their husbands to cultivate cash crops threaten women's traditional rights to grow food crops and sell the surplus for their own income. Women are still expected to grow the food that will nourish their families but, unless they resist cash-cropping schemes, they will have fewer and fewer resources to fulfil their responsibilities.[23]

In Gambia, a large government project, funded by international aid agencies, sought to convert 1,500 hectares of land into plots for growing hybrid rice. For generations, the land had been used by women to grow rice for family consumption and for personal income. Without consulting the women landowners, the village chief leased their land to the government for the new project. The women were promised other land, but they doubted that they would get it:

I think this project will distribute all the land to the men. It was the same with earlier projects when we helped build them — but they gave the men all the plots. It was the World Bank that gave the land to the men. . . . We think this will happen again.[24]

Again and again, national and international elites are leading the way in imposing these top-heavy, bureaucratic projects which often encourage local leaders to deny women's traditional rights in favour of chimeric benefits promised, but not delivered, by aid officials. They have refused to listen closely to or collaborate with rural people who best know their areas and abilities and who have demonstrated a willingness to work toward local and national interests if mutual respect and understanding are forthcoming.

Grassroots ecology

African environmental knowledge also has much to teach outsiders. For rural Africans the natural environment is an integral part of daily life. It is not a separate component, to be considered only when a new project is proposed or in times of natural disasters. Soil, weather, plants and animals provide the means for living, for drawing reward from nature without destroying it. An effective understanding of the environment and its behaviour has been essential for overall food production and livestock raising. People recognize that careful preservation of the environment is crucial for their own well-being and conservation has been practised for centuries.

Farmers have an intimate understanding of the types of trees which grow in their area. The forests offer many types of resources — foods and oils, building materials, firewood and charcoal for energy. In Zambia, farmers recognize that different trees are associated with different soil types on which crops would respond in various ways once the trees were cleared. In areas of shifting cultivation, trees are partially cut to clear land for planting. The trees regenerate after ten to twenty-five years, and during that period the area provides shelter for small animals. Sahelian farmers recognize that the pods of the acacia tree enrich the soil and crops grow better around such trees. The pods also provide a valuable food for livestock. In several instances, farmers themselves incorporated these trees into projects designed by outsiders who had ignored or not known of their value.[25]

In rural Tanzania, both government and international aid agencies had tried, and failed, to rid a Masai area of the tsetse flies which infect and eventually kill cattle grazing there. Cynical about outsiders' solutions, villagers came together and discussed how to burn off the trees and other vegetation where tsetse flies breed so that roots too would be destroyed. 'They knew that dried manure was a source of sustained heat. They concluded that using dried manure to burn the trees and brush might just kill the roots.'[26] The success of their efforts encouraged villagers to plan other community improvement actions, building upon their own wisdom and adapting it to problems which arose.

Soil conservation is regularly practised by rural people. For example, the intercropping techniques described earlier are not only productive for crops but also provide ground cover which reduces erosion. A study in rural Zambia found that small-scale farmers were far more efficient conservators of their soil cover than the large, commercial farmers who tended to mine the soil beyond easy repair. In a number of countries, land terracing and contouring has been practised by rural people as a way to conserve soil from run-off, retain soil fertility and hold moisture for crops. The construction of terraces requires heavy work and the systems began to break down in the colonial period as men left rural areas for work elsewhere or devoted more time to cash crops. Increased erosion and greater susceptibility to drought followed. Colonial governments sought to counter cases of extreme erosion by resettlement and compulsory hillside contouring — rules which were often but not entirely resisted. Recently, more sensitive attempts to deal with erosion have been tried. An OXFAM-UK sponsored project in Burkina adopted traditional contouring methods to help stabilize the degraded soil. The practice is now spreading beyond the original pilot area as people recognize its value and organize to devote greater attention to preserving the communities' resources. The project discovered, however, that legitimizing the traditional practices was not enough to assure that everyone in the community took part. Poor households have been unable to take part in building the contours because they must divert their limited labour to working for cash. A food loan component was introduced into the project to assist poorer farmers to hire labour for construction purposes, but the poorest people 'are still afraid to borrow food when they habitually fail to produce enough for themselves'.[27]

In Senegal, Keur Momar Saar lies at the northern edge of the Sahel. For years, because of drought, people in the area could barely meet their subsistence needs. Many herders had lost their livestock. Beginning in the mid-1970s, people of Keur Momar Saar began revitalizing their villages. Utilizing the annual fluctuations of a neighbouring lake, irrigation systems were created to provide more food. Trees were planted to restore the fertility of the soil and hold it in place against wind erosion. As of old, manure was applied to fields. New community services were created to meet local needs, thereby linking villagers together in larger political and economic units.

The rejuvenation of this marginal land by the people of Keur Momar Saar is of interest not only because of the application of peoples' knowledge to restoring their environment, but also because their success has attracted the interest of larger and richer landholders. The struggle now is to preserve their development against this elite covetousness.

These examples of utilizing environmental knowledge are important, yet it cannot be assumed that all rural Africans have a complete understanding of integrated environmental control. The Green Belt

Movement in Kenya — organized by women, primarily for poor women and now internationally recognized — found that much of the knowledge of the links between forests and agriculture which people had possessed in the pre-colonial period had been lost because European farming methods were 'erroneously considered superior. Now the scientists are recommending this agroforestry approach and unfortunately the current generation has to be taught to intercrop all over again.' In the interim between the breakdown of the holistic systems of the pre-colonial era and the rediscovery of their relevance and appropriateness for development, the poor in Kenya have been the major victims of the ecological decline. Soil erosion and deforestation are well advanced in many parts of Kenya and both contribute to an energy and food crisis for the rural poor — a relationship well understood by the women most affected. This rediscovered knowledge, combined with the knowledge about the wider causes of poverty, has produced a dynamic programme that addresses the immediate need for tree planting, while promoting community organizing and reflection and action upon the situation of women in contemporary Kenyan society.[28]

The Green Belt Movement encourages the protection of Kenya's natural vegetation from irresponsible citizens and investors who continue to cut down indigenous trees to make way for exotic pines and eucalyptus trees. . . . It is worth remembering that by the time we shall have cut every tree to make wooden antelopes, giraffes and wooden Maasai standing on one leg, Kenya will have turned into a desert.
— Wangari Maathai, founder of the Green Belt Movement, 1985.

If the knowledge is there, why such crises?

The examples of the women's Green Belt Movement in Kenya and of the people of Keur Momar Saar in Senegal are instructive, for they demonstrate the conflicts now existing between the regular application of people's knowledge, skills and resources, and the economic, political and social realities within all African countries. The colonial experience did much to discredit popular knowledge and skills. Christian missionaries attacked the religious beliefs and leadership of societies. The mission and other colonial forms of education promoted an individualistic alternative to the social and community relations of Africans. It is to their credit that a number of Africans have adapted Christianity to their own social and theological needs, but the process has not been easy nor is it complete.

Other factors also undermined the structures which had provided for social well-being. The economic demands of colonialism for cheap labour, land and cash crops set in motion a process that has undermined food security. Women's economic and social power has been particularly weakened by the codification of European sexism into African law and elite behaviour. Men have acquired greater control over the exclusive use of land and the earnings from agriculture than had existed previously. Denied their traditional land rights, women have been widely excluded from farmer cooperatives and have had only limited access to credit or other inputs to improve their own crops. The 'development' process has passed them by:

> During the anticolonial campaigns we were told that development would mean better living conditions. Several years have gone by, and all we see are people coming from the capital to write about us. For me the hoe and the water pot which served my grandmother still remain my source of livelihood. When I work on the land and fetch water from the river, I know I can eat. But this development which you talk about has yet to be seen in this village.[29]

In the post-colonial world of international development, the massive influx of outside experts and their many plans and their money has been accompanied by a zeal and righteousness that in many ways match the narrow evangelism of the early colonial religious missionaries. The deep and expansive African understanding of the world has been ignored, disputed and discredited. African governments that sought to promote models of development at odds with the patterns of Northern contributors have been isolated or overthrown with Northern intervention or compliance. The development models proposed and funded by the international and national 'experts' have sought to remove control of agricultural production from the producers. Commercially produced fertilizers and pesticides have been combined in technical packages for farmers to buy or to receive on credit to be repaid with one's harvest. Mechanized settlement schemes and plantations have also been promoted using peasant participants as labourers and massive projects for the production of cash crops have been planned and created. Nevertheless, these expert-designed programmes to create labourers where independent producers exist have been widely resisted by peasants.

These national and international strategies have assumed that national development plans and individual projects will be designed by 'experts' and managed by bureaucratic technicians during implementation. 'People's participation' has been added to many of these centrally run projects as an afterthought, but the elements of control have remained in the hands of outsiders. People — and this almost always has meant men only — have been able to participate so long as they followed the instructions of the managers. What has emerged within modern Africa are two systems of development activity: one is the 'official' system, which is advocated, financed and run by national governments and international development organizations; the other is the 'people's' system with its own sets of priorities, resources, organizations and support networks. Often this is the only system which addresses the disenfranchisement particular to women. The two systems do not exist independently of one another. They are closely related but often antagonistically so. The official system has suffered grave setbacks. Its credibility is badly strained because it has failed to match accomplishments with its rhetoric and, in a number of cases, is overtly corrupt. Desperately searching for ways to achieve a degree of success, some governments and development agencies have blatantly lied about the outcomes of their projects, have become more oppressive in seeking conformity from people, have funded extremely expensive projects in order to reward themselves, and have jumped from one magic solution to another.

The victims of failures of official development are well known: devastating famines and chronic malnutrition have ravaged millions of people; people's communal identity has been officially denied and threatened; initiatives to assert their rights have often been brutally crushed. Yet, people have continued to assert their rights by defining their own problems and designing their own solutions. They have adapted new structures to best meet their own needs or have created new structures when the official system is too slow, corrupt or inept to respond. One Zairean scholar calls attention to the survival and creative attributes of people:

> Coping with the crisis involves not only a strategy of self-reliance, exemplified by the recourse to either the subsistence or the 'underground' economy, but also a strategy for dealing with the state's violation of human rights through economic neglect and mismanagement, repression, and extortions of all kinds.[30]

It is fairly rare that we in the North have the opportunity to hear what ordinary African people are saying about their conditions. In the next chapter we will look more closely at the silent revolution in Africa: the means people use to adapt and to turn crises to their advantage, to assert their rights, and to organize themselves in order to apply their invaluable knowledge and skills to a new future.

Notes

1. The four quotes are from: H. Crawford Angus, 'A trip to Northern Angoniland', *Scottish Geographical Magazine*, Vol. XV (1899), pp. 74–79; E.D. Morel, *Nigeria: Its People and Its Problems* (Smith Elder, London, 1911); William Allen, *The African Husbandman*, revised edition (Oliver & Boyd, Edinburgh and London, 1967), p. 4; Paul Richards, *Indigenous Agricultural Revolution* (Hutchinson, London, 1985), p. 63.
2. Richards, *op. cit.*, p. 79.
3. Constance M. McCorkle, *et al.*, *A Case Study on Farmer Innovations and Communication in Niger* (Academy for Educational Development, Washington, DC, 1988), p. 40. I wish to thank Mike Yates of USAID for bringing this study to my attention.
4. Jennie Dey, 'Women in African rice farming systems', in *Women in Rice Farming* (Gower, London, 1985), p. 439.
5. Hartmut Brandt, *Food Security Programmes in the Sudano-Sahel* (German Development Institute, Berlin, 1984), pp. 24–28; Sankung Sagnia, 'Pest control in millet farming', *ILEIA Newsletter*, Vol. 4, No. 3 (October 1989), p. 15.
6. Gill Gordon, 'Research on rural women: feminist methodological questions', *IDS Bulletin*, Vol. 15, No. 1 (January 1984), p. 43.
7. Richards, *op. cit.*, pp. 60–61.
8. William Duggan, 'Irrigated gardens, Molepolole, Botswana', *Rural Development and Women: Lessons from the Field*, Vol. 1 (International Labour Office, Geneva, 1985), p. 11; Patrick P. Molutsi, 'The state, environment and peasant consciousness in Botswana', *Review of African Political Economy*, No. 42 (1988), pp. 40–47.
9. John W. Harbeson, 'Integrated agricultural development and agricultural policy in Liberia', *Rural Africana*, No. 22 (Spring 1985), pp. 3–24.
10. Jack Keller, *et al.*, *Project Review for Bakel Small Irrigated Perimeters*, WMS Report No. 9. (Utah State University, Logan, Utah, 1982), p. 5.
11. Duggan, 'Irrigated gardens', *op. cit.*, p. 17.
12. Ann Waters-Bayer, 'Soybean Daddawa: an innovation by Nigerian women', *ILEIA Newsletter*, Vol. 4, No. 3 (October 1988), pp.8–9.
13. Ben Wisner, *Power and Need in Africa: Basic Human Needs and Development Policies* (Earthscan, London, 1988), pp. 256–257.
14. Bill Brownell and Jocelyne Lopez, 'Women are the backbone', *Women and Development*, reprinted from *Development Forum* (DESI/UN, New York, 1985), p. 39.
15. Personal communication from Mark Auslander.
16. R. James Bingen, *Food Production and Rural Development in the Sahel: Lessons from Mali's Operation Riz-Segou* (Westview Press, Boulder, CO, 1984), p. 118.
17. Bjorn Beckman, 'Bakolori: the menace of a dam', *Development*, No. 3 (1985), pp. 24–32.
18. Catharine Newbury, 'Ebutumwa Bw'Emiogo: the tyranny of cassava. A women's tax revolt in eastern Zaire', *Canadian Journal of African Studies*, Vol. 18, No. 1 (1984), p. 49.
19. Elizabeth A. Eames, 'Why the women went to war: women and wealth in Ondo Town, southwestern Nigeria', in Gracia Clark (ed.), *Traders Versus the*

State: *Anthropological Approaches to Unofficial Economies* (Westview Press, Boulder, CO, 1988), pp. 81—97.

20. Guy Belloncle, *Non-Formal Education and Farm Cooperatives in West Africa* (Non-Formal Education Information Center, Michigan State University, East Lansing, MI, 1982), pp. 12—23.

21. Adrian Adams, 'The Senegal River Valley', in Judith Heyer *et al., Rural Development in Tropical Africa* (St. Martin's Press, New York, 1981), p. 332.

22. *Ibid.*, pp. 339—340.

23. This argument is forcibly made in *Man-Made Famine*, a film produced in 1986 by the *New Internationalist* magazine.

24. Sarah Hobson, 'Bulldozed', *New Internationalist*, No. 131 (January 1984), pp. 21—22. For an up-dated, but no more hopeful, report of the struggle of women to control land and rice production in The Gambia, see Judith A. Carney, 'Struggles over land and crops in an irrigated rice scheme: the Gambia', in Jean Davison (ed.), *Agriculture, Women, and Land: The African Experience* (Westview Press, Boulder, CO, 1988), pp. 59—78.

25. Nigel Twose, *Drought and the Sahel* (Oxfam, Oxford, 1984), p. 15.

26. *Sharing Experiences in Development* (Silveira House/IRED, Harare, 1984), p. 15.

27. Nigel Twose, *Fighting the Famine* (Food First, San Francisco, 1986), p. 38. See also Chris Reij, 'Soil and water conservation in Yatenga, Burkina Faso', in Czech Conroy and Miles Litvinoff (eds), *The Greening of Aid: Sustainable Livelihoods in Practice* (Earthscan, London, 1988), pp. 74—77.

28. Wangari Maathai, 'Kenya: The Green Belt Movement', *IFDA Dossier*, No. 49 (September—October 1985), pp. 4-12.

29. A woman in rural Kenya, quoted by Achola O. Pala, 'Definitions of women and development: an African perspective', *Signs*, Vol. 3, No. 1 (Autumn 1977), p. 13.

30. Nzongola-Ntalaja, 'Crisis and change in Zaire, 1960—1985', in Nzongola-Ntalaja (ed.), *The Crisis in Zaire* (Africa World Press, Trenton, NJ, 1986), pp. 10—11.

11 The People Organize

Creative and stirring events are occurring in Africa. A revolution is under way — organized, run by and for people long excluded from the 'official' development process. It is a silent revolution arising from the grassroots and one which is increasingly influencing organizations and policies at other levels of power. Not surprisingly, national governments and international contributor agencies have taken credit for improvements in food supplies and economic activity, citing their policy reforms which have been designed to regain control over the wealth and productivity of majority of rural and urban people. But these claims are spurious and distort the reality of peasant and worker initiatives.

Peasants, workers, low-income consumers and others have lived with and confronted the food and development crises by devising new organizations which spring from their own knowledge and experiences. They have felt the anguish of lost hopes and opportunities, the pain of hunger, and the misery of being deprived of the services for basic humanity. They have chosen to redefine development and in the process have begun to create institutions that serve their needs.

We are not an organization of professional people, but we are a people's organization, the people doing those things for themselves which are not catered for. Any person who seeks to fight oppression is welcome. We want to be assertive and fight for our rights. We recognize oppression of women by the law, our men, and discrimination by society and set out to fight against it. Our yardstick is democracy.
— Vaal Women's Organization, South Africa, 1984.

As with any revolution, there is strong resistance from the elite to these popular initiatives. The struggle is young, but it has begun. In this chapter, we document some of the popular organizational forms that people have used to further their needs. Thus, we try to reflect some of the creative activities now occurring in Africa, making the revolution somewhat less silent.

Coping with crises

As is seen throughout this book, the Northern media image of African people as helpless victims, passively accepting events around them, is false. It is an image which African people do not recognize and which draws their anger and disgust when used by Northern relief agencies to raise funds. Because of their experiences with their world, Africans have developed a variety of alternative means to deal with food and water shortages, with economic contractions and governmental neglect or abuse.

The seeds and the farming methods used by farmers are adapted to respond to variations in rainfall. Drought-resistant millet and sorghum seed, for example, continue to yield even when rainfall is well below normal. Peasants stagger planting times to take advantage of differences in micro-environments and soil types and to accommodate the labour required for all farming chores.

However, in severe, prolonged drought situations, social coping mechanisms begin to take over. Households and communities begin to make decisions for further conserving food and water, reducing demand and acquiring food from non-traditional sources.[1] McCorkle discusses five areas where changes in behaviour reflect food insecurity and people's adaptation to those situations. Changes are seen in the market (increases in prices but decreases in sales of grains, while livestock sales increase but prices decrease), in non-market exchanges (barter), in the diets and nutritional status of children, in use of labour (declines in work parties), and in gifts and tribute (with cutbacks). Some of the responses reflect long-term strategies, others represent adaptations not only to natural constraints but to the economic constraints of contemporary society. Among the Taita in Kenya, for instance, a complex agricultural system is capable of producing food year round under even the harshest conditions. However, land and labour shortages for producing food crops have more recently caused households to rely upon non-farm employment to survive. During the 1984 drought, non-farm jobs became far more important. Cash incomes were used to purchase food as a supplement to that which had been lost through drought. Over half of all households had a member who migrated out of the area for work, remitting a portion of his income. Women who headed households — usually among the poorest households in most African communities — increased their work for wealthier people in order to get food or cash. Households with livestock sold more of their animals than usual. Other poor families turned to the environment, increasing their sales of charcoal and honey. Beer brewing and sales nearly tripled. Dietary changes also occurred. In the Kenya case, bean consumption declined. Instead, people prepared less substantial meals and at 10 per cent of meal times there was no food at all.[2]

An extensive study of the impact of the 1982-84 drought on the Dogon of Mali showed responses broadly similar to those of the Taita. Out-migration by young men occurred as a result of food shortages. Normally, migration is not encouraged by Dogon elders, but the loss of food crops forced a change in that social condition. Money was needed to supplement the badly depleted food crops and seed supplies. Thus, in many cases young men left with specific instructions from their villages on where to go. They were sent with the expectation that they would send money home to ensure the survival of those who remained. This system of controlled emigration has created other problems, however, as many young men have remained away for two or more years, depleting villages of needed labour. Food preparation methods also changed. Millet chaff, usually reserved for animal feed, was retained and mixed with other foods to provide greater bulk. Livestock and other commodity sales increased. The cash from these sales and from remittances by the young migrants was used to buy food and/or seed. Many households preferred to retain their seed if they could afford to buy food or had access to relief supplies because the locally adapted seed was too valuable to eat. Families that had seeds shared with those who did not, thereby ensuring the survival of the community.[3] Evidence from Ethiopia adds to this picture. Food management by women becomes critical in the early stages of shortage situations and the values of society place priority on providing for children, pregnant women and the elderly. Gathering of wild foods is common, and women utilize their botanical knowledge to identify and collect edible plants that contribute to the diet. Men, in turn, are expected to arrange inter-family deals — the barter or pawning of assets in exchange for food.[4]

Following a drought, there is a major effort to restore food, seed stocks and livestock. Restoration is not easy. Households may have lost most or all of their seed and many lack the labour needed to resume full production. Yet the dramatic increase in food production in many places in Africa in 1985 and 1986 — following devastating famine conditions in areas of the eastern Sahel — demonstrates that the survival mechanisms which people had employed to carry them through a period of hardship were often successful.

When we discussed food shortages and wondered whether this problem has always been with us some of our parents said that they felt that the traditional seeds that used to be grown were far more drought resistant than these modern hybrid variety. So what we have done is try and gather as much of the local seeds as possible and encourage our groups to try them again. Unfortunately the

rains failed again but even with only four rains our fields with local seeds will at least produce enough seeds for next year whereas the maize fields have failed completely and if we wanted to do maize again next year we would have to buy new seeds.
— Zimbabwean rural community leader, 1984.

The crisis in Africa is very much connected with food. Across the continent over the past ten to fifteen years, people have switched from production of crops which would enter the export market to food crops for consumption and for sale within local markets. In many areas of the Sahel, market gardening has become a major activity and petty commerce has increased as people trade their foodstuffs in order to obtain cash needed for other purchases. In many countries, parallel economies, sometimes referred to as the 'black market' or 'underground economy', have been created as sources and outlets for a variety of commodities which are illegal or otherwise unavailable. These commodities can include distilled alcohol as well as many basic items, from soap to cooking oil. The parallel market has long provided jobs for many people. In recent years, the informal sector has employed tens of thousands of people and is often larger in terms of employment than the formal sector. One of the innovative characteristics of the parallel economy is the recycling of throw-away products: soft drink cans are reworked into cooking pots and utensils; discarded tyres are transformed into shoes; and used oil drums are hammered into cook stoves.[5]

Many independent churches have emerged, offering a theological and social support as well as an explanation for people whose lives have been disrupted. Many of the established churches have responded to popular directions and have become more involved in development activities. In eastern Zaire, for example, two local clergy promoted a series of health, reforestation, literacy and income-earning projects for their parishioners. A distinctive feature of the programme 'was the parishioners' strict adherence to Zairean law, including their mutual support for each other in this goal'.[6] This has been particularly important as villagers resisted the corrupt activities and interference of local officials who have flagrantly ignored and violated the law. The power of the state and local officials remains pervasive, however, requiring constant struggle. Efforts to establish a consumers' cooperative to sell basic goods at prices lower than in local shops were defeated by merchants who were in close collaboration with government officials.[7]

Popular responses to the African crisis are diverse and innovative. In some cases, the coping strategies arise or are instituted because of adverse conditions, such as drought, famine, war or oppression and may be confined to dealing with those events. In other cases, people's actions become a positive approach to problem solving, an assertion of human dignity and determination not only to survive but to create new social orders.

People's organizations and cooperative structures

The instances of rural resistance described in the previous chapter all required forms of social and political organization and cooperation. The often given official explanation that resistance is instigated by outside 'agitators' holds no credence; it is an excuse used to disguise the failure of elite enrichment. The innovative character of African development is often preserved in and supported by people's own indigenous organizations and institutions. The Sarakolle villagers of eastern Senegal have been able to sustain their own identity and sense of locally directed development over two decades because of their collective and well-organized efforts. Community and labour organizing in South Africa has occurred in spite of extraordinary official efforts to prevent or co-opt such initiatives. Across Africa, women's traditional social and savings clubs have expanded their scope, and their members' skills, to meet new needs and challenges. Both Islam and Christianity have been adapted to merge with local cultures and conditions, and these new religious forms offer the security of belief and community. While well-known within African communities, collaboration, networks and formal organizations are infrequently reported outside. Yet these organizations have sustained people over the decades and centuries and have provided the means to create new social orders which offer the most meaningful opportunities for development within Africa.

Labour organizing is spreading as a way for workers to protect and expand their rights. In Ghana, women agricultural workers, recognizing that they are working within a labour-scarce market, negotiated to shorten their work days while demanding the same wage. They argued that they still had their many domestic responsibilities to perform after work, and reducing their labour time was more important than seeking higher wages. Also in Ghana, young people, unable to obtain jobs in urban areas, have formed work groups in order to obtain contracts for specialized farm tasks, the various 'groups being known as expert in cleaning, sowing, weeding, harvesting or bagging paddy [rice]'. Not only did the unemployed young men find work, but they were able to use their collective bargaining position to command decent wages and to resist employer cheating.[8] In cotton growing regions of Cote d'Ivoire, some women and young men devised work groups based on the principle that one member of the group would receive all of the group's daily income. Members of the group had to continue working until each member received the daily wage at least once. The attraction for group members was the large lump-sum payment — a form of enforced savings which can be used for major expenditures — not available to individual labourers.[9]

For resource-poor households, labour sharing on household fields remains an essential production strategy. Women, who are estimated to head 20 to 50 per cent of all rural households in Africa, depending upon the area, have been especially active in cooperative labour sharing. In southern Africa, women's labour sharing and cooperative organizations have enabled women to cope with the absence of men who may be working in urban areas or who have abandoned their families altogether. In Kenya, nearly all rural women are reported to belong to labour sharing groups which also offer mutual aid in times of need. In recent years, some of these groups have taken on social welfare and income raising activities, often based on one or more agricultural activities. In Murang'a District of central Kenya, women are collectively involved in livestock and poultry rearing, crop production and firewood and charcoal sales in order to increase their incomes. Some groups have purchased and allocated land to members as a means of ensuring the women members greater control over their production and income.[10] However, it is necessary to distinguish those women's groups from the high profile women's groups in Kenya and elsewhere which are controlled by and for elite women (and occasionally by men). These national women's organizations often receive government funding and their pro-grammes often exclude the vast majority of women who must turn to their own community resources.[11] Poor women must struggle to protect the sharing and survival mechanisms which they have developed against co-option or repression by elite women or groups.

Another form of labour cooperation is exemplified by the Rural Artisans Group of Yatenga in Senegal, abbreviated as GARY. The GARY groups are composed of several dozen young artisans who learn, on the job, the various skills for construction and maintenance of wells in drought-affected villages. Members govern themselves cooperatively. GARY's work is based on the belief that only villagers themselves can define and resolve their own problems. GARY has been able to implement the kind of educational programme that many national governments have only talked about. Its programme enables young people to learn, in the village context, and thus find employment without moving to the city. In its ten years, GARY has learned that a water project not fully desired and approved by village authorities will not succeed, and is thus now able to insist that financial help from outside the village will be subject to total village control of the donated resources.[12]

Some cooperative structures have broken down under the influence of the commercialization of human relations, some Christian teachings and elite-sponsored patronage. Other cooperative forms have emerged or adapted to these pressures. In Ghana, the rapid rise of wealthy rice farmers alienated poorer farmers and urban-based field workers who found themselves exploited. This unjust situation was not passively accepted. Utilizing their increased political consciousness, the farm labourers began collective action to protect their economic and social rights, including withdrawing labour at crucial times or occasionally engaging in sabotage in order to reinforce their demands.

Insufficient labour to produce rice is a major constraint among rural people in Sierra Leone. As a means to solve this problem, an estimated 20 per cent of all agricultural labour is organized in six different types of cooperatives which evolved out of earlier peasant-run work associations. The farmer-run cooperatives maintain their own constitutions and records in order to facilitate their activities in an efficient way. In western Cameroon and elsewhere, 'working bees', or rotating labour sharing arrangements, allow women to contribute to and draw upon their friends and neighbours to complete agricultural chores. According to one member, 'we have joined together to work because we are not strong. If we work together, we finish very quickly.'[13]

Communications and networks

Other cooperative structures have emerged among professional Africans who are using the media to encourage respect for traditional knowledge and local people's control of their own lives. The *African Women Link Newsletter* is produced by women journalists to serve as a channel for news on women's self-help efforts throughout Africa. In another example, the widely circulated magazine *Famille et Developpement* is produced by the African Association of Education for Development and regularly features information on effective traditional medical treatments. *Living Otherwise* (*Vivre Autrement* in French) is a newsletter published by Environnement Africain (ENDA), an African environmental organization headquartered in Senegal. Among its activities, ENDA demonstrates how urban dwellers can use local products rather than imported, expensive and wasteful ones. Produced by the West African Federation of Associations for the Promotion of Handicapped Persons, the quarterly journal *Solidarité* reports on medical rehabilitation and job creation programmes which are appropriate to local economies and which use local resources. The West African Social and Economic Centre in Burkina Faso runs training courses in grassroots development for villagers; its publication *Building Together* (*Construire Ensemble* in French) features interviews with farmers who are solving agricultural problems on their own. These and many other examples indicate the growing collaboration between urban and rural Africans to build upon indigenous African values and resources.

Across Africa, workers responsible for community-based, self-help activities have organized themselves into networks that facilitate exchanges of information, ideas and techniques generated by Africans themselves. These networks seek to learn from each other, rather than accept the handed-down assessments and solutions of elite outsiders. One example is SINA, the Settlements Information Network-Africa, which since 1981 has grown to include 300 members in 26 African countries. Members are involved in activities that improve the quality of life in different kinds of settlements and are committed to working with local communities to make the most of available resources. Also, exchange study visits among village development workers in Africa and throughout the Third World are organized by IRED (Innovations et Reseaux Pour le Developpement/ Development Innovations and Networks), a coalition of more than 600 community groups which also publishes the *IRED/FORUM*, a journal in which the groups report on their ideas and new activities, and ask for advice. Another valuable instrument for this kind of networking and learning from each other is the *IFDA Dossier*, produced by the International Foundation for Development Alternatives, which publishes articles and announcements from locally controlled groups in Africa, as well as other regions of the South.

There are also increasing instances of dedicated, charismatic individuals who have returned home from technical studies abroad to use their new skills to help facilitate community-controlled progress. One such example in Rwanda is instructive. Working in his home area, with approval and support from a national ministry, a Rwandan who returned from overseas studies held many discussions with villagers to understand how they analysed their own problems. Emerging from those analyses was an emphasis on self-help cooperative activities, rather than externally funded 'projects' which were felt only to encourage the passivity that results from lack of control. Since 1979 villagers have formed ten cooperatives which are joined together in the Tuzamuke Twese Union. The Union uses a portion of the groups' income from agricultural and other revenue-producing activities to support loans for new start-ups and speaks with a strong voice in beginning negotiations for credit with commercial banks. The original promoter has withdrawn as villagers have increasingly taken control of the Union. He now works through a technical assistance support organization which helps the Union as well as other villages wanting to create a similar structure. It is especially interesting to examine the reactions of local elites who have felt threatened by the increasing control of villagers over their own activities. An observer of the Union noted some of the conflicts.

> When the programme first started the attitude of local officials was one of expecting it all to fail, but as it became successful and spread widely, hostility grew and spilled over into serious conflicts. Projects were sabotaged, particularly the brickmaking units which were directly competing with certain local influential authorities. The watchman of the Cooperative was attacked and killed and there were threats to withdraw the registration of the Cooperative.... Despite these conflicts and setbacks ... they have ... had a positive effect in that the people have become more determined and confident in their ability to consolidate what they have already achieved.[14]

As in this case in Rwanda, cooperative structures are often a means for local people to gain experience for further organizing.

Vusanai: 'support each other to get up'

In Zimbabwe, independence prompted a range of responses by rural people to changing political and economic opportunities. A number of marketing cooperatives and associations emerged in response to governmental encouragements and the peasants' own perception of collaborative development. Access to agricultural credit and markets was the motivation behind the formation of many cooperatives. Producer cooperatives were less frequently formed, but some do exist and provide models for others while reinforcing mutual learning among members about agricultural methods and crops.[15]

Village development associations have been formed by local initiative and provide mutual support while people examine their conditions and seek effective ways to deal with the wider world and its constraints. The Matsvaire Village Development Programme, located 80 kilometres south of Harare, is a case in point. These Zimbabwe villagers initially bought into the technical production package of hybrid maize seed, chemical fertilizers and pesticides which is promoted by the agricultural extension service and major Northern funding agencies. However, doubts soon arose. One villager later noted that 'continued drought [in the early 1980s] proved these packages a failure. Acute food shortage ... pushed villagers to question this package and to seek alternatives.' The alternatives have included a new respect for the tested, traditional seeds and crops as well as the methods used to produce those crops. New credence is being given to cereal banks for cooperative grain storage for distribution throughout the year. Community services are being created where none had existed under the colonial government. Perhaps equally as important for organized village development, Matsvaire has become associated with other villages in the district, and the leader of the Programme has been brought on to the

District Council which deals with development programmes and financing. It is clear that these village initiatives have provided an example to which government officials and local political leaders look for ideas and direction.[16]

We don't call ourselves groups but rather *amalima*, which means meeting together for working and helping ourselves. Groups are built around that idea, and then we go to ask for help from outside. We know what we want. We did not come into being as beggars: we have something to contribute to development ourselves.
— Group leader in rural Zimbabwe, 1984.

Another example from Zimbabwe of local organization is the case of ORAP (Organization of Rural Associations for Progress). ORAP began as a series of women's clubs which rapidly expanded to over 600 affiliated groups of women and men engaged in a variety of essential, village-based development actions. ORAP's staff takes its lead from village-level analysis of problems and offers to assist in determining solutions, including negotiating with external contributors for working capital and appropriate technical advice. ORAP's own strategies grow out of the difficult environmental and political conditions in western Zimbabwe, as well as the decades of exploitation and neglect suffered by people during the colonial era. Among its many village-sponsored activities are the propagation and use of indigenous seeds, rain water catchment, inter-village food marketing and community grain stores. The village grain stores date from the pre-colonial era and existed to provide food for public distribution in times of need and celebration. It is interesting to note that community grain banks and grain stores are re-emerging in villages in the Sahel, also. In these cases in southern and western Africa, a popular recognition of the value of former methods has been translated into contemporary and practical programmes.[17]

In the Sahel, popular structures and organizations have responded to two of the major problems in that region: food security and environmental integrity. Both concerns have been factors in the actions of farmers in the Segou region of Mali. An exchange of labour has commonly assisted farmers to concentrate on necessary farm operations at crucial times. However, the cooperative labour is being denied to neighbouring farmers who have adopted mechanical equipment. Cooperative members recognize that the deep ploughing by the equipment hurts the fragile soils, causing them to lose their fertility more quickly and erode more easily. Farmers using such equipment would have to leave their land fallow more frequently than those who farm with hoes. When their land was fallow, the equipment-owning farmers would demand more land, thereby threatening land over which the community as a whole has an interest. By withholding access to cooperative labour, villagers hope to discourage the use of destructive and threatening mechanized tools.[18]

In Kenya, as in most African countries, wood and charcoal provide the major sources of energy for cooking. Urban population growth has accelerated demand for wood and charcoal. To meet this demand, trees as much as two and three hundred miles from urban centres have been cut. Environmental concerns are not a top priority of the Kenyan government, but in 1981, with financial backing from USAID, the government began a programme to introduce more fuel-efficient cooking stoves among lower-income urban residents. The programme stalled under government indifference and inefficiency, but was picked up by a local NGO. After nearly twenty years of repeated failures in the international community to produce inexpensive, acceptable energy-efficient stoves, the Kenyan NGO adopted a participatory approach with users and manufacturers. The improved stoves were of a design long used by people and relied upon components largely manufactured in the informal sector. The new addition was a heat-retaining ceramic liner, again produced from local materials. The dissemination of over 200,000 of the new cook stoves has had several positive results. It is estimated that reduced charcoal demand saved 1.5 million tons of trees in 1985 alone, representing a saving to the national environment and to individual households. The experience with the manufacture of the new stoves provided a viable example to the Kenyan government which finally revised antiquated policies that had discouraged small, unregistered businesses, thus opening the way for more rapid production and distribution.[19]

The liberation movements of both Tigray and Eritrea, in north-eastern Africa, seek to transform traditional community structures in which large landholders exercised feudal powers over other villagers into truly representative associations. These associations have been especially effective in realigning land ownership and in granting access to agricultural inputs to women. Erosion control and water harvesting are improved in the process. Pilot projects relying upon collective involvement have harnessed river beds to collect water run-off. The water is used for irrigation and the crops produced demonstrate that the land so often described by outsiders as degraded and lost can bring forth abundance.[20]

One of the most interesting examples of the adaptation of traditional social forms to contemporary Sahelian problems has been the use of the *Naam* groups to organize young people. The *Naam* are traditional cooperative work associations for young people in Burkina Faso. Outside financing for village improvements has been arranged to complement the *Naam* concept and structures without disrupting community solidarity. The funding source is another indigenous organization, known as the Six S. The Six S organization provides local communities with a wider organizational and financial base than may be found in any one village in order to address and solve problems in a cooperative way. Villages now design their own development activities and can request an unrestricted loan for their use. Six S is organized so that it can both respond to local needs without intimidation and engage in discussions with government officials. Thus, the organization crosses many of the barriers which normally inhibit outside involvement, much as ORAP has done in Zimbabwe. The success of the Six S association and concept has enabled it to spread into rural Mali and Senegal.

Another community structure has evolved out of the especially severe disenfranchisement felt by people with disabilities across Africa. More and more dissatisfied with the paternalistic attitudes inherent in colonial and then national organizations acting 'for' them, disabled persons have created their own associations and are engaging in both advocacy for better government policies and practical economic activities to benefit their members. The association of blind people in Niger trains villagers with visual impairments in farming techniques adapted to their special needs and helps families negotiate with village leaders for land. Fuel-efficient cook stoves that use small amounts of wood are manufactured for sale in urban markets by the physically handicapped association in Mali. In Mauritania, local business people train young disabled workers in such trades as tailoring and typing, and then help set them up in their own micro-businesses. The success of such programmes has helped erode the negative image of blind people, for example, being trained to make myriads of baskets with nowhere to sell them. In turn, these organizations have begun to influence how governments and inter-national organizations perceive and treat people with disabilities.

Savings and credit: people's capital mobilized

Another set of supportive indigenous institutions is the variety of savings and credit systems which exist throughout Africa. The lack of credit is often cited by development organizations as a major constraint to smallholder agricultural production and to rural and urban entrepreneurs. However, numerous officially sponsored credit programmes have failed. Because banks and other formal financial institutions largely ignore small, rural customers, this does not mean that such people have not devised savings institutions and pro-grammes of their own. One study in Ethiopia in the mid-1970s estimated that about eight per cent of the national income is handled by 'informal' savings institutions.[21] In eastern Cameroon, each adult is a member of at least one savings and/or loan association. Some of the associations are particular to specific ethnic groups, others have wide regional connections. In West Africa, traders maintain savings associations in order to facilitate trading and transportation needs. In Cameroon, savings societies offer technical and managerial assistance to businessmen. Women in western Zimbabwe collectively save in order to pay school fees for their children. Fixed fund accounts bearing interest and rotating fund associations also offer a range of services to savings group members. The dramatic contraction in formal employment opportunities in urban Nigeria in the early 1980s gave greater impetus to savings and loan schemes used by many women operating in the informal economy. Their daily and monthly contributions enable the women to both meet basic needs and gradually increase the size of their businesses.[22] These rotating funds provide a pool of money contributed by members to select individuals. Savings are a key factor in these mutual groups, providing members with a way to accumulate and draw upon cash when most needed. The default rate is low because, as a number of formal project-based credit programmes have also discovered, community and peer pressures as well as sanctions are a prime way to ensure individual repayment.[23]

The uses of informally obtained credit are similar to those promoted by many development projects, ranging from purchases of major consumer durables, to investing in profit-making ventures, to meeting everyday needs such as food, clothing, school and medical expenses. A formal credit programme in Kenya found that the women involved used their credit to invest in micro-businesses which provided them with enough cash to live.[24] For many poor people, credit, no matter how obtained, is a means of meeting immediate survival needs. More secure farmers utilize informal savings to finance agricultural production and expansion, but we have also noted how women pool their savings and labour to expand and better control agricultural production.

In Sierra Leone, women's membership and leadership in highly structured religious secret societies, called 'Sande', has provided a starting point for the creation of other associations focusing on economic activities. The 'Sande' have used traditional rotating credit associations as a basis for raising funds for community improvement projects.

A welfare-oriented women's nutrition club in southern Zambia started out by purchasing nutritious food such as dried fish, beans and milk from the National Food and Nutrition Commission and reselling it at a small profit to club branches. Members became increasingly aware, though, of their dependent status, since the National Commission itself depended on food donated from outside Zambia and thus was not able to control the availability of its own food supplies. The nutrition club began to grow and market its own food and transformed itself into the Chikuni Fruit and Vegetables Producers' Cooperative Society. Open to both women and men, the Society now controls its own vegetable marketing, operates two vegetable-processing industries and has increased members' access to credit through encouraging their participation in the Chikuni Credit Union.[25]

The colonial legacy of assigning land ownership to men continues to express itself in current national policies. As a result, women in Africa own little land and thus do not qualify for membership in the farmer cooperatives which grant their members the credit they need to purchase agricultural inputs. The evolution of women's associations into credit-granting entities is thus particularly significant for enabling women to better control their own means of production. In some communities, landless women have organized to convince credit unions to lend cash with a future crop, instead of land, being used as collateral. In many other communities, as reviewed above, women's traditional rotating funds are linked with other social welfare functions, such as child care, support networks in difficult times, and work sharing. These activities resemble in many ways the welfare associations which were organized in the mid-colonial period, providing security and services primarily to men employed in urban areas. In time, those welfare associations became the impetus for organized political action, in some cases being transformed into political movements which pushed for national independence. To be sure, the historical climate is different at the end of the twentieth century than in its middle decades, but it may not be unreasonable to presume that popular women's associations will become the basis for wider political and economic influence in the coming decades. We have already seen, for example, in the case of ORAP in Zimbabwe, how a group of social clubs was transformed into a dynamic and creative development organization. The demands by women for support and knowledge especially in their domestic concerns is probably the best indicator that broader political action will follow from their organizing.[26]

In some cases, informal savings associations are beginning to influence more formal credit programmes. The first rural bank in Ghana opened in 1976; rural peoples' enthusiasm for these banks has led them to apply for local branches throughout Ghana, of which there are now nearly one hundred. Designed to be accessible to small producers, rural banks serve an area within a twenty-mile radius, are owned and controlled by local people, loan only to farmers cultivating fifty acres or less, and accept collateral based on the community's knowledge of the borrower.[27] The successful characteristics of Ghana's rural banking system are largely based on the factors in village savings and borrowing systems that work the best.

The success of people's credit for small businesses has inspired a number of NGOs and some large donors to begin small credit programmes. Too little is known about complementary relations between formal and informal credit activities; it is an area requiring further study. What does seem obvious is that the informal savings and credit programmes are likely to be both more pervasive and more flexible in meeting local needs than many of the top-down, donor-funded programmes which also carry the burden of external accountability and design. Many donor programmes assume that the 'support is often granted in the form of a gift, [but] a gift rarely mobilises the person who receives it.' With this reality in mind, a group of African development association leaders joined with European colleagues to create the RAFAD Foundation (Research and Applications for Alternative Financing for Development) which administers an international loan guarantee fund designed to enable grassroots groups in Africa to obtain credit from their local banking systems. RAFAD works through local umbrella organizations on whose behalf letters of credit are granted to local banks. The umbrella organization identifies the beneficiary groups who will use loans drawn against the bank, and administers the loan guarantee on its own.[28] This system seeks to enhance informal credit practices by making more financial resources available.

Another example of the blending of formal and informal credit systems occurred in eastern Niger. The traditional *tontine* association has been adapted to a small-scale credit programme being run by a U.S. NGO. The *tontine* association is a rotating savings/credit fund which, in its adapted form, has become a way of enforcing savings in order to provide small loans to women for food marketing and processing and weaving businesses.[29]

Many groups in Northern countries have been attracted by the potential of offering credit to small-scale enterprises. However, the experience of USAID with micro-enterprise credit suggests the risks faced by potential recipients who may look to external expertise and funding for assistance. In 1987, the U.S. Congress provided $50 million for credit to individuals with very low incomes in countries in which USAID operated. Eighty per cent of the money was to be targeted in small loans of $300 and under to people in the poorest 50 per cent of the population, especially women and the very poor. An evaluation found that only about 10 per cent of the money actually was targeted by USAID to very poor people, contrary to the intent and direction of Congress. USAID's record has demonstrated its political bias toward wealthier groups and an unwillingness to work with groups of low-income people.[30] The risks in similar large, ideologically motivated credit programmes include: increased competition among groups for funds; the diversion of money to wealthier people, thereby increasing inequalities; and dependence on the vagaries of the 'aid' givers. On the more hopeful side, several NGOs — mostly European-based — are adopting some of the rationale of African informal savings associations and offering funding to African development organizations to use as the latter groups decide, without project prerequisites which have characterized giving in the past, and for the most part still do. The simple rationale of meeting human and community needs and drawing upon collective savings has guided the structure, organization and practice of Africans in mobilizing resources through their own institutions. Clearly, these examples of people's initiatives are a part of the legitimate basis for grassroots development which will spring from within Africa itself.

National structures

The recent attention given by African governments and international contributors to agriculture is a policy triumph for grassroots efforts. Through their withdrawal from the standards and demands of official programmes and their courage to offer alternatives, the great majority of African people have drawn overwhelming attention to the destructive policies of the development establishment. Peasant action and self-protecting measures have resulted in hundreds of failed projects, and the reduction of food sales to urban areas and of other cash crops for sale abroad. Governments and financial contributors have been stranded by their own exploitative approaches to the mass of African people. Unfortunately, their responses — as we noted in Chapter 8 — have misjudged the determination of African people to define and promote forms of development that are integral to their needs and social welfare.

Africa's food crisis is far less one of production — although all major development agencies and many governments cite the low productivity of farmers as the cause of declining output — than one of control over decisions about whose knowledge counts and whose needs and interests prevail. The power to allocate and control the direction of resources has enabled international and national elites to create the myth that their knowledge is superior to that of local peoples. The elite have claimed a monopoly on the knowledge to carry out 'development', and under the guise of that knowledge have justified their accumulation of Africa's agricultural, mineral and human resources for their own uses. As many African states now discuss the need to provide greater attention to agriculture, the underlying assumptions about who will control the finances, tools of production, and decision-making power have not been widely questioned. There is little evidence that decisions and funds will be effectively decentralized, which would open up the possibility for greater local control. Some lip service is paid to the value of 'traditional' knowledge, seeds and cropping patterns, but the investment trends in research and agricultural production continue to focus on quick technological fixes through large-scale, mechanized projects. Despite strong evidence that large irrigation projects are destructive to the environment, farmer productivity and peasant collaboration, many Sahel countries — with international support — are pursuing large dam and irrigation programmes.[31]

The mistaken view that peasants are an unreliable producer group, if potentially a powerful political force, makes many national bureaucracies and political parties reluctant to pursue agricultural and rural development policies based upon direct rural concerns, abilities and resources. Popular participation — the term widely touted by 'development' enthusiasts — has come to mean the peripheral inclusion of people in one or two components of a project. Only very rarely has popular participation as practised by the development establishment meant popular control over all aspects of a project, let alone over the policies that gave rise to projects. The term as it is used does not mean the enjoyment of popular benefits from participation. The discrepancy between rhetoric and reality is seen in a submission by African governments to the UN Special Session on Africa in May 1986, in which the document spoke about the limitations of 'traditional technology' and the 'small quantities of modern inputs' in use by farmers. Other macro-policy constraints are described, but nowhere in the document is the potential of full participation by poor rural and urban people addressed as a means of redefining Africa's priorities and programmes.[32]

Despite the general omission of people's knowledge, initiatives and organizations in national and continent-wide plans, these popular forces have nevertheless made themselves felt within some states' policies. The Green Zones of Mozambique, formed by women around Maputo, are now an integral part of Mozambique's agricultural strategies. The Green Zones began in the mid-1970s with small, independent gardens in the Maputo suburbs. Food shortages in the city induced a rapid growth of these gardens, 90 per cent of which were and remain controlled by women. The women began to organize, to share resources and to gain greater security. Cooperatives were formed, and by the early 1980s, a Union of Green Zone Cooperatives was formed. The success of these production cooperatives has given them great legitimacy in the eyes of the official institutions. For example, Mozambique's Development Bank now provides low interest loans to many of the 181 cooperatives which make up the Green Zone union. Also, the success of the production cooperatives around Maputo has led to the official establishment of an agricultural 'green zone' around other Mozambican cities, in direct emulation of the Maputo experience.[33]

Furthermore, both Angola and Mozambique have responded to farmers' disillusionment with state policies which had provided far greater resources to state farms than to private farmers and co-operatives. Angola is now moving to greatly reduce the number of state farms, handing over the land and resources to tenants' and workers' associations. During the preparations for the fourth party congress in Mozambique in 1983, the popular discontent with government priorities was openly aired and resulted in changes in official agricultural policy. New investment in state farms ended and many of them have been broken up into smaller units. Cooperatives and small-scale farmers were encouraged under the new policy, although the level of government assistance to these groups was left vague.[34]

In Burkina Faso national development policy has been reformed to address national problems more directly within the context of rural transformation. In part, Burkina policies have looked to village-level knowledge and organizations as models for broader public action. For example, during the 1982–84 drought in the Sahel, the Burkina government supported local efforts at food security by allocating funds to build 440 thirty-ton village grain storage banks. Also, government-determined prices paid to small farmers for millet were increased by 20 per cent in 1985, and the proportion of the budget spent on agriculture was raised from 2 to 40 per cent.[35]

In Zimbabwe, one of the major goals of rural people in their struggle for independence was to regain their land. Consequently, the independence government has sought to broaden and strengthen the base of the nation's agricultural economy. Prior to independence in 1980, the colonial government highly favoured the 5,000 large commercial farmers. At independence, Zimbabwe did not radically reorient services away from the commercial sector, but intentionally set out to buy up and redistribute unused commercial farms. In a two-pronged approach, the government sought to respond to popular demands for land redistribution and increase agricultural production by providing assistance for resettlement and credit, along with an extensive marketing system and favorable prices for both inputs and crops. Following the 1983–84 drought, the priorities of the government and many rural producers effectively coincided, for Zimbabwe's small-scale farmers — including a growing number of women's cooperatives — produced 50 per cent of the nation's marketed corn, the major staple. This gradual reorientation of government policies and services toward small-scale farmers has enabled households to grow food for both home consumption and sale, and they are now aggressively expanding production of other cash crops, without having to sacrifice family food crops.

Despite these policy achievements, there is a significant portion of the Zimbabwe population which feels much more remains to be done in order to improve conditions for the poorest people. The war for economic liberation is now being pursued by rural people across Zimbabwe, as seen in the rural groups associated with ORAP, in the cooperative movement and in the continued demands of rural people for return of the land. There are signs that the government is responding to these continuing pressures from below. Women are being hired as agricultural extension agents, thereby providing peasant women with wider access to information. Male extension agents also learn lessons, as many of them assumed that they already knew all of the problems and concerns of peasant women. A nation-wide decentralization programme began in mid-1987. What sets Zimbabwe's programme apart from similar, but incomplete, efforts in other countries is a major sensitizing campaign which uses popularly designed training materials and precedes the actual implementation of the programme. If rural and urban people grasp hold of the programme and continue to make it their own, the potential exists for major transformations in the economic and political control of the country.

Independence and alternative development

These national initiatives are important acknowledgments of the value of popular organizing, and of governmental policies oriented toward the people's concerns, but to date such national experiences have been fairly limited and do not indicate a trend toward building upon the people's needs and skills. The conflict between popular and elite control remains to be resolved and will be an on-going feature of Africa's political and economic environment during the next several decades.

Movements arising out of and retaining legitimacy through people's actions are also seen in the struggles against Ethiopian oppression, especially in the well-organized liberation movements in Eritrea and Tigray, in the struggles against the apartheid regime in South Africa and Namibia, and in the war for independence waged by the people of Western Sahara against Morocco. These movements are for the most part nationalistic, with the exception of Tigray, which seeks major changes in Ethiopian relations with the provinces. These liberation movements seek to alter the structures of society in order to remove many internal constraints to effective, long-term development. The movements directly address the issue of conflict between elites and the people; their legitimacy is found in seeking to promote the interests of the people. For example, the people in Eritrea and Tigray are already well on their way to placing decision-making power as well as the resources for development firmly under popular control.

It is unfortunate that many people's organizations must arise out of and attempt to exist in climates of oppression. For example, South

Africa's overt involvement in the anti-government wars in Angola and Mozambique has cost the lives of an estimated 1.4 million people, about 60 per cent of whom were children, in those countries. South Africa's destabilization of the independent states of southern Africa cost those countries over $60 billion in the years between 1980 and 1989.[36] Military and police actions in South Africa itself resulted in the deaths of over 2,500 people between late 1984 and early 1988. Poverty, ill-health, insufficient land, unemployment — all products of apartheid — have killed tens of thousands of other people. The human costs of transforming Africa have been and continue to be high — not to the 'development' experts, not to the business interests which invest in Africa's resource extraction, but to the people of Africa. Many of the examples of positive responses we have cited in this book have occurred not within a supportive national or international environment, but in opposition to hostile economies, repressive internal and external policies and elite self-aggrandizement.

Eritrea

Nearly thirty years of warfare against Ethiopia have partially contributed to Eritrean solidarity and self-reliant attitudes. But it has not been only a response to the conditions of warfare and oppression that has shaped Eritrean political and development policies. The Eritrean People's Liberation Front (EPLF) — now the only significant liberation movement in Eritrea — has carefully analysed the conditions of oppression and underdevelopment and has sought through its representative structures to transform social, economic and political relations in response to human needs and national development goals. A major factor in this process has been land reform which includes redistribution of the land to all rural people through village-level People's Assemblies. The Assemblies are composed of elected representatives from 'mass organizations' of peasants, women, youth, town workers and professionals. In the past, neither women nor landless people were allowed to participate in village assemblies; the new Assemblies are fundamentally different. The results are impressive and instructive of how popular democracy can lead to creative problem-solving:

> EPLF statistics record that by 1981 land redistribution had been achieved in over 160 villages, resulting in nearly 50,000 families gaining additional land and 12,500 landless farmers acquiring plots for the first time. Clearly, landowners and peasants with large holdings lost out in this process. In densely populated areas, land reform has led to the fragmentation of land into small parcels. In these situations the EPLF has encouraged a second stage land reform where larger plots are farmed by cooperatives and mutual aid groups. During the recent drought [in 1983–84], such organization has become important for poorer peasants who lack tools or must hire oxen for ploughing.[37]

Continued progress on land reform is limited by the war and the flight of tens of thousands of people because of military action, drought and famine. However, the EPLF has placed a priority on food production for local consumption and has encouraged mutual assistance among farmers as one step in increasing the productivity of available land, labour and tools. Local blacksmith cooperatives have emerged to provide basic farm equipment which is distributed free to the poorest farmers through the mutual assistance groups. 'Barefoot vets', environmental protection schemes, training programmes and newly legislated women's participation have emerged to support the inherent agricultural strength of Eritrea.

Many observers have been struck by the inventiveness of the Eritrean movement as people have sought to solve technical and health problems through their own ingenuity. The concept of self-reliance, building upon people's collective needs and utilizing the skills and resources of the Eritrean people themselves, has guided policies and problem-solving. Light industrial manufacturing and repairs occur throughout the liberated areas of Eritrea, including the production of spare parts for vehicles, machines to make the parts, shoes and sandals, sanitary pads for women and food processing. Health facilities provide both preventive programmes and curative treatments, mainly to treat people affected by the war. Some hospitals are mobile and rehabilitation patients receive special treatment. A number of people disabled during the war have received technical training and continue to serve their society. Shortages of drugs and equipment have, as might be expected, been dealt with by the establishment of manufacturing facilities within Eritrea itself.

All of these activities have generated a tremendous pride and dedication among Eritrean people. In order to expand and pass on the knowledge which has arisen from their own experiences, the Eritreans have designed a variety of educational programmes. Practical work is built into school curricula; literacy and adult education have also become a part of village life. 'An astonishing system of informal "technical colleges" has been established in Eritrea, held in concealed underground workshops or classes under rocks,' creating a trained work force which 'would be the envy of many an African state'.[38]

Observers of the EPLF's achievements cite them as a possible model for other African countries, but also note three conditions which have existed in Eritrea and have promoted its development. First, Eritrea has avoided the aggressive penetration of corporate capitalism. In health services, for example, Eritrea's isolation has shielded it from 'aggressive marketing by Western companies of baby foods, sweet soft drinks, and harmful drugs ... which often have such a negative impact on health and health care.' Second, the decision to work without expatriate advisers and 'experts' has left the EPLF to devise, evaluate and modify its own solutions without the imposed control of outsiders. And third, Eritrea 'has had to meet the needs of a rural population without having to satisfy the competing demands for resources and expertise of an urban population.'[39] Rural people and their self-sufficiency have remained of first priority.

I wake up thinking about what is distinctive and common in all the countries I've been to, and what occurred first to me is the new vehicles. In Ethiopia, Sudan, Eritrea and Chad, the only new vehicles are those of ... the relief agencies. In these impoverished countries, these shiny, very shiny new vehicles jump out, speaking of external wealth and capacity completely foreign to the lands they have been dropped into.

And who controls the vehicles? In every case, save one, the Westerners ... the new vehicles that symbolize power, and are real power, are directed in their travels by the West. Only in Eritrea was the power over transportation, and everything else, clearly in the hands of Africans.

— Nick Mottern, from a journal kept during travels in northeastern Africa, 1985.

The people of Eritrea are well on their way to creating the egalitarian, democratic state which they so desire, which they themselves have determined as their goal. To be sure, there are questions being addressed in Eritrea itself and among its exile community about sustaining the spirit and institutions of transformation once the war with Ethiopia is over. Other nations have faced similar dilemmas — Mozambique and Zimbabwe being two recent examples. The opposition faced by both of those countries has simultaneously proven to be both disruptive and a stimulus to on-going and effective transformation. Both countries, like Eritrea, had policy statements and some opportunities for in-country organization prior to independence, but subsequently they have faced strong bureaucratic, elite and international pressures to soften the commitment to true popular progress and participation. The hope and reality for progressive change is that the mass of people recognize that development is within their hands, to be shaped by their struggles.

South Africa

While political conditions in South Africa are highly fluid, it is obvious that alternative views of the future already exist. Africans in South Africa have a century's experience of modern political and economic organizing. It is not unreasonable to expect a popular, black majority government in South Africa within the not too distant future. Alternative organizations are already evident in many areas such as community government, education, religion and economic affairs. The initiative for determining events in South Africa is often in the hands of African people and their leaders and organizations. The resistance and positive alternatives offered by Africans in South Africa have become the guide for many pressure groups in other countries seeking to influence their own governments and businesses, such as the sanctions and divestment movement in the United States.

Among the strongest alternative groups in South Africa have been formal and informal associations of urban youth — people under twenty-five years of age who represent half of the country's black population. One of the major student organizations, the Congress of South African Students (COSAS), was banned by government in 1985 because of its success in challenging the inferior education policies and services of apartheid. COSAS had been successful in organizing students long disenchanted with apartheid education. An Education Charter defining a unified, democratic system of education was issued. COSAS harnessed the energy of urban youth who increasingly have determined what will and will not be taught in schools. School issues, in turn, have merged with local community issues and organizations, almost all of which deal with local concerns within the context of broader class, national and international issues.

Youth, school, community and worker organizations have joined together to form the United Democratic Front (UDF). The UDF was banned by the government early in 1988 after having established itself as the most visible anti-apartheid coalition in South Africa. Its successor, The Mass Democratic Movement, continued to provide support and organizational skills to local groups, taking direction from them. Local communities engaged in actions to redress immediate concerns, such as high rents, increases in transportation fares, inadequate water services and refuse removal. These initiatives were a part of a wider campaign not only to make the black townships ungovernable by the apartheid regime and its stooges, but to seek new forms of services and institutions to meet the needs of people there. Further, within townships many informal and loose organizations came into existence to pursue changes. These groups were especially important during the periodic crackdowns and mass arrests carried out by the police and military. It is the breadth of African alternative organizing which provided the liberation struggles in South Africa with internal dynamism, cohesion and strength.[40] The pressure from African organizations was a major factor in the government's decision early in 1990 to negotiate with the African National Congress for majority rule.

The rapid growth, aggressiveness and sophistication of African trade unions, many of which are now a part of the Congress of South

African Trade Unions (COSATU), has sustained pressure on the white-dominated economy. COSATU and individual unions have evolved in the past several years and now effectively represent workers and organize their production and productivity. A number of white business leaders have broken ranks with the white minority and responded to the unions' demands for control over labour by calling for major government policy reforms.

Politics is not about the changing of governments. It is about eliminating poverty and unemployment. The wealth must be shared by all the people in this country. It is important for us to make our politics the politics of the oppressed people of this country.
— Cyril Ramaphosa, head of the National Union of Mineworkers in South Africa, 1985.

To credit the African independence movement, and all its diverse elements, with creating constructive alternative visions and organizations is not to suggest an easy end to apartheid and class inequalities. What the South African experience does confirm in the context of alternative development for Africa is that the knowledge, skills and institutions of African people can and do provide the means for dramatic change within the continent and between Africa and the rest of the world. The South African situation also demonstrates the lengthy process of transformation which faces the entire continent of Africa. It is little wonder, then, that governments of the North and their 'development' agencies, including most of the multinational agencies, have sought to discredit, ignore and resist the people's abilities and struggles to bring their interests and approaches to development to the fore.

Notes

1. Constance M. McCorkle, 'Foodgrain disposals as early warning famine signals: a case from Burkina Faso', *Disasters*, Vol. 11, No. 4 (1987), pp. 273–281. This is one of a growing number of studies to focus on survival mechanisms of people under stress. The results of these studies are finding their way into the early warning systems of relief agencies, enabling them to respond to crises more quickly and with greater sensitivity.
2. Anne Fleuret, 'Indigenous Taita responses to drought', paper presented to the American Anthropological Association, December 1985.

3. Sarah Breet-Smith, 'Report on the agricultural situation on the Dogon Plateau, 5th Region, Mali', 1985. Also see the previously cited and extremely informative study by Alexander De Waal, *Famine That Kills: Darfur, Sudan, 1984–1985* (Clarendon Press, Oxford, 1989).
4. Dessalegn Rahmato, 'Peasant survival strategies in Ethiopia', *Disasters*, Vol. 12, No. 4 (1988), pp. 326–344.
5. Martin Wright, 'Letting nothing go to waste', *Panoscope*, No. 15 (November 1989), p. 15.
6. Catharine Newbury, 'Survival strategies in rural Zaire: realities of coping with crisis', in Nzongola-Ntalaja (ed.), *The Crisis in Zaire* (African World Press, Trenton, NJ, 1986), pp. 105–106; Churches Drought Action in Africa, *Report on the Root Causes of Hunger and Food Insufficiency in Africa* (World Council of Churches, Geneva, 1985).
7. Catharine Newbury and Brooke Grundfest Schoept, 'State, peasantry, and agrarian crisis in Zaire: does gender make a difference?', in Jane L. Parpart and Kathleen A. Staudt (eds), *Women and the State in Africa* (Lynne Rienner, Boulder CO, and London, 1989), pp. 95–96.
8. Nicholas Van Hear, ' "By-Day" boys and Dariga men: casual labour versus agrarian capital in northern Ghana', *Review of African Political Economy*, No. 31 (1985), pp. 48, 49.
9. For this and other forms of agricultural labour groups see Thomas J. Bassett, 'Breaking up the bottlenecks in food-crop and cotton cultivation in northern Cote d'Ivoire', *Africa*, Vol. 58, No. 2 (1988), pp. 163–64.
10. Fiona Mackenzie, 'Local initiatives and national policy: gender and agricultural change in Murang'a District, Kenya', *Canadian Journal of African Studies*, Vol. 20, No. 3 (1986), pp. 392–397.
11. Kathleen Staudt, 'The Umoja Federation: women's cooptation into a local power structure', *Western Political Quarterly*, Vol. 33, No. 2 (1980), pp. 278–290.
12. Jean-Louis Chleq and Hugues Dupriez, *Métiers de l'eau du Sahel, Eau et terres en fuite* (Environnement Africain, Nivelles, Belgique, Terres et Vie and Dakar, 1984), pp. 120-123.
13. Phyllis Kaberry, *Women of the Grassfields*, cited in Kathryn S. March and Rachelle L. Taqqu, *Women's Informal Associations in Developing Countries* (Westview Press, Boulder, CO, 1986), p. 57.
14. *Sharing Experiences in Development* (Silveira House/IRED, Harare, 1984), pp. 14–15.
15. Barry Munslow, 'Prospects for the socialist transition of agriculture in Zimbabwe', *World Development*, Vol. 13, No. 1 (1985), pp. 51–52.
16. *Sharing Experiences in Development, op cit.*, pp. 43–47; for a West African example of villagers developing alternatives to chemical pesticides see Kudzo Agbeve, 'Searching for alternatives', *ILEIA Newsletter*, Vol. 4, No. 3 (October 1989), pp. 3–4.
17. *Ibid.*; and Lloyd Timberlake, *Africa in Crisis* (Earthscan, Washington, DC, 1985), p. 212; Nigel Twose, *No Shortcuts: Sustainable Development in the Sahel Region of Burkina* (Euro-Action ACORD, London, 1986).
18. John Van Dusen Lewis, 'Small farmer credit and the village production unit in rural Mali', *African Studies Review*, Vol. 21, No. 3 (December 1978), p. 40.
19. Monica Opole, 'Improved charcoal stoves programme, Kenya', in Czech

Conroy and Miles Litvinoff (eds), *The Greening of Aid* (Earthscan Publications, London, 1988), pp. 118–123.

20. Max Peberdy, *Tigray: Ethiopia's Untold Story* (Relief Society of Tigray UK Support Committee, London, 1985), pp. 48–54.

21. Bagashaw in Marvin Miracle *et al.*, 'Informal savings mobilization in Africa', *Economic Development and Cultural Change*, Vol. 28, No. 4 (July 1980), p. 701.

22. O'seun Ogunseitan, 'Working to defeat the Nigerian squeeze', *Panoscope*, No. 13 (July 1989), pp. 6–7.

23. For a series of case studies on the impact of community and group savings on more formal banking systems see *Banking the Unbankable* (Panos Books, London, 1989).

24. Douglas Hellinger, *et al.*, 'The small business scheme of the National Council of Churches of Kenya (NCCK)', in *The Pisces II Experience*, Vol. 2 (USAID, Washington, DC, 1985), pp. 119–122.

25. Filomina Chioma Steady, 'Women's work in rural cash food systems: the Tombo and Gloucester Development Projects, Sierra Leone', pp. 47–70 and Mabel C. Milimo, 'Chikuni Fruit and Vegetable Producers' Co-operativexh Society, Zambia, a case study', pp. 21–36, in *Rural Development and Women: Lessons from the Field*, Vol. 1 (International Labour Office, Geneva, 1985).

26. Kathleen Staudt, 'Women's political consciousness in Africa: a frame-work for analysis', in Jamie Monson and Marion Kalb (eds), *Women as Food Producers in Developing Countries* (UCLA African Studies Center, Los Angeles, 1985), pp. 71–84; Olivia Muchena, 'Women's organizations in Zimbabwe and assessment of their needs, achievements and potential', in Kirsten Jorgensen (ed.), *Women's Programs in Zimbabwe* (KULU, Copenhagen, 1982), pp. 34–35. Also see Ruvimbo Chimedza, 'Saving together, spending together: Zimbabwe's rural savings clubs', *The Courier*, No. 99 (September–October 1986), pp. 75–77.

27. Gloria Nikoi, 'Rural banking on the rise', *Women and Development*, reprinted from *Development Forum*, (DESI/UNU, New York, 1985), pp. 85–89.

28. '1985 Progress Report and Presentation of the FADEP Guarantee Funds' (RAFAD, Geneva, 1986).

29. On *tontine*, see Melinda Smale, *Women in Mauritania* (USAID, Washington, DC, 1980), pp. 80–82; Laura Tuck, 'Appendix' to John Waterbury, 'The Senegalese peasant: how good is our conventional wisdom?' in Mark Gersovitz and John Waterbury (eds), *The Political Economy of Risk and Choice in Senegal* (Frank Cass, London, 1987), pp. 85–87.

30. Danielle Yariv, 'Where credit is due: report on AID's compliance with 1988 Microenterprise Earmark' (RESULTS Educational Fund, Washington, DC, 1989).

31. Jon Moris, *et al.*, *Prospects for Small-Scale Irrigation Development in the Sahel* (Utah State University, Logan, Utah, 1984); Gunilla Andrae and Bjorn Beckman, *The Wheat Trap* (Zed Books, London, 1985).

32. Organization of African Unity, *Africa's Submission to the Special Session of the United Nations General Assembly on Africa's Economic and Social Crisis* (Addis Ababa, March 1986).

33. Mozambique Information Office, *News Review*, No. 57 (31 July 1985) and No. 69 (24 January 1986); Stephanie Urdang, *And Still They Dance: Women, War and*

the *Struggle for Change in Mozambique* (Earthscan, London, 1989), pp. 144—150.

34. *West Africa* (19 May 1986), p. 1063; Philip Raikes, 'Food policy and production in Mozambique since independence', in *Review of African Political Economy*, No. 29, pp. 95—107; Bertil Egero, *Mozambique: A Dream Undone* (Scandinavian Institute of African Studies, Uppsala, 1987).

35. Nigel Twose, *Fighting the Famine* (Food First Books, San Francisco, 1986), p. 38; FAO, Office for Special Relief Operations, *Burkina Faso: Assessment of the Agriculture, Food Supply and Livestock Situation* (Rome, 1984), p. 36.

36. United Nations, *South African Destabilization: The Economic Cost of Frontline Resistance to Apartheid* (New York, 1989).

37. James Firebrace, *Never Kneel Down: Drought, Development and Liberation in Eritrea* (The Red Sea Press, Trenton, NJ, 1985), pp. 36-37.

38. Twose, *op. cit.*, p. 90.

39. Firebrace, *op. cit.*, p. 115.

40. Martin Murray, *South Africa: Time of Agony, Time of Destiny; The Upsurge of Popular Protest* (Verso, London, 1987).

12 No Longer Playing the Game

> Development is a process of articulation and participation. This is the starting point, and the end product of development is the persons themselves; knowing what they want and acting to get it.
> — Sithembiso Nyoni, Executive Secretary of ORAP, Zimbabwe, 1985.

For hundreds and thousands of years, African societies managed their affairs so as to grow and prosper, to become and remain self-sufficient in food production, and to develop elaborate cultural, ritual and political systems. Values of sharing, cooperation and respect for the forces that remain unseen but central to peace, harmony and well-being have guided social relations. Complex economic relations — ranging from long distance trade across the Sahara to daily labour management — evolved in ways that provided most people with the necessities of life. And life was usually accepted as good by most people. To be sure, there were wars (although not on the scale to which we have become accustomed today), disease, hardships due to drought and pests. Slavery existed and further divided Africans into separate groups. There were periods of food shortages and of famine. Yet, throughout the centuries, the skills, knowledge and organizations existed that enabled most African societies to retain balanced systems that promoted stability, change and, usually, food self-sufficiency.

The intrusion of the world economy, through contact with Western European nations, began to alter the conditions Africans had created for themselves. The slave trade, followed by the era of colonial rule and now the period of national independence, in turn progressively integrated Africa into the world economy. Indigenous skills and know-ledge of crops, soils, environment, manufacturing, labour relations and religion were challenged and widely discounted by outsiders. In recent decades, Northern-defined concepts of development have replaced African concepts of well-being; Northern technical expertise has come to be seen as more legitimate than African scientific experimentation and observation. Internal management of social relations for the social good has given way to external and elite control for their self-enrichment. And although Africa retains the ability to produce food to meet the needs of its people, policies which favour food production and agricultural growth for broader economic expansion, as largely existed 100 years ago, have been replaced by policies that promote production of agricultural crops for export and the commercial advantage of outsiders.

It is against this background of colonial and neo-colonial intrusion and disruption that the various solutions proposed for dealing with Africa's problems need to be placed. The prescriptions of Northern contributors must be assessed not only in terms of their current impact but against their origins in colonial perceptions of Africa and the advantages derived by Northern businesses from the dominant definition of development. The popular attempts to redefine development, too, can be measured for their validity from this historical perspective as well as against their ability to express, act upon and fulfil people's needs. In this book we have tried to provide both the historical context of Africa's food and development crises and a range of examples of responses — official and popular — to those crises.

> I believe the Third World must realize that these institutions [i.e. the IMF, the World Bank], originally meant as institutions of cooperation among the developed countries, are now being used as instruments of control over the developing countries. They have become instruments for a new kind of empire . . . they are being used as instruments of power to dominate the Third World.
> — Julius Nyerere, President of Tanzania, 1984.

Confronting the course of history

There is little doubt that processes for substantial and sustained change are being discussed, designed and implemented by African people across the continent. In this study we have sought to provide an initial hearing for popular direction in promoting these changes and to give outsiders some sense of the on-going dynamism within African communities, organizations and popular structures.

Popular analysis and actions in Africa have generally been ignored or discredited by the major Northern development agencies and even by many African governments. The World Bank, USAID, the EEC and other 'donors' have used their financial and political power to prescribe and enforce programmes for African countries which pose direct threats to popular control and well-being. The programmes of major contributors serve to increase the power of elite groups (both in Africa and in their home countries) which generally control central governments, channelling that power into self-serving structures at the expense of decentralized decision making and popular control. It is this nexus of international and national elite interests which popular movements and organizations reject.

As most African people know, the programmes that emerge from the 'development dialogues' between national and international elites are frequently self-serving. For example, the great emphasis on increasing agricultural producer prices is a primary goal of the contributors' policy dialogues with African governments. The goal sounds worthy, on the surface. However, peasants know all too well that their crops provide the foreign exchange which fills stores in the cities of their countries with luxury imports, which pays for the cars and fuel used by the elite and which sustains an exploitative lifestyle only a small minority can ever enjoy. This knowledge provides producers with the power to withdraw products and labour from the markets controlled by governments. Despite the enticement of promised higher producer prices and wages, peasants and workers know they have been victimized and are demanding more than higher prices for crops. Their demands now include a more equitable distribution of national wealth and resources and greater participation in local and national policies as requisites for restoring popular legitimacy to governments.

The knowledge people have long used to feed themselves and their communities, to support one another with credit, labour and encouragement, and to organize for the common good is now the basis for a forceful African voice. Peasant farmers know they can produce food and cash crops efficiently; they know the forms of organization and social services that best meet their needs; they know they can face problems and devise meaningful solutions. These experiences offer the basis from which African people call for economic and political democracy and social justice at all levels, from their local communities to the international scene.

The collective consciousness among Africans of the validity of their own social systems and knowledge has become the lever for change. Governments which have ignored the welfare and needs of workers and peasants now find themselves isolated from their constituents and dependent upon international organizations whose self-interest is served by perpetuating the 'development' status quo. The ability of peasants and workers to influence and guide national policies requires more research and attention. But the indicators now exist to give their influence credibility. The recent orientation of the new governments in Ghana, in Burkina Faso under the late Thomas Sankara, and in Zimbabwe has promoted national policies which begin to respond to popular concerns. In other cases, such as in Mozambique and Tanzania, governments have revised policies under strong popular pressures. But peasants and workers are still unconvinced of government sincerity. At this stage, the struggle continues within Africa — the struggle for popular legitimacy and popular democracy.

A place for outsiders

In this book we have sought to increase readers' awareness of some of the major forces of change in Africa and to reflect some of the events and views within Africa which give hope for a new future. This knowledge is important in itself and should provoke questions about how we normally view Africa.

Accurate knowledge about Africa should be the first object of Northern citizens who wish to support long-term transformation in Africa. The way to acquire knowledge about Africa is to follow the advice normally given to us by African groups: listen to their analyses, to their solutions, to their struggles. The temptation for outsiders concerned with African development too often has been to assume that we know the best path to a development which resembles our own experiences. Thus, programmes and strategies for Africa are devised in Washington or London, for example, without any African input and very often without any assessment of local interests and concerns or local tensions and constraints.

African people regularly urge North American and European citizens to take advantage of their political and economic systems to help alter the conditions contributing to underdevelopment. The challenge for concerned citizens of Northern, industrial countries is to open their own political and economic systems, just as African people are demanding the expansion of democracy and equity in their own countries. Where better to learn about these issues than from people who live within and have struggled against the institutional oppression of underdevelopment? The opportunities and resources exist to learn from the experiences of African, Asian and Latin American peoples and adapt them in order to debate and promote changes in the policies and institutions which constrain our own well-being and that of others throughout the world.

A commmon response among people in Europe and North America when presented with the problems facing people in Africa is to ask, 'How can I help? Where can I send money?' We have suggested in this study that money is secondary to substantial rethinking about and redirection of development policies and economic and political interaction. However, the question of financial support to African (and other Third World) non-governmental organizations and popular movements is legitimate. For the past 40 years, Northern organizations have provided the means for channelling money to the South (often retaining substantial portions for administration costs, further fundraising and salaries for staff), but those channels have largely been ones defined as appropriate by people in the North. Some of the Northern organizations have made substantial efforts to alter their programmes so as to incorporate African needs. However, it is now time for financial supporters to send their money directly to African groups. That money will be used in ways that support the efforts of African people to redefine development and to create the organizations and structures for moving forward in ways that they themselves determine.

International voluntary agencies express the desire to fund grassroots projects in which the people participate and which will enable the people to have a greater control over their lives etc. They, however, often seek to do this while exercising total control over the purse strings and also avoid becoming involved in the wider political issues that have to be tackled in the search for total development.
— African grassroots leader, 1984.

Policy initiatives

There are indications that such openings for forcing policy changes are gradually occurring. The movement to impose and enforce comprehensive economic sanctions against South Africa has demonstrated citizens' power in the United States and Europe. The movement has responded to repeated appeals by South Africans and has mobilized popular opinion in Northern countries to pressure the national legislative and executive bodies to consider and pass sanctions legislation. In the United States in 1986, well-organized popular pressure not only caused Congress to pass a sanctions law but to overturn the presidential veto of that legislation. The sanctions legislation of 1986 was not perfect and its implementation has many loopholes, but its passage was a vital step in the long struggle to involve U.S. citizens in setting a foreign policy that responds to the legitimacy of African views and concerns.

The legislative process provokes caution among many people, and rightly so. For example, the U.S. Congress is largely populated by wealthy white males whose knowledge and concern about Africa is minimal. Congressional acquiescence to the provision of tens of millions of dollars in military aid to UNITA, the rebel force in Angola, by the Reagan and Bush administrations indicates the difficulties involved in promoting the peaceful conditions necessary for effective development.

These difficulties are real, suggesting the need for greater citizen involvement in selecting our representatives and holding them accountable to equity and justice issues. An approach to creating a more representative Congress is to create and define legislation that provides dual benefits for U.S. citizens and Africans. For example, an end to the U.S. practice of using much of its food aid to create and maintain markets for commercial food imports can save billions of dollars annually in subsidies while reducing an artificial price and demand structure which facilitates food imports by African countries at the expense of their own farmers. Legislation to curtail the flight of multinational corporations to countries which repress workers and wages may save jobs in the U.S. and European countries while avoiding exploitative and repressive conditions in African industry. Legislation remains to be fashioned and effectively implemented which assures that bilateral development assistance reaches grassroots groups in responsive, responsible and supportive ways.

We are suspicious, America: suspicious that the White House is blinded by the whiteness of the oppressor in southern Africa and has no enthusiastic, practical concern for the oppressed because of their blackness. We think it is in your long term interest — it is in the interests of justice, peace and order that instead of exporting Stinger missiles and intelligence to the oppressors and their surrogates, you should be exporting support to progressive freedom lovers in South Africa and Namibia, and the Frontline states. We expect Uncle Sam to export democracy, justice and peace.
— Simon Tshenuwani Farisani, South African Lutheran pastor, from a speech on the steps of the U.S. Capitol, 1987.

U.S. and European military aid is a common means to interfere in African affairs. There have been minor efforts to reduce U.S. military aid to Africa, but the prevailing emphasis in U.S. foreign policy has been to expand military and security alignments with repressive, anti-democratic and reactionary regimes. What are the benefits of such aid to U.S. citizens? The most often cited benefits include military-industrial jobs, alliances to protect far-flung 'strategic interests', allies among repressive governmental leaders as in South Africa and Zaire who hold up the threat of communism as a means of perpetuating U.S. aid. Are these 'advantages' reasonable trade-offs against the suffering, hunger, unemployment and hardship experienced by millions of people on a daily basis? The U.S. public has indicated 'no', but translating that good sense into viable political action remains an imperative for the future. Assuring reductions in arms shipments and ending military alliances remains an imperative for European groups concerned about peace and economic justice in their own countries and in Africa.

Accountability

Just as our legislatures and parliaments need to be held accountable to popular opinion and interests, so too do aid agencies. Such a statement assumes that aid agencies will continue to ply their trade, despite the many problems we noted in Chapter 8. Currently, aid serves important political and economic functions for governments and elites and will not be readily reoriented or abandoned. Thus, whether we seek the end of 'development' assistance as it now exists or its reform within the Northern industrial context, critical assessments of aid are necessary building blocks.

USAID evaluates itself and then offers watered down summaries to the public. Even this is better than what is offered by the World Bank. Its evaluations are also 'in-house' but are not published for public review. Many PVOs/NGOs have only just begun to evaluate their programmes from the perspective of African well-being. OXFAM-UK and War on Want have published several incisive accounts of how deteriorating economic and social conditions caused by debt and structural adjustment have a negative impact on people in countries in which they work. These are important steps for holding agencies like the World Bank accountable. However, other parts of their programmes must also be held up for public review. Also, will the results of Catholic Relief Services and CARE (PVOs in the U.S.) development and food aid programmes, for example, be widely publicized? Accountability of public money spent in the name of development is essential for on-going understanding of the changing nature of development problems and opportunities, of the reaction of various groups of people, both within and outside a project framework, and of assessments of the ability of programmes to fit and meet people's real needs.

Criteria for assuring the accountability of aid agencies must also include demonstration that those agencies are addressing the structural causes of hunger, poverty and developmental failures which originate in the North. Accountability is not a mechanism for assuring that monies are spent, but a political tool for assuring that public monies are being used by the people we say we want to help 'develop'. Thus, more than anyone, people within a local area must decide upon the timing, approach, relevance and processes by which development programmes are funded and implemented. This is more than participation; it requires turning over the control for change to the major participants and trusting their judgments. At this point, very few development agencies are willing to make that form of commitment.

Responsible citizens are like responsible investors — seeking to ensure that their investments of time, money, service and concern bring the expected returns. The United States public has an expectation that their giving will support an African continent that builds upon its human and natural resources within a framework designed by and for people there. To help ensure those returns, Northern citizens can become active in the debate about their governments' foreign policies, as well as the development and military assistance programmes to Africa and the motivation behind these programmes. The debate is still young and there remains vast scope for citizens to determine the course of behaviour by our governments, our corporations, our churches and our development establishments.

Three steps will help facilitate an effective challenge to the aid establishment. First, independent evaluations of USAID, the World Bank and United Nations projects and programmes are needed. These will generate information about the strengths and weaknesses of most aid. The evaluations will provide citizens with clear and meaningful information about the use of their money. At the same time, they will provide activists with a solid base from which to suggest alternative development models. Some of this information is already available to the public,[1] but more is needed.

Second, a coalition is needed to build upon this information and field experiences and to offer practical alternatives for using aid. The NGO Working Group on the World Bank, representing twenty-six Southern and Northern NGOs, is one such coalition. For several years the NGO Working Group has been engaged in dialogue with the World Bank. One aim of the Group has been to increase the flow of information to Third World NGOs about Bank plans and another is to expose the Bank to the realities of 'development' as experienced by most Third World people. The Debt Crisis Network, with its office in New York, offers a model for coalition-based analysis, education and advocacy.[2]

A third step is to work for alternative structures in which aid is given. In the process, the very term 'aid' will be called into question. It is likely that proposals will be made to significantly reduce the level of aid so long as it remains linked to short-term security issues and elite corruption. Holding donor agencies accountable to criteria of development envisioned by the vast majority of rural and urban poor people in the South is largely impossible so long as aid remains a tool of the wealthy. Alternative structures for U.S. and European support for African initiatives and alternative models of development are requisites for realigning USAID, the World Bank the European Development Fund and the programmes of other contributors.[3]

To be sure, aid is but one segment of a wider network of constraints inhibiting grassroots development in Africa. Trade, militarization, racism, sexism, agriculture and economic ownership require similar introspective work by Northern citizens.

Direct action

There will be occasions when formal education, advocacy, accountability and investing will not adequately address the harm being caused by negative policies and institutions. Direct action must be a factor in supporting African liberation and developmental goals. Such action may take many forms. Some current examples are:

• The Africa Peace Tour, sponsored by thirteen religious and secular organizations in the U.S. which have carried directly to the public in big cities and small towns the issues of war and hunger in Africa. The five tours held in the late 1980s have joined African and U.S. speakers. Some have reflected on direct personal experiences in Africa; others have demonstrated the repercussions in people's suffering of repressive negative policies; and yet others addressed the role of the U.S. in those policies and suggested ways to alter them. The 1989 tour added to the drama of the talks by also using a replica of a Casspir, the armoured personnel carrier used by the South African military forces in African townships, Namibia and Angola. The tours have drawn together and energized social action groups at the local level and have facilitated the creation of a network of Africa peace activists in the seven southeastern U.S. states.

• The Central America and South Africa Solidarity Day, held early in 1987, produced a major demonstration in Washington against common U.S. policies in two battered regions of the South. This creative linking of issues helped focus people's attention and action across what had been generally divided constituencies.

• Solidarity and fund raising has occurred in support of striking mine workers in South Africa. Work stoppages by mine workers provided an opportunity for U.S. citizens to offer legitimate moral and material support to the liberation struggles in South Africa. In Britain and Europe, similar actions have been taken to support the liberation struggles in Eritrea and Namibia.

• The major street demonstrations in Berlin during the IMF-World Bank annual meeting in 1988 showed the solidarity of numerous popular groups in the North with people in the South suffering from the impact of debt and Northern structural adjustment programmes.

What remains to be done, as situations and conditions demand, is more direct and effective action in support of African popular and liberation movements. For example, will a shipment of South African steel be stranded in a port as longshoremen and others refuse to handle the cargo? Will an effective boycott of oil firms sustaining South Africa be enforced by public pressure? Will production and shipment of Stinger missiles and Claymore mines now being routed to Angolan anti-government forces be ended by blockading U.S. military depots? Will travel agencies promoting tourism to South Africa be boycotted? Will donors to private development agencies demand that those agencies appoint boards of directors and staff inclusive and representative of grassroots groups in Africa?

The war in Vietnam is but a symptom of a far deeper malady within the American spirit. . . . During the past ten years we have seen emerge a pattern of suppression that now has justified the presence of U.S. military 'advisers' in Venezuela. This need to maintain social stability for our investments accounts for the counter-revolutionary action of American forces. . . .

I am convinced that if we are to get on the right side of the world revolution, we as a nation must undergo a radical revolution of values.
— Martin Luther King, Jr, 1967.

Catching up with Africa

The challenge for citizens in Northern industrial countries, and their representatives, will be to catch up with African thinking and actions. The North has to face the reality of U.S. imperialism which thrives on racial stereotypes and corporate and elite domination. It is necessary to confront the growing inequalities in our own societies in order to reduce the burden of exploitation at home and abroad. An alternative, Southern view of development has emerged; no longer can development be defined in terms of corporate welfare, military security and cheap consumer goods. Instead, development will be measured in terms of social equality, human dignity, popular democracy and economic sharing.

For those of us in the North, the struggle for change will not be an easy one. It will involve a lengthy debate about the nature of U.S. and European societies and priorities, not unlike the debate and struggle within African countries over the last three decades about similar questions. As in Africa, that debate will be manipulated by powerful political and economic groups to advance their own interests. Further repression will result. However, the course of Northern history is also filled with instances of successful popular organizing and action. Thus, the struggle for change will involve seeking ways for disparate groups to coalesce around core issues and avoid being diverted by the rhetoric of exclusive policies. It will entail a willingness and sense of organization to act on a variety of fronts.

Asserting greater popular control over major economic and

political decisions may take even longer. Again Africa offers many models, such as the struggle of the people in South Africa to overthrow the forces of racism and colonialism. There are the examples of the struggle of people in other parts of Africa to transform the patterns which cause underdevelopment, or in the dignity of people to forgive centuries of exploitation. Models of popular control and development can be seen in the determination of farmers to bring forth an abundant crop to feed themselves while sharing with their neighbours and in the creativity of the people who can weave grass into intricate baskets capable of holding water.

In assessing our own responsibilities and formulating our own futures, we see that the challenges facing most people in Africa and in the North overlap and are often very similar. Mine workers in Africa, Europe and the United States have in common a desire for economic security, dignity and respect in their work, control over their lives and a supportive and responsive government. The paths taken to reach these goals may be different, but there is a commonality in the struggle to make development applicable for all people which unites us in pursuing these goals.

Notes

1. 'A critical look at World Bank and IMF policies', draft report of the Bank Information Center, Washington, DC, 1989; Frances Moore Lappe, *et al.*, *Betraying the National Interest* (Grove Press, New York, 1987); Bade Onimode (ed.), *The IMF, the World Bank and the African Debt*, 2 Vols. (The Institute for African Alternatives and Zed Books, London, 1989).
2. The Network's major publication is *From Debt to Development: Alternatives to the International Debt Crisis* (Institute for Policy Studies, Washington, DC, 1985).
3. An excellent analysis of structural alternatives for aid is Stephen Hellinger, Douglas Hellinger and Fred M. O'Regan, *Aid for Just Development: Report on the Future of Foreign Aid* (Lynne Rienner, Boulder, CO, 1988).

Appendix 1
Listening to the People

The following organizations and their publications can help you remain in touch with events and processes of change in Africa.

ENVIRONNEMENT AFRICAIN (ENDA)
B. P. 3370
Dakar, Senegal

Publications and newsletter, in English and French, which often include voices and activities of peasant, cooperative and other grassroots groups.

AFRICAN NGOs ENVIRONMENT NETWORK (ANEM)
P. O. Box 53844
Nairobi, Kenya

Provides policy and programme coordination, training and assistance between environmental non-governmental organizations.

FORUM FOR AFRICAN VOLUNTARY DEVELOPMENT ORGANIZATIONS (FOVAD)
B. P. 3476
Dakar-Colobane, Senegal

Begun in 1987 to provide an umbrella organization for African non-governmental organizations. Publications are planned, in both English and French.

IRED
3, rue de Varembe/Case 116
1211 Geneva 20, Switzerland

Facilitates information exchanges and innovative programme funding for Third World non-governmental and popular organizations. *IRED Forum* ($25/year in either French or English) contains a wealth of information on those organizations and their acitivities.

INTERNATIONAL FOUNDATION FOR DEVELOPMENT ALTERNATIVES (IFDA)
4 Place du Marche
1260 Nyon, Switzerland

Publishes *IFDA Dossier* (in English, with some articles in French and Spanish; $30/year) which includes news, analysis and resources from popular organizations and individuals in the Third World and some comparative references to U.S. and European experiences.

ICVA
13 rue Gautier
1201 Geneva, Switzerland

Secretariat for the NGO Working Group on the World Bank. Provides up-dates on negotiations with the World Bank for redefining development.

ORGANIZATION OF RURAL ASSOCIATIONS FOR PROGRESS (ORAP)
P. O. Box 877
Bulawayo, Zimbabwe

One of the most successful popular organizations in southern Africa. ORAP does not have a regular newsletter nor a publications list, but its staff can answer specific questions.

SIX S ASSOCIATION
B. P. 100
Ouahyiagouya, Burkina Faso

Promotes locally designed rural development projects in the Sahel region of West Africa. Widely recognized for its effective organizing among rural communities.

PAN AFRICAN INSTITUTE FOR DEVELOPMENT (PAID)
B. P. 4056
Douala, Cameroon

A training and research centre, with a branch in Zambia, PAID also publishes to a limited extent. Its reports and training materials are available in English or French.

CENTRE D'ETUDES ECONOMIQUES ET SOCIALES DE L'AFRICA DE L'OUEST
(CESAO)
B. P. 305
Bobo-Dioulasso, Burkina Faso

Offers short-term training to development groups and peasant leaders.

MATCH INTERNATIONAL CENTRE
401–171 Nepean
Ottawa, Ontario K2P 0B4, Canada

Publications include a newsletter and reports on issues relating to Third World women.

BREAD FOR THE WORLD
802 Rhode Island Ave, NE
Washington, DC 20018

A Christian citizens' movement of over 40,000 people in the U.S. which seeks to alter U.S. national policies to alleviate hunger. Regular publications available with S25/year membership.

INSTITUTE FOR FOOD AND DEVELOPMENT POLICY
145 Ninth Street
San Francisco, CA 94103-3584

Maintains a regular publications programme, based upon research, which both critiques USAID, World Bank and other donor policies and highlights positive and innovative initiatives of Third World people.

UNITED NATIONS NON-GOVERNMENTAL LIAISON SERVICE

DC 2-1103	Palais des Nations
United Nations	CH-1211 Geneva 10
New York, NY 10017	Switzerland

Both offices of NGLS produce newsletters, reports and studies relating to grassroots development.

PANOS INSTITUTE
8 Alfred Place
London WC1E 7EB, UK

Publishes *Panoscope* (£15 or $18/year), a news feature magazine which focuses on the initiatives of Third World people.

Appendix 2
Famines in African History

1543–44	Major famine in Ethiopia
1560–62	Drought in Ethiopia
1631–87	Drought and famine in Sahel region
1738–56	Massive drought, famine and epidemics in Sahel region
1786	Drought and famine in Darfur region of Sudan
1888–92	'Great Ethiopian Famine' — one third of population dead. Drought compounded by rinderpest killed 90 per cent of cattle. Warfare in Sudan caused severe famine
1890–97	Rinderpest, locust, disease, drought and famine across eastern half of Africa. Many people die; cattle and some wildlife affected
1895, 1896–98	Drought in northern Nigeria and Chad
1908	Crop failure in Mozambique
1909–22	Prolonged drought and crop failure in Bostwana
1911–12	Drought and famine in Somalia
1911	Drought and famine in southern Angola and Namibia
1912–13	Crop failure and starvation in southern Mozambique
1913	Famine, due to absence of men from villages, in southern Zaire
1913–14	Drought and famine in Ethiopia and Sudan
1913–15	Drought and agricultural changes leading to famine in Sahel region of western Africa; c. 200,000 dead
1915–17	Famine in northern Zambia due to requisition of food by military
1930–35	Locust invasions and drought lead to food shortages in East-Central Africa
1931	Famine in Niger, due to government requisition, taxes, cash cropping and drought
1933–34	Drought in Lesotho, major losses of livestock
1942–43	Famine in northern Nigeria due to military requisition of food

1943	Famine in central Tanzania
mid-1950s – late 1960s	Generally good rains, perhaps above normal, in Sahel/Sudan zones of West Africa
1968	Beginning of drought in West Africa; hunger in parts of Mali, Senegal and Niger
1970	Food shortages in many parts of Sahel
1971	Food shortages reported in northern Ethiopia; reports ignored
1972–74	Famine in northern Ethiopia; estimated 50,000 to 200,000 people die
1973	Widespread famine in Sahel; estimated 250,000 deaths; major cattle losses
1974	Major food shortages in Tanzania, due to drought and population resettlement
Late 1970s	UN agencies predict food crisis in Africa due to declining per capita food production
1981–84	Drought in southern Africa; food shortages widely reported; South African attacks affect relief efforts
1982–85	Drought and massive famine in seccessionist and other northern regions of Ethiopia; estimated 1 million dead, often due to disease in relief camps
1982–84	Drought and food shortages in Sahel region of West Africa
1983–90	South African-directed war in Mozambique disrupts food production and distribution, leaving one million people dead
1984–85	Drought and famine in western Sudan; estimated 100,000 people die from health-related causes
1986–87	Drought and famine in Eritrea
1988	War-induced famine in southern Sudan; estimated 250,000 people dead
1989–90	War in Eritrea and northern Ethiopia; widespread crop failures and famine

Index

Zed Books Ltd

is a publisher whose international and Third World lists span:

- **Women's Studies**
- **Development**
- **Environment**
- **Current Affairs**
- **International Relations**
- **Children's Studies**
- **Labour Studies**
- **Cultural Studies**
- **Human Rights**
- **Indigenous Peoples**
- **Health**

We also specialize in Area Studies where we have extensive lists in African Studies, Asian Studies, Caribbean and Latin American Studies, Middle East Studies, and Pacific Studies.

For further information about books available from Zed Books, please write to: Catalogue Enquiries, Zed Books Ltd, 57 Caledonian Road, London N1 9BU. Our books are available from distributors in many countries (for full details, see our catalogues), including:

In the USA
Humanities Press International, Inc., 171 First Avenue, Atlantic Highlands, New Jersey 07716.
Tel: (201) 872 1441;
Fax: (201) 872 0717.

In Canada
DEC, 229 College Street, Toronto, Ontario M5T 1R4.
Tel: (416) 971 7051.

In Australia
Wild and Woolley Ltd, 16 Darghan Street, Glebe, NSW 2037.

In India
Bibliomania, C-236 Defence Colony, New Delhi 110 024.

In Southern Africa
David Philip Publisher (Pty) Ltd, PO Box 408, Claremont 7735, South Africa.